Reference G

Under the Editorship of

GARDNER MURPHY

REFERENCE GROUPS

Exploration into Conformity and
Deviation of Adolescents

MUZAFER SHERIF

AND

CAROLYN W. SHERIF

Institute of Group Relations
The University of Oklahoma

Henry Regnery Company
CHICAGO

Gateway edition published by Henry Regnery Company
114 West Illinois Street, Chicago, Illinois 60610
by arrangement with Harper & Row, Incorporated

Printed in the United States of America
LIBRARY OF CONGRESS CATALOG CARD NUMBER: 64–10594
First Gateway edition, 1972

Contents

Foreword

Youth problems, adolescence, group structures, and intergroup conflict are lively issues foremost in the minds of practitioner and scholar, government official, parent, and teacher. The future of our society rests in large part upon a better understanding of these topics and the development of action programs to cope with the social problems of adolescents, not only in America but throughout the world. The authors of *Reference Groups* could not have picked a more timely or urgent subject for study than the nature of conformity and deviation of adolescents within their self-chosen reference groups.

In 1958, Muzafer Sherif accepted a visiting research professorship at The University of Texas, supported in part by the Hogg Foundation for Mental Health. It was our hope that the Sherifs would find an opportunity in several Texas cities to try out their latest ideas for combining a variety of techniques in the scientific study of naturally formed groups of adolescent boys. Pilot studies in San Antonio, El Paso, and Houston led immediately to more sustained investigations that continued for several years after the Sherifs' return to Oklahoma. Studies sponsored by the Foundation are still in progress in San Antonio under their close supervision and will probably continue as long as the research workers in San Antonio find fruitful leads for further investigation.

The initial goals of the Sherifs and the hopes of the Hogg Foundation have been more than realized in the studies and findings reported herein. In the relatively short period of five years, a number of groups have been studied intensively by young men who, themselves, had grown up within the local neighborhoods and have since developed into highly competent youth workers under the skilled tutelage of the Sherifs.

Unlike the usual research grant in which funds for a number of years are approved on the basis of a fixed research blueprint, the pattern of relationship between the Hogg Foundation and the Sherifs stayed close to the way in which field research of this kind actually develops. Flexible funds in small amounts were provided as needed, together with close, informal support by the Foundation staff in arranging for consultation, community contacts, and resources. Although a total of less than $15,000 has been provided by the Foundation to date, a relatively minor part of the total support received by the Sherifs from various sources, these particular funds were sufficiently informal in timing and purpose to prove crucial, particularly in the all-important early stages of the field research.

In one sense this book is a progress report of a highly original approach to the intensive study of naturally formed groups, an approach that will undoubtedly be rapidly adopted by other workers soon after its publication. The Sherifs themselves are continuing their research along these same lines, doubling their efforts to complete the last two stages in their programmatic design—the experimental testing of hypotheses by the study of group members interacting with new persons, and the study of individual differences in behavior within groups by extending their investigations to include personality characteristics. We can look forward to future publication of this work in progress to complete the picture. In another sense, however, this book is a finished product, a report of a new comprehensive approach to the study of small groups. A single, multifaceted method, it is the culmination of a lifetime of work on such related though distinct topics as the psychology of ego-involvement, social norms, intergroup conflict and harmony, reference scales in social judgment and attitudes, and the social ecology of behavior.

There have been many studies of individual behavior in small groups, of the immediate environment surrounding adolescent gangs, and of the commonly shared values, opportunities, and experiences of the American culture in which youth develop. But these have generally been segmental approaches which choose to ignore some aspects of adolescent group behavior while focusing upon others. The Sherifs have succeeded in skilfully combining all three sets of influences into one study, achieving a genuine integration of research methodology drawn from psychology, sociology, and anthropology. Such a fusion of laboratory methods with the natural life setting while dealing with naturally formed groups of adolescents on their own terms is a welcome relief from the plethora of studies using artificial groups in contrived, hypothetical situations. The highly consistent results and unusual insights obtained by the Sherifs across a wide variety of adolescent groups provide clear evidence of the rewards to be gained by putting forth the extra effort and ingenuity required to employ measurement techniques in real life situations without in any way disturbing the process under investigation. The detailed procedures are spelled out in the Appendix for those who are interested.

On the one hand, the research methodology, formal hypotheses, and empirical findings bearing upon theory will be of special interest to psychologists, sociologists, anthropologists, and other social scientists. On the other hand, the rich case material uncovered about adolescent behavior and the attention given by the Sherifs to the practical implications of their findings will be of particular value to anyone concerned about youth programs or juvenile delinquency, be he parent or teacher, probation officer or public administrator. The book begins and ends on a practical note—the urgency of reforming outmoded and inadequate approaches to youth problems, and some timely suggestions as to how to go about it. The need for such reforms is now generally recognized; the specific action to be taken is still being debated throughout the country. Here is one set of findings, criticisms, and recommendations that deserves special attention.

WAYNE H. HOLTZMAN

Austin, Texas

Preface

This book deals with individual behavior and group processes in differentiated social settings. The individuals are adolescents. Both socially acceptable and socially objectionable behaviors are explored, for it is our conviction that each can best be articulated relative to the other. The groups in question are those of the individual's own choosing under conditions of contemporary urban life.

Our major focus is on interaction processes in reference groups over a time span and their consequences for the individual. His problems of conformity and nonconformity are often concentrated in these groups, and usually deflected by them. However, neither the groups nor person-to-person interactions within them are insulated from their surroundings. They are not closed systems. The concerns of the members, their activities in concert, their individual claims and aspirations take place within reference scales provided by the physical and cultural character of their settings. Hence, the properties of the setting become an integral part in studying behavior of individual members and their interactions.

For these reasons, the behavior of individual members, their motives and goals, the preoccupations of the groups, their organization and values, and the characteristics of their settings were made interrelated aspects of study in a single research program directed by the senior author. The procedures and findings in this research up to early 1962 are incorporated in this work along with representative studies by others pertinent to the various aspects. Comparison of behavior as a function of group processes and their settings obviously requires study both of different groups and different settings. Therefore, groups have been studied from different socioeconomic levels (low, middle, and high); different cultural backgrounds; and geographically separated urban centers. The various aspects of the inquiry required utilization of relevant findings, procedures, and techniques both from psychology and sociology.

The scope of the undertaking has necessarily made us heavily indebted to several agencies for understanding, counsel, and implementation; to various colleagues for calling our attention to relevant literature and ongoing research in both psychology and sociology, where we sought procedures and skills necessary in such an inter-disciplinary research effort; to collaborators in various cities; and to those younger colleagues who engaged in data collection.

The research program started in several cities in Texas while the senior author was a visiting professor at The University of Texas in 1958-1959. Initiation of pilot exploration and study of the first groups were made possible through the close interest and financial support of the Hogg Foundation for Mental Health of The University of Texas. The authors are genuinely grateful to Dr. Robert L. Sutherland and Dr. Wayne H. Holtzman, officers of the Foundation, for their understanding support and encouragement. We are fortunate to have Wayne Holtzman's active and continuing interest in the project and the benefit of numerous conferences with him on matters of research strategy.

The continuity of the research program during an interim period was insured through small research grants from the Rockefeller Foundation and the Human Ecology Fund of New York, for which we are grateful.

During the last two years, the major support came from the National Science Foundation. This support made it possible for us to extend the research program into more adequate proportions—an effort still continuing—and to concentrate most of last year on assessing the procedures and data obtained up to early 1962, as well as writing this book. The senior author is grateful to Dr. Henry W. Riecken and Dr. Robert L. Hall of the National Science Foundation for several conferences on different aspects of this multifaceted undertaking. These conferences raised stimulating questions about operational research strategies which have been used and are still being refined. Challenging problems were articulated in the way of bridging "the gap between field studies and laboratory experiments in social psychology," which is ultimately one of the main objectives of the research program.

The book owes much to the editorial comment and suggestions of Dr. Gardner Murphy of the Menninger Foundation, our never-failing friend in various research and writing activities through the years. The material in Chapter 1, concentrating on the background and actualities of interaction in one group for each socioeconomic level, was enlarged chiefly because of Dr. Murphy's insistence on including more "flesh-and-blood" interaction among the adolescent boys. Likewise, the discussion on implications of the research findings in the last chapter was expanded at his suggestion.

We appreciate the helpful conferences on sociocultural (ecological) settings and measures with Dr. Walter Firey of The University of Texas; Dr. Eshref Shevky and Dr. Wendell Bell of the University of California at Los Angeles; Mr. E. G. Luna of Inman Christian Center, San Antonio; Sister Frances Jerome Woods of Our Lady of the Lake College; and Dr. Robert Talbert of Texas Christian University.

In view of the generous support, counsel, and encouragement from those mentioned above, we should absolve them from any responsibility for omissions and commissions in this book. The authors alone are responsible for its content, as well as the design and conduct of the research.

It is a pleasure to extend again our sincere appreciation to the administration of the University of Oklahoma and especially to Dr. Pete Kyle McCarter and Dr. Lloyd E. Swearingen who, in line with the farsighted policy of President George L. Cross, instituted the framework of the Institute of Group Relations which makes possible the needed time and facilities for an expanding program of research with young collaborators.

Our indebtedness is boundless to colleagues who were interested in the research and gave of their skills in their communities to help its translation from plan to action, especially Mr. E. G. Luna, Sister Frances Jerome Woods, and Mr. J. Robert Weber of the Veterans Administration in El Paso. Professor Henry Bullock of Texas Southern University was most generous of his time in the early period of exploration. Mrs. Marie MacGuire, then Executive Director of the City of San Antonio Housing Authority, now Commissioner of Public Housing in Washington, D.C., procured data not otherwise available to us and inspired us with her enthusiasm. Other resource persons who opened paths to us include Dr. Bernice Moore, the Hogg Foundation; Dr. Charles Burrows, Trinity University; Sister Mary Immaculate, Our Lady of the Lake College; Alvin R.

Eggeling, Director of Recreation, Oklahoma City; Mrs. Catherine Simpson, Superintendent of Programming; and Dr. Virgil Hill, Oklahoma City.

Those with the difficult and indispensable tasks of collecting and tabulating data summarized in this book are Dr. Kenneth Dick, Eduardo Villarreal, Joel Garza, Gregory Luna, Aurelio N. Navarro, Ben Mata, Mrs. Ofelia Sanchez, Mrs. Josephine Valencia, Paul Burns, Mel Coose, Gerald Foster, John Nordquist, John Rodrigues, George Concha, Alfonso Velarde, Jr., Tom W. Carter, George Kirkland, Dan Medina, and Jesse R. Ybarra.

Our sincere thanks go once again to Mrs. Betty Frensley who, as in several past endeavors, has shown both skill and patience in preparing the manuscript through several revisions. We appreciate the assistance of Samuel S. Shurtleff of the Institute of Group Relations in preparing the name and subject indexes.

M. S. and C. W. S.

Norman, Oklahoma
November, 1963

PART I

Introduction

1 *Grist for the mill*

In this book we deal with adolescent behaviors. Some are socially acceptable, and some objectionable. We are attempting to relate these behaviors to adolescents' daily give-and-take with one another and with adults. We also want to locate the give-and-take of behavior in terms of the concrete social settings in which it is enacted. Through examining person-to-person interaction, we will attempt to uncover urges and self-pictures to be fulfilled, as these provide characteristic goal-directedness in what the individuals talk about and do. For this purpose, the interactions of adolescents are particularly appropriate. The period is one of throbbing existence in a changing and maturing body, with the image of full-fledged adult man or woman dramatically in the making, as the transition from childhood is made in a social setting itself in the process of change.

When everything is said and done, the give-and-take between adolescent and adolescent, and with adults, is grist for the mill. Through it we study a social process in which are revealed individuals' urges, their self-pictures as formed and changing at the time, and the impact of appraisals meted by others in the social milieu. This first chapter presents pictures of the give-and-take among adolescents before we turn to the more difficult tasks of processing them. The reader can then judge for himself whether the products of the milling process in the rest of the book do justice to their ingredients.

First, the general outlines of the task undertaken need to be drawn.

Exploration into Conformity and Deviation

In this rapidly changing and shrinking world of our times, problems of conformity and deviation acquire great complexity. To enhance their ages-old significance modern times have speeded the proliferation of human groupings with specialized interests and goals, while, at the same time, bringing increasingly larger numbers of people into interdependent modes of existence.

What do "conformity" and "deviation" mean? They refer, respectively, to behaviors appraised in a favorable light and to behaviors condemned as inappropriate, wrong, objectionable, even punishable, by *other people*. Conformity is always conformity *to* something. Deviation is always departure *from* something. And the objective definitions of those "somethings" are the actual or anticipated evaluations of some set of people.

Regulation of one's behavior with respect to *some* specific other people is an axiom of human social life in any place or time. Departure from established, accustomed, or expected ways of behaving is a prominent feature of human historical process and change. Glorification or denunciation of all conformity or all nonconformity may be an effective political tactic or literary device. But neither will advance our understanding of social behavior or process. It is easy enough to think of conforming deeds which promote human well-being, and nonconforming deeds which do likewise. Conversely, nonconformity can endanger human life (driving down the middle of the road), as can conformity (staying on the right side of the road, no matter what).

In this book, we explore critical questions concerning *who* the people are whose appraisals count for the individual, *what* defines a deed as conforming or deviating, and *why* the individual does or does not conform to it. Compliance to the demands of others through sheer force and physical coercion, or their threat, are not our major concern, although they are important and striking instances of conformity. Such instances usually bring the individual face to face with a direct choice between physical safety and survival, on the one hand, or following paths he believes right, on the other. Such a choice is no simple affair. However, the probable outcome is so taken for granted that individuals who actually do follow their "conscience" are recognized as exceptional, even heroic.

The deliberate choices of exceptional individuals who defy punishment, even death, to follow what they see as "right," have an important feature in common with the great bulk of conforming behavior by people in ordinary circumstances: Pressure experienced to act as they do comes more from *within,* rather than from the immediate, overt urgings of others. When Polonius, a rather conventional court politician, in Shakespeare's *Hamlet,* instructed his son on how to get along in the world, he could sum up "To thine own self be true" in recognition of these *inner* promptings to regulate one's behavior within the bounds socially defined as acceptable at the time for one in his son's station.

All social behavior cannot be classified as either conforming or deviating. There are areas of social activity in which acceptable behavior is poorly defined, if at all. In others, long-established imperatives are fading. And human individuals frequently face novel situations lacking clear relevance to the familiar. Such are characteristic of our times.

To determine whether or not an action is conforming or deviating, we have to know *what* there is to conform to or depart from. In other words, there must be something *external* to the individual's experience and actions which has demonstrable connection with his behavior. This *something external* is the actual or most probable evaluation by other people of the range of behavior which is acceptable, appropriate, respectable, even ideal, under the circumstances.

But the fact that the *something*—the social norm—consists of the appraisals of other people immediately links the question of *what* to the question of *who* the people are whose appraisals count for the individual. Certainly, these other people need not be immediately present when the individual acts. Those who originally made the appraisals may be long dead. They may be people whom our individual has not seen, but with whom he strongly desires to belong. The problem of *who* the other people are is enormously complicated in modern societies, where one individual belongs to or may identify himself with a number of different sets of people at the same time, or in different circumstances.

For example, he may be an American boy attending a certain school with other boys and girls in his neighborhood, but belong to a Spanish-speaking family whose members have encountered social and economic obstacles to improving their lot. He goes to church, spends his leisure with other Spanish-speaking boys in his neighborhood, and belongs to an athletic club run by the city. Whose appraisals count for him? Those of his schoolmates? His teachers? His parents? Those who discriminate against his kind? The church authorities? His neighborhood friends? The athletic staff? Fellow team members? Or are his sights set beyond the present toward images of successful, more prosperous persons he sees on the printed page, television, and movie screen? These are all identifiable sets of people whose appraisals we can ascertain. But which are his *reference groups*—which are the sets to which he feels he belongs, wants to belong, relates himself, psychologically?

Suppose we can relate the social norms prevailing among different sets of people to the individual's reference groups, taking into account their relative importance in his scheme of things. Then we would have a factual basis for determining whether his behavior is conforming, in some degree, or deviating, in some degree; or whether it is neither. This alone would hardly be sufficient, however. What are his actual relationships to his reference groups? Does he belong to them as a member? Is he *with* them? What is his place or position in their scheme of things? How do these different sets of people regard and treat him? How do they regard and treat one another?

To sum up, the regulation of social behavior termed *conformity,* and its converse, termed *deviation,* are by definition relative to the shared or agreed-upon appraisals of others (social norms). It is perfectly feasible to assess conformity or deviation in terms of any standards to which an individual has been exposed. But the meaningful relationship, from a psychological point of view, aimed at understanding and *prediction* of behavior is between the norms of the individual's reference groups, his place or position with respect to people in them (their *organization*), and his words and deeds in concrete situations. Such relationships are our problem in this book.

GRIST FOR THE MILL

Without a moral, without theorizing, without even going deeply into how we investigated, let us look at adolescent behavior, adolescent groups, and different social settings which we have studied. Of course, there are morals: Important public figures discuss them in terms of "juvenile delinquency"; "discovering creative potential"; "school dropouts"; "disillusioned youth"; "values of the younger generation"; and "adolescent subculture." Of course, there is theory: It cannot help intruding somewhat in the way we summarize the stuff of our research and the questions we pose. And, of course, there are ways and means by which we obtain this grist for the mill of social science: We report them later. Now we need only say that what follows are pictures obtained slowly and painstakingly over months, primarily through direct observations made without these individuals knowing they were being studied. After observations were completed, then and only then were these individuals, and many others who knew them, interviewed or questioned. Information on the neighborhoods in which they lived and on other teenagers living there was secured independently of these observations.

In the pages to follow, we summarize three groups of adolescents and their members, illustrative of a dozen studied so far. We start near the top of the social ladder—in a neighborhood of high social rank—then go to a middle rank setting, and finally to a group in a low rank neighborhood with a large Spanish-speaking population. These groups and the boys in them are in no sense distinctive as cases. In fact, we trust that those who know adolescents well will find themselves in familiar territory.

All names of individuals and places are changed out of respect for individual privacy. Actions and events are real.

UPPER RUNGS OF THE
SOCIAL LADDER

On an arterial street dividing the most established residential area of a large southwestern city from the even more luxurious

homes and spacious lawns of the newer and most exclusive suburban area, there is a restaurant called the Wing-Back. The food—
whether charcoal-broiled hamburger or steak—is excellent, and the
prices higher than average. During the noon hour the Wing-Back is
crowded with students from three large high schools located from
a few blocks to several miles distant. They come in groups of three
to six by car. They are orderly, but boisterous, and the cars create a
traffic problem. Therefore, a policeman is on duty during the rush.

An observer begins to frequent the Wing-Back. He is a well-
dressed university student who grew up and works in the city. He
drives a stunning late model car. He appears to have a passion for
charcoal-broiled hamburgers, which he satisfies at noon and in the
evening just about the time that high-school ball games and dances
are over. During the course of a month he sees five boys, 16–17 years
of age, who reappear frequently, in pairs, threesomes, or quartets. By
watching as they leave, he learns to identify their cars. Once, while
waiting for his order, one of the boys speaks to him, but in the
casual way of strangers facing the problem of service in a crowded
restaurant.

The boys were neatly and well-dressed in clothing favored by
the collegiate set. Two of them wore "letter jackets" denoting membership on high-school athletic teams. Their hair was trim. Their
cars were three to six years old, one of them a very expensive make.
One car was a convertible, another of foreign manufacture. At different times during the first month, the observer saw the cars and
combinations of these and other boys at Peaches Drive-Inn and at
the Old Stone Coffee House near a local college campus.

One of the boys first talked to the observer when they emerged
from the Wing-Back at the same time to enter adjacent cars. The
boy—Whitney—admired the car and asked about its performance.
Soon afterward, one of these boys saw the observer in the coffee
house, an informal "beatnik" place, and asked him: "Have you by
any chance seen Whitney?" The observer replied: "Who?" The boy
reminded him that they chatted recently in front of the Wing-Back
about his car. Then the observer told him he thought he had seen
Whitney and a girl leave shortly before.

A week later, four of the boys were sitting at a table in the coffee house when the observer came in. They asked him to join them. One of them—Elliott—suggested a poker game, but the others did not bother to reply. Jack asked Elliott to tell "the joke about the pigs," but interrupted Elliott to correct a detail, and ended up telling the joke himself. Phil, a sturdy, attractive boy, almost seventeen, who had "lettered" in track, asked about the observer's car: "How does it run? Is it outside?" He said he certainly would like to ride in it sometime. About 15 minutes later, they all left for a ride.

The observer drove toward the main business area. Returning, Whitney asked if they could go to the highway and drive faster. Halfway there, the observer turned over the wheel to Whitney, who drove out along the highway. All of the boys admired the car's performance. Whitney offered to return the wheel, but to the observer's reply of "Go ahead," he asked the others where he should go. Getting no suggestions, he drove through the parking lot of Peaches Drive-Inn, then said, "Let's go by that ol' girl's from Smithville" (a nearby small town). The others laughed, but consented.

On the way, Phil explained that this "ol' girl" was really an ugly slob who lived in an apartment nearby. He knocked on the door when they arrived. The girl was surprised, and to the boys' merriment, they found two others there—Hutch, whom the observer had seen with them before, and a new face (Jim). Hutch and his companion were clearly embarrassed. They sat down and began to read magazines, Hutch making derogatory faces behind his magazine for the boys' benefit while the girl sat on a bed and talked. In a few minutes, Whitney said they had to leave. The unknown boy stepped outside the door to explain that *he* hadn't wanted to come, and that he and Hutch were going to leave to go bowling.

Back in the car, Whitney insisted that the observer drive. The boys were overcome with mirth. Each had a remark about the girl. Phil asked Whitney if he thought Hutch was "doin' any good with her." Whitney replied that he knew a lot of fellows who said they had.

What Adults Thought and What the Observer Saw. School authorities and parents in this part of the city said that there really were only a few "groups" of teen-agers there, certainly no "gangs."

These groups were just a few trouble-makers whose identity they knew and who could be controlled. In fact, they said, most boys belonged to so many special-interest groups and activities, such as athletic teams, school plays, the band, the Anchor Club (a social service club that held car-washes and dances to raise money), that with school and home obligations, the boys were very busy. Each had one or two good friends, it is true, and other friends in his interest groups. But, said the adults, the friends were not together as a group outside of school functions; the boys were just too busy. There *had* been a high school fraternity which caused "trouble." The school had abolished it by requiring members to resign on pain of expulsion. Most parents supported the decision.

There was some truth in the adults' conclusions. Over a period of five months, the observer found all the nine boys he studied together at one time, outside of formal, institutional settings, on only a few occasions. They were highly active in school and community affairs. Hutch and Phil were athletes. Whitney, Jim, and Jack practiced for baseball, but did not make the team. (Whitney was sure that he would not, so he stopped practice. Then Jim and Jack lost interest, although they were better players.) Sterling, Don, and Hutch were cast members in two school plays during the period. They all attended school functions, the Anchor Club activities, churches, and various private parties at homes and country clubs. Late in the spring, Phil was elected President of the Student Council by popular vote.

However, the observer found a number of things that parents and teachers could not have known. First, the high school fraternity existed underground. Sterling was not known as a member when it was broken up, and he still belonged. The other boys regretted their separation from the brotherhood. Sterling was actually to be seen more frequently with these boys than with his fraternity brothers; nevertheless, he prized his membership. When Whitney and Jim were invited for a week end to a college fraternity on a nearby campus as "younger brothers" of members, Sterling (who was not a younger brother) deemphasized the experience by saying that his high school fraternity was far superior to any college fraternity he had heard about. No one challenged his statement.

Second, in terms of sheer frequency and regularity, these boys were together, in varying combinations, more than they were with others. Indeed, there were at least six other boys who were friends with one or more of the bunch and were seen with them on numerous occasions. However, there was a difference between these and the regulars. When some boys were absent, these occasional companions seldom knew where they could be located. In contrast, the regular set invariably knew the whereabouts of most of the others, including whom they were with and where they could be expected to turn up at particular times. They kept in touch by telephone. Sterling, Whitney, and Don had coffee and sweet rolls at Sterling's house every Saturday morning. The late breakfast was served by Sterling's grandmother, who enjoyed the preparing and serving for these attractive boys. The ritual gave them, in Sterling's words, a chance to "plan the week."

Third, the patterns of influence among these boys were not immediately obvious from their standing in school or their parents' standings, although the instrumentalities afforded by these undeniably affected a boy's position. Phil was elected President of the Student Council with the active campaigning and support of this bunch. He was conscientious in his studies and was a letter athlete, but he was not among the most influential in determining what they would do. He was almost always in on their activities. But he was too strait-laced to swing much weight: he did not drink or smoke, and was known as having "strong principles." But he was a good fellow in a pinch, and could be counted upon to see that others got home safely after a drinking party.

Don, whose father was the prominent owner and head of a large business, was unparalleled in carrying out the details for a party. He provided his home complete with maid service for dinner on one occasion. He was good at securing liquor (a false identification card was used only when absolutely necessary). But he always went along with Sterling's plans.

Hutch had very little say in what happened, even though he had one of the better cars and a very "good" family. He worried a lot about what might happen. Yet his car certainly counted. Chuck worked as an usher at a movie theater with the specific intent of "getting a car like Hutch's." When he did get the car, he dashed out before work to call, not Hutch, but Whitney about it.

Sinclair ("Ol' Oil Can") had the least money and "family." Among boys who took many things for granted, he held his own by personal charm and never being apologetic. If he sacrificed pride in hearing what they took for granted, he liked being one of the bunch, and they liked him. In any case, the gap was not so great that in appearance he could have been singled out as different.

On the other hand, Elliott had money and a car. But his weekly five-dollar allowance came on Saturday and was invariably gone by Monday. His frequent references to being broke and his attempts to get the boys to play cards for money to refill his billfold were sufficiently annoying to bring him the cold shoulder on several occasions.

Whitney, the first to speak to the observer, was among the most favored, in terms of family circumstances. He had one of the oldest cars, but it was his own. After Chuck got his car, Whitney's parents promised to chip in for a better car if he would earn part of the money by working on some of their real estate. Whitney was always in on things, until he and his girl had a falling out, and he had trouble getting dates. On one occasion, Sterling and Jim called girls to get Whitney a date, but it was too late. Twice after that, Whitney and Elliott were at loose ends on week ends because all the others had dates for parties. They asked the observer to go with them first to a rock and roll concert at the city auditorium, and, the second time, to Blatt's Dance Studio, where pick-ups were easy. Then Whitney got a fail slip in math, and his parents "slapped the lid on." By the end of the year, he had started to pass, made up with his girl, and was back with the crowd again.

It was Sterling whose word counted most. His father was a dentist; his car a 6-year-old yellow convertible. He had flunked algebra and was taking it over (he passed). But the only time he got into real trouble at school was when he cut a required assembly and was expelled for two days. This was not real trouble, for his father reinstated him. With a lecture from parent and principal, he was back.

Sterling was aggressive in his relationship with others, but jovially so. He was fun. When he made suggestions they sounded like polite orders, and were received that way. His decisions were usually on matters of substance. For example, it was his idea to get two adjoining motel rooms for an end-of-school party, and he figured the cost at $3.00 a boy. Don and Jack worked out the details, collected the money, arranged for refreshments. Sterling interfered only when he had a better idea: "We need a case of beer for the afternoon to get tanked up for the party."

There were some details, however, in which Sterling was highly skilled and very attentive. He was the best one to ask if you needed a date for a party, and he would really try. His reputation with the nice girls was okay, but he also knew which were "easy makes" and passed the information around for individual use. Sinclair appeared at the observer's apartment with such a girl—a very attractive teen-ager—to. request use of the apartment. The observer had a good excuse for refusing. When Sterling found out about Sinclair's request, he chastised him. Sinclair apologized to the observer and accepted the rebuke gracefully because: "Sterling lined me up with my first piece." Sterling was helpful in other ways too. He even offered to introduce a pal to his father for dental work at a "friend's price."

Sterling found an eighth-grade girl who welcomed attention and offered no objections when she was baby-sitting in the evenings. He was very annoyed to find Whitney there one night. As he said, "Whit is definitely not a cocksman and just ruined everybody's evening." But on another occasion, he found the girl with another schoolmate—not a member of the crowd. It was a different matter: he was outraged. He called all the boys together, telephoned the culprit, then went to his house and hurled challenges to fight up to the second-story window. With the others backing him, he confronted the boy's father with the charge that he had a yellow streak for a son. The astonished and, by now, angry father offered to fight, but forbade his son to come out. (Probably Sterling accomplished his purpose. The boy was not allowed out at night for weeks.)

An Important Event. Throughout the winter and spring, these boys spent a lot of their free time in and around cars. Much of their conversation was about cars. Sterling and Whitney had definite plans to get better ones, others had hopes. The boys were scarcely ever idle, but were very occupied youths at school and its functions, in the community, at private parties. All of them planned to go to college, but only two had explicit professional aims. Whitney and Jim planned to go to the same school and become architects.

If it appears that Sterling led these youths astray, it must be said that he was among those who understood what the others wanted and was most effective in proposing appropriate activities. Phil, now Student Council President, was enthusiastic about Sterling's plan for an end-of-the-year party. The observer was present when things reached the planning stage, because they hoped that he, as a safe adult, would sign for two adjoining motel rooms. Don had arranged with his parents for a dinner served by their maid. Sterling suggested that each fellow bring his own liquor or buy a share of someone else's. Phil thought they should not tell the girls of their plans for a swim party at the motel until they got to Don's. Sterling objected that the girls would then have to go home for their swimsuits and someone would be more likely to spill the beans. The thing was, as Don clearly saw, to call the girl just before dinner to tell her to bring her swimsuit. This eminently logical plan was immediately endorsed.

The boys understood the observer's reluctance to sign at the motel, and it could be managed. They asked him, nevertheless, to drop out sometime after 10 P.M. He found not just them, but several similar parties in progress, held by students from three different schools. Everyone was drinking but Phil and some of the girls. Sterling, Don, and Jim told him they hoped to keep their girls there after the others left. The problem was to get rid of uninvited guests.

Later, Whitney got in a fight with a boy from another school who persisted in splashing his white coat and dark trousers and his girl's evening dress as they sat by the pool. The management intervened. Phil took home two boys and their dates whom Sterling classified as "stoned." At about 3 A.M. they all left, partly because several chairs and the thermostat in their rooms had been broken. Sterling and Don agreed to reimburse the management, who set the damages at $25. Don collected this sum the next day, contributing himself, although the observer knew that the previous day he had spent $9 on liquor alone, $3 for the motel room, and had bought his girl a corsage. He was a junior in high school, going on seventeen. He was a very responsible boy.

MIDWAY UP ON A LOOSE RUNG

The middle rungs of the social ladder are thought to be more comfortable than the lower ones, more stable than the upper. The middle rungs we will look at are not representative of the journalistic picture of the "stable middle class," but they are located in this region.

The neighborhood is in a large city. Its residents move about a good deal, often to the suburbs. Many live in duplexes and apartments, comfortably equipped with appliances and television, but shabbier than the plush, new buildings going up in the city. In this neighborhood, we will look at seven boys whose families are more favored than the average. Their incomes are a bit above the city median, their parents are high school graduates, and some relatives have college degrees. The fathers are employed in sales or in small businesses they own. The mothers work, too, as bookkeepers, business machine operators, teachers. (Only one family breaks the pattern. The mother works as a file clerk; the father is in a penitentiary.) They dress well, have nice cars, and some money on the side.

Our observer is an athletic young man, a graduate student who tells the boys, when occasion arises, that he is studying to be a teacher. But he doesn't like teaching much and is thinking of going into recreational work. He needs experience. He meets the boys at a recreation center located in a city park. It is staffed by two officials who know his purpose and cooperate to create his chosen identity, one without authority in the center. The boys are 16–18 years old. They appear at the center every afternoon, when allowed to come in.

There are Ike and Mike. They resemble each other, but it takes the observer nearly a month to ascertain that they are twins. Presumably, their parents were touched at having twins, or had a sense of humor, to name them thus. Some four months later Ike explains in halting and confused words that his parents were divorced when they were seven. Both remarried. The father had another child, a younger boy whom they both get a kick out of now. Two years ago their parents were divorced again and remarried each other. The father's former wife married again, to a man with a substantial upholstery business. This is not irrelevant to what happened with these boys. And though it was a tangled web, it was not unconcerned with the children.

Ike and Mike are attractive boys, very neatly dressed in slacks and sweaters (or jeans for games), well-mannered to adults, good athletes. The observer notices that Ike is the more outspoken, usually the one to suggest what to do next, and that Mike goes along enthusiastically.

At first appearance, Fox seemed very different from them. His hair was long and greasy. He was a homely one, neither very clean nor neat. But he was very well coordinated, an excellent player. Ike, Mike, and Fox had been friends for five years, since they were thirteen. Three years later they had been dropped from school for excessive absences and failures. School test scores showed, however, that they were all well within the normal range on intelligence and achievement tests. Teachers at their school recalled Ike and Mike as most amiable, courteous, and cooperative in listening to suggestions. They even promised improvement; they just never did. Fox, on the other hand, was regarded by former teachers as a "minor irritant." Only the physical education teacher praised his interest and ability. Other teachers confessed that he never caused real trouble, but irritated in little ways. But this was long behind them. All three were 18 years old.

With the three, the observer found four other boys, although a combination of four or five was more frequent than the total seven. Sonny, tall and good-looking at 16, wore his hair long, like Fox. Promptly on his sixteenth birthday, the school had dismissed him for repeated absences, failing grades, and (as the teachers said) a sullen disposition. He had not taken part in school activities, preferring two close friends—Mitch and Bobbie. With the boys, Sonny was apt to joke too long, or make sexual remarks at the wrong girls. Ike, Mike, and Fox told him so, and usually, he drew in gracefully.

Sonny's friend Mitch was nice-looking too. He was blond and had never been a discipline problem at school. In fact, his school records contained test scores well above the average range. But at school he just sat, did not do homework after hours, and frequently missed school. His mother and stepfather were solid citizens—the mother worked as a cashier, the stepfather owned a service station. They sent him to stay with his grandfather in another town with the explicit hope of separating him from "those boys." A few weeks later Mitch returned to the city, alone, and went to reenroll in his former school. The counsellor called his mother, who expressed her surprise and gave permission not to enroll him. It was at this time, some weeks after the observer met the others, that Mitch appeared on the scene.

Bobbie had a superior score on intelligence tests, and his teachers said he had considerable capacity; but his grades were just average. At 17, Bobbie was tall, skinny, had acne and a high-pitched voice just beginning to change. At an early age, he and another orphan had been adopted by a teacher. He was, obviously, a late maturer.

Finally, there was Bo—a rather unattractive boy, though above average height and well formed. His father was a real-estate broker, and his mother a skilled business machine operator, yet his long hair and generally unkempt appearance resembled Fox's—the poorest of the lot. His uncle was a school principal in a fair-sized city nearby, and last year he had been sent to live with him. His uncle at last despaired and returned him home. He was still in school, physically at least.

With these boys, very frequently, were three girls. All were attractive and one even pretty. At the Center, they played card games, Ping-pong, attended social dances, parried Fox who bit their ears, and paid a lot of attention to Ike and Mike. They drove around in cars together. At the girls' homes, they ate, watched television, and drank beer.

At various times, Ike, Mike, and Fox had other, "steady," girl friends, whom they dated and brought to dances. Mike said that he'd almost "had to marry" his girl, and was intensely relieved when it had proved to be a false alarm. Only Bobbie did not have a girl. He had a date once during five months. Donna, Jody, and Sylvia— the frequent companions—sometimes had him over when the other boys had dates. Perhaps his late development at seventeen left them free to indulge publicly in play that otherwise they would have evaded and, otherwise, would have been dubbed sexual. For example, with Bobbie, there were games, publicly, of smoking a cigarette together. One smoker would transfer the smoke to the other lip-to-lip, the recipient exhaling. Bobbie was a vehicle for actions provocative to the others.

On one occasion, Donna left the group before they took off for the usual car ride when the Center closed. One of the boys explained: "Donna has the idea she's a sosh." *Sosh* is the well-known and nationally common name for those in the "good" crowd in a high school. "A 'sosh' boy asked for a date last week end, and she can't get over it. If he got what he wanted, she'll get over it."

The Center was a gathering place for the boys, a pleasant location to meet, play card games or Ping-pong, see girls, and make plans. It had athletic equipment which few boys have individually. And these boys liked sports.

Despite this, every so often, one or all of them were barred from the Center. The pattern was fairly established. Sonny (or Bo or Mitch) would curse in the presence of the Center supervisor or *at* him in response to a command. The supervisor would invariably reply: "You're barred from the Center for two days." In response, the guilty party and others of the boys would swear again, or, if an order had been violated ("Don't kick the volley balls, you know it's against the rules"), they would continue the forbidden act (kick more volley balls). With each act of defiance, the supervisor would add time from the Center. The most aggressive behavior the observer witnessed occurred when a new supervisor apologized for being "rigid" after such an incident, and asked to join the boys in football. It was as though they thought—"Let's see how far he will go."

Ike and Mike were at no time barred from the Center for such active rebellion. They were first to protest a decision to oust another. On occasion, they explained to higher authority sent to investigate these local difficulties that the guilty party had *not* cursed at first, but that the supervisor was a little hot-tempered for one in his position. Ike told the observer that they were trying to wear the supervisor's patience thin, so that he would commit actions requiring his removal. Ike claimed that they had gotten rid of one official that way.

During six weeks of the months they were studied, the entire group was barred from the Center as punishment for behavior on the lawn. All of them had been drinking. The observer saw them rolling about, shouting and scuffling. The impression was that none could walk steadily. Yet, in pairs and individually, they showed a more sober state to the observer. He could not help feeling that this great drama was somewhat similar to their replies, early in their acquaintanceship, to his question "How-ya been?" when each replied (with elaboration and individuality): "We've been in jail."

When not at the Center, the boys were in cars, at one of their homes, or in a pool hall near the Center. Then the policeman on the beat kicked them out of the pool hall for excessive boisterousness. Riding about in cars, racing, cutting corners over the curb, shouting out the window to other cars and passersby was a regular pastime.

Ike and Mike had the use of their parents' cars—nice automobiles of recent vintage in the low-priced field. Bo was given use of his parents' new car (in the middle price range), but kept it for over thirty hours without returning home. During this time, he succeeded in knocking the wheels of this extremely handsome car crooked, by going over curbs. With his promise that he would return it promptly henceforth, Bo's parents promised him a car of his own. Whereupon Bo did, indeed, return the new car promptly.

Fox worked as a delivery boy until 3:30. During the study, he saved and bought a 25-year-old car. He was tremendously proud of it, though he said it had no brakes. The observer, at his invitation, drove it, and found this to be true. Some six weeks later, Fox got a 7-year-old model, without trading in the old one. His mother signed the note. These cars were the only ones always readily available—really their own. They became a center for group activity, without Fox taking over from Ike, however. When the car needed repairs, the entire group would become concerned, go to the garage, discuss the matter. Certainly, Fox acquired greater importance in the group as a result. When he decided to have his hair cut short like Ike's, the barber misunderstood and cut it all off. Ike—appearing with a similar "butch"—reported he had said, "Oh, what the hell!" and had his shaved too.

It was Ike's word which counted, and Ike who masterminded the plans. He was attractive, and better in some sports even than Fox. Much more than Fox, Ike knew the ways to get along with adults and girls. Ike stood and walked with a slight slouch, tipped his head at an angle, and looked at you from the corners of his eyes when he spoke. It was not without charm. It took the observer some weeks to trace the peculiar way all the boys stood and talked to this rather charming mannerism of Ike. Each, in his own way, had emulated Ike's slouch and oblique gaze. It was strange that it made Fox seem shifty.

Ike, Mike, and Fox had accumulated large traffic fines. When they first began to talk of them, the observer equated the talk with the "I've been in jail" routine. They did worry about these fines. Mike's amounted to ninety dollars. Fox managed to pay for his from his wages, and he got Ike a job delivering with him—after Ike refused to work any longer for his father in his restaurant.

The parents were insisting that the boys discharge their responsibility to the traffic court. Unlike Ike, Mike did not take effective action—and his fines were larger. At last he was sent to live with his father's ex-wife and her husband, who gave him a job in his upholstery business. He now lived several miles from the Center, but he continued to drive over after work to be with the boys. But it would be 5:30 or 6 before he could make it. His frequent absences resulted in Mike's fading as "something" in the group. At last, Fox said he thought Mike had changed. He seemed to think he was too good for them. Ike seldom referred to his brother these days.

One day they hailed him in the upholstery shop truck and urged him to come have a hamburger with them. Reluctantly, he explained he had to be back to the store by five. Their appraisal of the change in him from the free-wheeling Mike they knew was confirmed.

Sonny caused a lot of trouble one night. At a dance at the Center, he started making sexual remarks about the girls in a loud voice, and he didn't stop. Outside, Ike told him to stop or he would stop him. Fox said, "Lay off him. I'll get him to stop." Ike insisted that he was the one to stop him. An internecine fight broke out, splitting the group right down the middle. The police stopped the fight.

The next day Ike and Fox were quiet, and not speaking. Even the girls regretted this state of affairs: "They are such good friends." Reconciliation occurred the following day, when Ike told Fox he had been overcome when his mother had told him about a phone conversation with Fox's mother. Each mother had blamed the other for her son's behavior. Ike and Fox laughed until their sides ached. They were old buddies again.

Here is a fairly typical afternoon in these boys' lives, starting at 3:30 and lasting for three hours. If they played ball, something like this followed—ball, Ping-pong, and cards could be forgotten because of car trouble.

Only Sonny was missing this day. Mitch and Bo were playing Ping-pong. When they saw the observer, Bo said: "Hey man, have you seen Fox's car?" To the negative, he continued: "They should be here any minute. Fox has had a lot of trouble with his new car, and we're going to take it to the shop." Then followed an explanation of the malfunctioning of the car, which was repeated in even finer detail by Ike and Fox when they roared up a few minutes later with Bobbie and Donna.

Mitch, Bo, and the observer were invited into the car. Fox gunned the motor, and away they went, taking every corner on two wheels. Fox explained that his new car had a defect which could be repaired for $168, which he had borrowed from another finance company (his mother signing the note) for $13 a month.

Ike said, "Fox, don't you think it'd be a good idea to go by your house and get your old car so we won't be stranded at the garage?" Without a word, Fox executed a sharp U-turn and drove to his house. Ike took the wheel of the old car, joined by Bo, Mitch, and Donna.

After leaving the new car at the garage, they drove to a drive-in for a drink. Bobbie, enjoying his drink outside the crowded car, said he had to go home. Fox said, "Hop on," and they sped away with Bobbie on the running board of the old car. Fox drove as close to parked cars as possible to see if Bobbie would "scrape off." This went on for ten minutes, though Bobbie's home was not far away. The observer, somewhat perturbed, asked if "the Law" might get them. Fox showed him three tickets received that day, one for speeding. (Fox said, "Fifty-five in a 30-mile zone," but the ticket said, "Forty-five in a 35-mile zone.")

After dropping Bobbie, Ike said: "Let's go to see Mike. I think he's off work by now." The drive took 15 minutes, and they waited another 15 for Mike. Mike joined them in a drive around the city streets, heading somewhere it seemed. Ike said they should get a baseball game with the McKinley boys, whom they had played before. Fox seconded the suggestion strongly, and they all discussed strategies to use to win this time. Mike complained that his job kept him until five every afternoon: "I don't like not being able to play ball with you guys." Ike said: "Fox and I got fired today," explaining that the boss they delivered vegetables for had said they were too slow, so they started throwing tomatoes at him and left. This was good for a big laugh.

Then Ike turned to plans to go to a statehood celebration in a small town where, he said, his sister was to be crowned "queen." Ike, Mike, and Fox planned to go and pressed everyone, including the observer, to join them. Ike warned: "You'd better not back out on us, or you've had it."

Bo asked to be dropped by his house for supper, and Mitch got out there too. Ike, Mike, Fox, and Donna left the observer by his car at 6:30. They had driven for an hour.

NEAR THE BOTTOM

The poor neighborhoods of large cities are usually identified with tenement houses, crowding, and impoverishment. The poor neighborhood we shall look at held impoverishment, and it was crowded, especially with children. But the large families of six to twelve lived in three- or four-room frame houses. Almost all of the adults were first or second generation from Mexico. Fathers and mothers worked, usually regularly and hard, earning a total of about $200 a month at the most. Only one boy whom we shall meet had no adult male head of his family. His mother had a good job as a waitress, earning $45 a week on which she supported her five sons.

An observer goes to a city park bordering the neighborhood. He is Spanish-speaking himself, having grown up in another part of the city. The park is full of children of all ages, couples, and young adult men who talk and play basketball or baseball. Everyone seems to know everyone else. The young men who frequent the park and the nearby pool hall—Perez Place—joke with the teen-agers, usually with insulting names: *"El Africano," "puto"* (homosexual, but also used with variations for anyone to be despised), and other sexual terms. The younger boys take the insults without reply. To be singled out for an insult is, after all, not to be ignored. They trade insults themselves, the younger and those with less prestige getting more than others. It is standard to return the insult, preferably with a worse or more humorous slander. But to the young men, only Juan (an almost ugly, short, sturdy teen-ager) hurls *"puto"* back.

The observer decides he has no chance with the teen-agers unless he is recognized by the young adult men first. He takes a ball to the park and works out near the young men. They join him, giving him chances over several days to explain that he needs to keep trim, that he would like to be a coach, too, but he has never worked with teen-agers—which is where the jobs are. He says he could get games with other teams outside the neighborhood if he found a group that wanted to play. He pays no attention to the teen-agers, although there are four or five bunches of them around.

Cutting a much longer story short, the upshot is that a teen-ager named Jesse, a good player, approaches him saying he hears that he could get basketball games for them. The observer is wary: "Why don't you fellows play in the church league with St. Anthony's?" "We tried that," comes the reply. "It's no good. We can't get along with the coach." The observer tentatively agrees, and makes a date to meet the fellows the next day.

At the appointed hour, no one shows up. At the nearby pool hall, the observer is challenged to a game by a lad of fifteen, who turns out to be Jesse's younger brother, Tony. Tony brings up the idea of team play, naming the boys who should be on the team. But it is Jesse who finally brings the boys to the park a few days later, the eight named by his younger brother. (Dompe was recruited later when they needed him as a player.) Juan, the tough one who was not afraid to answer the grownups, is the oldest, at 18. The youngest are 15, although Jesse's younger brother and Pinto are clearly considered too little. Only Lalo at 15 is regarded as a likely player. In height they range from 5 feet 2 inches to about 5 feet 10 inches. Some, like Rogelio, are good-looking, upright, and poised. Skin color ranges from Wero's light skin to the warm brown of Lalo's (whom the adults insult as *El Africano*).

Jesse said simply: "*El senor este nos puede consegir juegos con otros* teams." ("This man can get us games with other teams." Note the single English word.) The conversation, like all in this group, continued in Spanish, or more properly "Tex-Mex," the lingo of the area, embroidered with teen-age slang and invariably loaded with enormous curses. "Who would we play?" "Why don't you get fellows from some place else?"

The observer explained his reasons for being there, adding that he happened to see them play. Che, a short sturdy 17-year-old with dark brown skin, turned to Juan: "Do you want to play, Juan?" Juan answered: "Hold on, let him finish talking." The observer continued that it was kind of important for him to start with boys who played well, so that he might get a winning record right from the start. Juan said with conviction: "I'll play," turning to a self-confident attractive boy of seventeen: "Rogelio?" "I will. How about you Wero?" Wero said: "Hell yeah, *que si vacillo*," continuing in Spanish: "We'll all play and we'll all give hell to those damn guys." The others did not wait to be asked; they volunteered.

Juan said to Che: "You and Lalo will play in front and me, Wero, and Rogelio under the basket." Wero asked Rogelio if they wanted to practice now. Wero repeated the question to Juan. Juan said, "No, I'm tired. I've been here all afternoon and want to go home to eat." Che, Rogelio, and Wero said this would be best, Wero adding they could practice tomorrow. For the first time, Jesse, who had introduced the observer, spoke again: "Tomorrow night will be best for me." Rogelio said: "We'll be too tired at night to practice." Che added: "It's best in the afternoon—right Juan?" Juan said they would meet about two in the afternoon. Jesse said not a word.

The next day the practice was held, and the first match scheduled. The observer asked about Jesse. Juan said: "I don't know if he will play. Anyway, *el puto* doesn't rate any more." Some weeks later, the boys told the observer how Jesse had turned and run when another bunch of boys jumped them. He had run out on them, and the fact that he ran from a drawn knife did not alter the fact. In view of the almost complete exclusion that Jesse was subjected to by these boys and even the girls, it was surprising that the boys had let him introduce the observer to them. Apparently, getting a schedule of games was of overriding significance.

A Little History. What happened in this group of boys—eight regulars and two frequent hangers-on of fifteen—is difficult to understand without background. Before he got it, the observer had considerable difficulty in understanding why certain things happened. This poor neighborhood was also a "tough" one. There were known gangs of narcotics pushers, thieves, and auto strippers in it. Just a few years earlier, the older brothers of some of these boys were so tough that they had things their way, until tragedy hit. The owner of a small grocery had let the boys use his store to hang around, in order that he could keep an eye on his own son. What he did not know was that they used the rear of the store as an arsenal and cache for stolen goods. But when this came to light, two boys were dead and a third seriously wounded. One of the dead boys was his son. The man committed suicide.

The mantle of toughness fell to the adolescent boys as they got old enough to wear it—especially to Juan and his younger brother (16 years old), Pete. Their older brother, dubbed "El Joe Louis," had been sent to prison. He was out now, but not living in the neighborhood. Other older brothers and some of the parents were very concerned that the tragedy not be reenacted. *Machismo,* translated as manliness, was an admirable trait. It meant not being afraid of a fight, having sexual adventures but not being bossed by a girl or woman, even one's mother. But getting killed or going to jail was another thing. A social worker in the area some years previously had told them that the best way to prevent it was to get the boys interested in sports. So young adults and parents did encourage

their younger brothers and sons to play ball, which was not characteristic of the older neighborhood. Furthermore, times had changed
a bit. These boys were much more Americanized than their parents
or even their older brothers.

What the Boys Liked. Besides liking sports, the boys all watched
games on television. They greatly preferred rock and roll to popular
Mexican music, hot dogs and hamburgers to tortillas and beans,
modern dance steps to traditional ones, Hollywood movies to Mexican films. They played billiards, American style, and football. Yet
all of them were reluctant to go to a doctor or nurse, believing in
Mexican folk healing. They used English words only when they
could not be translated or adapted to a Spanish form (for example,
jukea for hook; *donguea* for dunk; *shotea* for shot). They adored
crime shows on television, such as *The Untouchables,* praising the
characters like Al Capone and his henchmen, rather than the police,
who, everyone knows, are *perros* (dogs). The attitude of local policemen, in turn, was expressed by one on seeing the observer with the
boys: "What are you going to do with those monkeys?" Upon the
reply that they would play basketball, he laughed: "*This* I want to
see!"

There was a strong sense of belonging to a community. When an
account of a stabbing was in the paper, the boys read with great
interest until the youth was identified as living in a different area.
The paper was tossed aside and not referred to again. If they lost a
game, their greatest worry was what other teen-agers and young
men in the neighborhood would say when they returned. They only
lost three games.

Yet none of the boys had been involved with police in recent
years, despite the presence of other gangs labeled "criminal" in the
area. They did joy ride in stolen cars, roll drunks, take money from
youngsters at knife point, occasionally smoked marijuana, steal soft
drinks, enter and steal from stores. But they were not caught. True,
Che had been charged with theft at a local Protestant church three
years ago, but he was just placed on probation. Juan was found in a
grocery store after closing, but he worked there and was simply dis-
charged.

Typically, their behavior together was so boisterous and tough that the observer feared for the interior of his car when he took them places. They admired the car greatly, and were most appreciative of the chance to ride. There was no deliberate action to harm it. Individually, they were extremely polite to him and other adults. Together, they acted like tough ruffians. To be with them in public was to be noted.

The observer felt, perhaps correctly, that the boys were not caught in illegal acts because they were intelligent and well-coordinated. Only Wero (17), Joel (18), and the three 15-year-olds were still in school. Wero's English reading achievement score was only at the seventh-grade level, but his intelligence test score was 100, average for his age.

The observations of this group of boys are full of evidence of the boys' attempts to avoid trouble with authority and with other groups. They took actions which might cause trouble only when circumstances were such that one had to be forthright or be labeled the equivalent of "yellow" by the others.

The Group as a Team. The observer could tell that the boys had had years of experience playing together. They could anticipate when a teammate was going to shoot, fake, make a fast break. They were highly coordinated, and a number were excellent players. The observer followed the practice of mapping out plays on paper without assigning positions. Juan would then take the paper and tell each fellow what position to play, how to execute the movements, etc. He praised their successes. When Lalo (the one 15-year-old who "counted") made an error, he cursed him strongly. Wero goofed once, and Juan threw the ball hard at his upper back. Wero turned in a fury, which he contained when he saw who had thrown the ball. Juan was never hard on Rogelio or Che, however, and accepted their suggestions on the starting lineup and substitutions. In fact, he did not seem to trust his judgment about the lineup.

The team was a good one. They won several games and chose a name, after their park. But it was Rogelio who began to explore the possibility of getting in the City Recreation League, the day before the deadline. The fee was ten dollars. Juan had all of them pool their money—the total was $1.18, of which he gave 55 cents. After the game that day, Pete suggested stopping to buy cold drinks. It was Rogelio who insisted the money was for "down payment" on the entry fee and who asked the observer if he could help them out.

Especially after entering the League, winning became very important to the boys. There was no doubt that Juan, the acknowledged leader, did not play basketball as well as the others, although he was a good softball player. Usually, there were several substitute players along. But one evening, a game was called at the last minute. The younger boys did not learn about it because they were at school, and Dompe did not turn up. He wasn't too reliable these days, because of his girl and because Juan did not let him play as often as he wanted. So there were six boys for the five-man game.

Who would start the game? Che asked the observer who should sit out first. The observer said he didn't know. Rogelio asked Che to choose five players. Che eliminated Wero, who protested that his position was indispensable against this team. Rogelio asked Juan, please, to decide. Juan thought a moment, then said he didn't feel too well and would sit out. So the game started. Juan's "illness" did not last long. Pete took himself out, then Che, and the others followed suit so Juan could play. They won the game and everyone had played.

Over the next month, Rogelio's words began to count more and more. This erect, self-confident boy had an almost uncanny ability to call plays and make selections which won the game, without hurting anyone's feelings. He never left Juan out, but Juan frequently volunteered to sit out when the team was in a tight spot, with no show of hard feelings, but for the sake of victory.

Juan was the best fighter in the group, by general agreement. But they knew Rogelio could hold his own, and would not take an insult from an outsider. Juan actually enjoyed a good fight. One evening, while spectators at a game between two rival church teams, the boys sensed open conflict arising. Even the pleas of two priests failed to quiet the vehemence of the rival cheering sections. The boys began to discuss the possibility of what to do if they were attacked. Juan said they should attack first. Rogelio, backed by Che and Wero, told him in no uncertain voice *not to start* anything. On the way home, they explained to him how seriously they could get in trouble if he did not stop looking for a fight. Later, Wero remarked that Rogelio was the best one to have along to keep them out of trouble. In two months' time, Rogelio was the acknowledged leader, though he had never competed or come into conflict with Juan. And Juan threw himself into group activities as heartily as ever; he wanted their team to win.

Since none of the boys worked regularly, those out of school habitually stayed up late and slept late the next day. Those who went to school regretted missing out on the good times the others had before four o'clock in the afternoon. This, added to the derogation of school as "kid stuff," created gnawing doubts concerning the wisdom of continuing, even for Joel with only a semester left before graduation, and for Wero, whose parents put great stock in a diploma, despite their own third-grade education. Tony and Pinto (fifteen-year-olds) had declared their intention of quitting promptly at sixteen. Then they too would have the pleasure of being together from late morning to the wee hours when Perez Place was closed to all but those in the neighborhood who knew about the rear entrance. Lalo's three older brothers had graduated, but it might be a struggle for his parents to keep him in school three more years.

Of the numerous occasions when boys had to make a decision between joining in a group activity and family obligation, or church duties (for example, attending confession), going with the group was by far the most frequent resolution. The really good members, like Wero, chose the group over steady girl friends. Even Dompe began to neglect his girl after Rogelio became captain. Whatever teachers', parents', or other adults' appraisals of this group, there was great pleasure in one another's company. Furthermore, group process had the effect of keeping individuals out of trouble with police and other groups, in a neighborhood where violence was not infrequent.

THE PLAN OF THE BOOK

This book reports research, initiated in 1958, on behavior of adolescent boys associating in groups of their own choosing. One reason for studying behavior during the adolescent period is that the individual faces a fairly prolonged period at this stage of life in modern societies, in which he is expected to reformulate his ties with others in society. He must change them from his childhood image toward those appropriate to adulthood, but for many years he is not an adult. Thus, during this period, the consequences of identifying oneself with a particular set of people and with small groups within it are far-reaching.

We could not assume that the reference groups of adolescents and their problems of conformity-deviation were identical in any social setting. Therefore, groups were studied in large cities in three types of neighborhoods: low, middle, and high in social rank. In addition to differing in social rank—that is, in economic and educational levels, standards of living and facilities—some neighborhoods housed residents from a different sociocultural background: Spanish-speaking Americans of Mexican origin whose cultural norms differ from those in other neighborhoods in a number of respects.

This book summarizes the research program to date. While the study goes on, the main procedures have been developed and a large quantity of data has been reviewed. These data pertain not only to the behaviors of adolescents over periods of several months, but to their groups, their neighborhoods, their agemates in school, their families, their relationships with adult authorities and institutions as well.

In studying adolescents in their groups and natural habitats, we encountered a host of problems concerning methods to use to secure both reliable and valid findings. Some of these problems and the ways of resolving them are decidely relevant to practical problems faced by adults who work with youth. Other problems of method, procedure, and research design are general problems in investigating human social behavior, regardless of the age of the individuals. Therefore, they are of significance to professionals and students actually concerned with evaluating or performing research. If research is to be assessed by standards of adequacy as a scientific endeavor, the theory, design, and methods of research become of primary concern.

We have grouped the discussions on research approach, methods, and design as Chapters 2–5, the design and main hypotheses being stated in Chapter 5. Chapter 6, on methods of observing groups of individuals who count in each other's eyes and who are engaged in activities they regard as important, is pertinent to problems faced by any adult working with adolescents. It is also essential for understanding the results of observation. Therefore, it is grouped with Chapters 7–10, which report the findings of the research to date.

It is possible to read the book, starting after this chapter with Chapter 6, and going through Chapter 12, returning to Chapters 2–5 with the actualities of behavior in mind. Whatever the order followed, we hope that the enormous problems in reaching valid generalizations and making accurate predictions about human social behavior will be more fully appreciated as a result. Such insight is essential for social scientists to meet the challenge of their fields, and for other readers concerned with the practical consequences of the behaviors described to assess the state of social science and its generalizations at this still early period of its history.

PART II

_Approach,
design,
methods_

2 *The problem*
and the approach

This book is concerned with the behavior of the individual as a function of membership in a group of his own choosing and of the sociocultural setting in which his group operates. It states an approach that takes into account the gamut of influences shaping the individual's behavior—whether the behavior is evaluated as good or as bad, as socially acceptable or unacceptable. And it presents research designed to take this gamut of influences into account.

The gamut of influences affecting behavior includes the individual's motives to be a part in the scheme of things with other persons who count in his eyes, and to be *somebody* in that scheme. It includes his strivings for attainment of earthly goods, sex partners, recognition, prestige, recreation, education, and work—as defined by his goals in these respects. The gamut of influences also includes the success picture prevailing in his surroundings through the living examples of persons within his reach and through the ubiquitous glamor of the picture, sound, and print to which he exposes himself day in and day out.

A list of all the influences affecting behavior would soon become long and boring. Therefore, it is preferable to pause for a moment on the two sets already mentioned—namely, the individual's own goals prompted by his inner desire to establish himself with a place under the sun, to be among those counted in that place, his needs to survive and enjoy the good things of life as others do, on the one hand; and, on the other hand, the particular goal objects and the pictures of achievement deemed desirable in his setting. These two sets of influences shaping his behavior are not insulated from each other; they are tuned to each other.

The individual's lasting and directive claims for acceptance, recognition, possessions, and enjoyment of good things in life are typically relative to other individuals. But who are the other individuals relative to whom the individual makes his claims for acceptance, to amount to something, to be a part in the scheme of things with them? Where does he stand in that scheme and where does he want to stand? Many studies in recent years have shown that the individual's personal goals are affected in no small way by the groups to which he belongs and aspires to belong—in short, by his reference groups. The gamut of influences, then, must include those groups in which the individual moves and has his being. It must include the patterning of relationships in those groups and the values cherished by members.

When the individual participates in a group of his own choosing, he contributes his bit—small or large—to its character, to the pattern of relationships, the standards for behavior, to mutual goals. But these, in turn, are also affected by the concrete conditions in which members interact and by the evaluations placed on behavior by others in the same setting.

In short, the gamut of influences affecting individual behavior is not composed of such-and-such a number of discrete items, each singly affecting behavior. It is composed of interacting influences coming from the individual himself, from his reference groups, and from his sociocultural setting. This is why the study of individual motives and characteristics as discrete objects of examination, or of groups and culture as imprinting mechanisms, are bound to fall short of a rounded and accurate account of the individual's social behavior. Thus conceived, studies of social behavior can do no more than support a continuing debate over individual *vs.* group (or cultural) determinants of behavior. At best, they show us that both are important, without telling us how to fit the pieces together.

What is needed is a conception of the individual *in* his group and cultural setting, and a conception of group and cultural setting relative to its members. This needed conception is not new. There have been such conceptions in social science for years, for example in the contributions of James Mark Baldwin, Charles H. Cooley, George Herbert Mead, F. C. Bartlett, and in the applications of Gestalt psychology by Lewin and others. Many writers have come to state the tenets of such a conception as an article of faith.

What we must do is to translate such conceptions into research operations based on the actualities of individuals coming together to form groups through repeated interactions over a *time span* and their participation, day in and day out, in these groups with differentiated status reciprocities which are lasting over time. The patterning of behavior is not only a patterning of contemporaneous events in cross section; it is also patterning of relationships and events in a temporal sequence. One can easily forget this today in the midst of the burgeoning literature on small group research.

What is needed today is the development of ways to link the study of behavior in small groups with the settings in which they actually function. There are numerous correlational studies in the literature showing actuarial relationships between characteristics of the setting and the relative frequencies of behavioral events, e.g., voting, suicide, delinquent acts, and crime. If our aim is the prediction of individual behavior, we have to go a step further. Individuals tend to set their goals and to regulate their behavior more in terms of some people than of others. Issues of conformity and deviation arise with reference to those whom they perceive to be in the same set as themselves, one way or another. This is why we need to go a step further than taking note of the generalized characteristics of an entire social setting. This further step involves specification of the values and social arrangements prevailing among those people relative to whom an individual actually gauges his own standing and performance in given dimensions.

Chapters 3 and 4 present the rationale and concepts which we have found useful in developing research strategies that accommodate the gamut of influences on the individual's social behavior.

On the basis of such considerations, a study plan was designed

(Chapter 5). Actual research was begun in 1958 and is still continuing. Chapters 7–10 review findings obtained thus far. The overall plan of this research can be outlined briefly as follows:

1. Areas of different cities were chosen, specifying their social rank as low, middle, or high in terms of indexes for socioeconomic level, urbanization, and ethnic composition recently developed by a group of sociologists.

2. The values and goals prevailing among the population selected for the research were assessed. Since the age-level chosen was adolescence, this step required assessment of the values and goals of youth in the settings of low, middle, and high social rank in pertinent dimensions. The Self-Radius and Goals Schedules developed for this purpose make it possible to ascertain the *overlap* across areas of low, middle, and high social rank in the society, and also the specification of *differences* among these areas. Furthermore, they yield data for construction of a baseline to evaluate the behaviors of specific individuals. Such a baseline is more meaningful than the appraisal of conforming and deviate behavior in terms of the prevailing values of an entire society, or a class within it, or some national average for the age-level in question. It reflects the standards and goals of persons who are peers in the same circumstances (Chapters 9–10).

3. Within each area, the attitudes and behaviors of individuals belonging to groups of their own choosing were studied intensively over a period of time. This intensive study of small groups was carried out under field conditions and was the focal concern of the research. The methods of study are specified in Chapters 5–8.

All of the data were collected for their bearing on the behavior of individuals in their small groups formed at their own initiative in the process of repeated interactions. Mindful of the fact that groups in actual life are formed under the common motivational promptings of their members—*not* for the benefit of social scientists who want to study them—one cardinal criterion of method has been to avoid cluttering the flow of interaction with procedures disruptive of the ongoing sequence of give-and-take among participating members.

The procedures and techniques of data collection were adjusted to the interaction of groups which, like any groups with unmistakable identities, have plans, have secrets of their own, and are likely to be suspicious of outsiders. In fact, the degree of suspicion and secrecy shown by the group—even to an observer who never posed as an investigator—proved to be among the useful indicators of group properties.

Procedures and techniques were abandoned that arouse the individuals's concern over how well he is performing, or whether he is behaving in ways that would be considered appropriate by the *investigator*. Indirect techniques were developed to obtain data without deflecting the direction, content, and continuity of the individual's behavior in ongoing interaction. What was missed in the way of detail by not imposing demanding and deflecting research techniques on the individual was recaptured through the use of a combination of methods (Chapters 5–7).

When research on interaction episodes within a group is not a one-shot affair, but is carried on over a time span focusing on characteristic recurrences, it has proven feasible to utilize a combination of field research methods and experimental methods. In field situations, it is feasible to introduce field and laboratory techniques at choice points in the form of problem or task situations at an appropriate time. From this point of view, our research aims at further demonstrating the feasibility of integrating field methods of social science and experimental methods of the psychological laboratory.

In the research program presented in this book, we have chosen to concentrate on adolescent behavior as a function of reference groups in specified settings. The choice of individuals at this age level is only partly due to its being in the limelight these days. Adolescent behavior is in the national limelight because of the grave picture of conforming and nonconforming, socially acceptable and unacceptable behaviors of the new generation. The grimly rising curve in the frequencies of socially unacceptable actions depicts this gravity, as duly noted by personages in positions to know the proportions of such offenses that get into the records (Chapter 12). The White House Conference in 1960 underscored the importance of the picture.

Our choice of adolescent behavior in the context of reference groups in different settings was determined mainly on theoretical and methodological grounds. One consideration was certainly the generality and relatively greater accessibility of informal groups at this age level. More significantly, the nature of the adolescent period in modern societies made this age level particularly suitable for the problem at hand.

Being in a period of transition in their lives from childhood to adulthood in a society which is itself changing at a relatively accelerated pace, adolescents are thrust betwixt and between the values of their own developing world and those of the older generation. This marginality plunges them into the throes of an unstable identity. Frustrated by the gap between their aspirations and what is afforded by the older generation, they gravitate toward one another to establish some identity in the image of their own time, as they perceive it. The product of interactions among individuals caught in the same predicament is formation of their own reference groups which serve as vehicles of reestablishing a stable identity and of mutual support toward more effective attainment of the goals defined by their personal experiences of frustration and deprivation.

The formation of informal groups by individuals caught in the same predicament of role conflict, and the same gap between expectations and what is afforded in the established scheme of things, is not a mere adolescent event. Such groups do form whenever a number of individuals are caught together in the same boat, whatever the age level, whatever the particular setting, including industrial and military settings.

Therefore, whatever we learn from the informal group formations of adolescents about the shaping of values, goals, and behavior of the individual members is applicable, at least in its essentials, to group formations at other age levels and in other circumstances. In short, conforming and nonconforming behavior in adolescent groups can be evaluated as a special case of the more general problem of the individual—group relationship and the influence of reference groups upon personal standards and goals. When research is conducted from this perspective, we may attain principles of behavior not restricted to this age level.

Our attempt in this project has been to place the individual in the context of the small group that counts in his scheme of things. The attempt has also been to place the small group in question within the context of its physical and social setting, including the formal groups and institutions in it. The study of small groups has been criticized for neglecting the reality of power relations and social control through effective sanctions so characteristic of formal organizations. The criticism is justifiable if a small group is studied as though it were an island in the midst of an ocean calm. When the individual is studied in the context of his group, and the group properties (its status hierarchy and its social norms) are assessed relative to its setting, the study of small groups does entail consideration of the larger organizations and institutions within whose bounds a small group operates.

3 *Behavior of group*
members in appropriate settings

I n this chapter, problems raised in Chapter 2 will be discussed
from the viewpoint of developing psychological theory adequate
to account for the behavior of group members interacting in different
settings over a period of time. We shall be particularly concerned
with developing operational tools for the study of such behavior.
After indicating some requirements of an adequate theory, we will
turn to the major features of the research strategy we adopted.

Then the main concepts used in developing operational methods
and procedures in the research will be presented for clarification,
without again reviewing the empirical literature on the basis of
which they were formulated (see Sherif and Cantril, 1947; Sherif,
1948; Sherif and Sherif, 1953, 1956). However, representative illustrations will be given.

PROBLEM: RELATIONSHIP BETWEEN
MAIN VARIABLES: INDIVIDUAL BEHAVIOR,
GROUP, AND THE SETTING

Our problem concerns the shaping of the individual's behavior in
terms of promptings from within himself and from other people
with whom he has traffic, day in and day out, either in person-to-
person relationships or through mediums of communication. In
other words, it involves the individual behavior-group-neighborhood

(setting) relationship—which problem is one of the most crucial in all social psychology. Especially prominent in the problem are the ways the individual comes to conceive himself as a person with definite goals for attainment, which henceforth become inner promptings for his behavior. These goals pertain to the objects he feels he must possess; the car he wants to own, the kind of house and neighborhood where he wants to live; to the people and groups by whom he wants to be accepted, whose approval or disapproval count for him; to the work he wants to accomplish; to the kind of sexual mate he wants to have; and to all of the allied achievements that these imply.

Despite the increased prestige and research funds accruing to the "behavioral sciences" in the country in recent years, it cannot be said that any one of them offers an adequate, rounded picture of individual-group-setting relationship. There is no dearth of theorizing. But some of the theories are diametrically opposed—attributing to "the individual" or to "the group" or to "the situation" or to "society" exclusive credit or blame for the plight of man. Hence the frequent reference to the "individual approach," "group approach," "culture approach," etc., in the controversies on these topics. Other theories, with varying success, attempt to reconcile or integrate all of the facts, including those which one-sided views of the problem inevitably ignore because of an exclusive focus on individual *or* on group *or* society *or* culture *or* subculture.

Discussion and critical evaluation of even the major current theories would take us too far afield from the tasks of this book. More pertinent here is sober consideration of what is needed to achieve an adequate and valid scheme to account for social behaviors of the individual and to predict them.

Needed Approach and Operations

The prerequisite for adequate theory, to be sure, is a basis in verifiable facts. Without question, there is a large body of research evidence available from the psychological laboratory, from experimental and field studies of small groups, from attitude surveys, from neighborhood and community studies, from studies of social organization and culture, from case histories, personal and public documents. The formulation of hunches (or hypotheses) about the significant variables to be included and their relationship must be guided by such facts at every step. Everyone seems to agree with this conclusion in the abstract.

What does "being guided by facts" mean concretely? It means a continuing process of checking hunches or hypotheses—checking them comparatively against findings in other settings and in other historical periods. For the researcher in any one academic or professional vineyard, it also means checking against the products of other vines. An adequate social psychological theory should not conflict with verified facts from sociology, anthropology, economics or history.

Our surveys of current theory and empirical research have pointed to another need for adequate theory: Tools which can be used in studying individual behavior *and* group *and* setting in their *relationships,* not merely one or the other separately. These tools include conceptual tools which enable one to generalize a variety of related facts. They include procedures and techniques for measurement which permit the concepts to be linked to one another as clearly and concisely as possible.

Historically and currently, those theories which handle the available facts best are those that formulate problems of social behavior in terms of individual *and* group (societal) relationships, rather than individual *vs.* group or society. If these theories are ever to be evaluated as scientific theories, they must be translated into operations, procedures, and techniques yielding data which can test hypotheses. In other words, an urgent need today is for tools to relate psychological data on individual experience and behavior, sociological data on group organization and functioning, and data concerning the settings in which these occur (ecological, physical, economic, cultural).

Several obstacles to the development of an adequate and rounded theoretical scheme for social behavior are immediately obvious. The first is that no one branch of human study has at hand the necessary tools and techniques. This obstacle is not insurmountable. Even though, in this age of specialization, "laboratory techniques," "survey techniques," "field methods," and "content analysis," for example, are usually employed by different investigators performang different kinds of research, it is perfectly feasible to bring any or all of them to bear which are appropriate for the problem at hand. By a *combination of methods,* new and more effective tools may emerge. Others can be devised. The findings obtained by one technique can be compared with findings obtained through another, to check the *validity* of conclusions.

A second obstacle lies in the extremely general nature of the problem. Broadly formulated, the problems in the individual-group-setting relationship include social psychology from birth to death, in all places and times. This staggering scope need not, however, force a retreat to discrete formulations applicable only to, say, sophomores of a small midwestern college, boys 13–18 years in one urban slum, or residents of Samoa. It does require a *strategy* to insure some generality to research results.

One feasible research strategy is to select a critical period of human development and to study behavior in groups during this period, intensively and comparatively, in relation to different settings. By using a combination of methods, bringing to bear the precision of laboratory techniques on the valid processes to be found in the stream of actualities in the field, some headway may be achieved toward developing an adequate and an operational theory.

Research Strategy Used

Since 1958 our research has specifically concentrated on a program studying behavior in groups which function in different settings. The strategy of the program, which is continuing, involves two major features.

First, for reasons we have indicated, the research represents an attempt to integrate conceptual tools and methods traditionally associated with experimental psychology, on the one hand, and with field work in the social sciences for study of groups and neighborhoods, on the other. Throughout, a combination of techniques has been used to cross-check the findings. For example, descriptive statistics on the neighborhoods were compared with the ways individuals living in them sized up their own neighborhoods and others'. Ratings of status in the groups were checked by ratings of independent observers, behaviors in special problem situations, and perceptions of the group members themselves.

Second, a strategic period of human development—adolescence— was selected because of the manifold evidence that the variables affecting individual-group-setting relationships can be seen in clearer focus during this period than, perhaps, any other. Adolescence, in any known human society, is distinguished as a period of change— a time of transition from the status of a child to that of an adult, socially as well as physically. It varies considerably in duration and in the manner in which the transition is achieved in different societies. But everywhere, this period of physical maturation is marked by a changed position for the individual, requiring of him a shift in loyalties, in his activities, in his demeanor, and in his conception of himself in a number of significant respects. Thus, problems of relationships among individual behavior, group and setting are thrown into bold relief in the adolescent period.

Our research program has studied behavior of adolescent boys in groups with which they associate by their own choice, whose activities were not directly initiated or programmed by adults, and which functioned in large cities in neighborhoods characterized as "high," "middle," or "low" in rank through the use of sociocultural indexes. Its design allows for needed checks and comparisons, taking variations in setting, groups, and individuals into account. It is not just another correlational study of behaviors and urban areas, nor a survey of a single community or socioeconomic level.

The Paradigm: Behavior in Small Adolescent Groups

As indicated in the above paragraphs, adolescent social behavior was selected for study, not for its own sake, but because adolescence is a crucial period of transition implying shifts in the scheme of the individual's relatedness to other individuals, changes in his claims as a person relative to the opposite sex, and to different tasks and responsibilities to be shouldered. Such changes require associated shifts in his outlook and behavior. The adolescent's regulation of his behavior in terms of the established grooves and expectations of the adult generation and his deviations from these grooves are significant problems for the social psychologist in studying individual-group-setting relationships.

Especially in complex and multifaceted urban areas, the study of the adolescent's acceptable and unacceptable behaviors, as appraised by the prevailing standards in the adult setting, may contribute significantly to the state of affairs in social psychology and the social sciences. His more serious deviations from established acceptable grooves and expectations of adults, referred to as "delinquent" behavior, are dramatic instances of unacceptable behavior, calling forth social and even legal sanctions. Delinquent behaviors, as dramatic instances of deviate behaviors, have implications for the problem of our research, even though it was not undertaken to tackle delinquency as the serious social problem which it is on the contemporary scene, as in studies undertaken by various agencies and action programs.

Any investigator engaged in basic research on formation and functioning of groups, the motivational bases of the behavior of members, their solidarity and morale, cannot help finding highly instructive leads for theorizing in the behavior of members in groups that engage in socially unacceptable ("delinquent") modes of behavior. Groups (such as some adolescent gangs) which engage in various types of socially unacceptable activities provide some of the clearest cases of tightly knit group functioning, with sharply defined leader-follower relations (status pattern) and a strict code with inescapable consequences for the behavior and outlook of individual members.

The statistical fact that the overwhelming majority of unacceptable behaviors of a serious nature committed during this transition period are attributable to members of adolescent groups makes it imperative for the psychologist interested in explaining social behavior, as well as the social scientist interested in the social problem, to study the formation and inner workings of such groups. For the psychologist, study of the formation and functioning of such groups involves basic problems of motivation—of deprivations of basic needs for food and shelter, frustrations, and aspirations to be accepted by other human beings.

Such groups also provide a singular opportunity to study the acquisition, or *learning,* by the individual of new goals on the basis of significant encounters with his surroundings, interpersonal relationships, and exposures to media of communication. This problem area is of general importance in psychology. Accounting for the particular goals individuals set for themselves related to belongingness, acceptance, worth of the school and achievement in it, occupational attainment, and the like, necessitates an understanding of stimulus conditions (including family, church, school, occupational, and social agents, heroes and villains, the success-failure models they encounter in their neighborhoods, through movies and television). A broadening of orthodox psychological schemes to include the study of these various conditions is indicated.

INDIVIDUAL MOTIVES AND GROUP TIES IN ADOLESCENCE

Empirical reports abound with cases showing the effective part played by adolescents' membership in groups in their participations in "antisocial" or socially unacceptable behaviors. In the literature on gangs, especially in the writings of those oriented toward practical programs to develop preventive and ameliorative measures through police action and agency intervention, there is a discernible tendency for some to view gangs as if they were pathological formations—in a class all their own. It is true that in common parlance, the label *gang* is used for formations whose members engage in antisocial or socially unacceptable behaviors.

In our opinion, the conception of gangs as unique formations in a class of their own makes advance in the analysis of their formation and the behavioral consequences of membership well-nigh impossible. We have noticed that school administrators and agency personnel are quick to deny the presence of gangs, even though they may be having problems with groups—which they usually prefer to call "cliques."

When an investigator conceives gangs as a unique type, he is blocked, by emotional fixations, from objective study of the underlying motivations and processes of their formation and functioning. Failing to see commonalities with other kinds of groups, he is forced into seeking a unique etiology of gang formation to account for the nature of their values or norms. Such typology restricts the perspective, preventing one from viewing formations such as adolescent gangs in the light of generalizations from a large body of factual evidence. Factual evidence indicates the following:

1. Group formations are a general phenomenon in adolescence whenever individuals with motives and interests conducive to interaction (regardless of their specific content) *do* interact over a period of time. This fact can be amply documented by the surveys of data contained in any standard adolescent text (*cf.* Blos, 1941; Bossard, 1948; Horrocks, 1962; Kuhlen, 1962; Zachry, 1940). These formations may be designated by various names, such as *friendship circle, peer group, cliques, buddies, clubs, "our set," "our crowd,"* or *interest group.* By whatever name they are called, whatever the spheres of activity the group customarily engages in, there are certain organizational or structural properties common to them all, which allow extraction of common principles concerning their formation and functioning.

2. Intensive study of adolescent group formations warrants the second important generalization, that the impact on behavior of membership in informal groups during adolescence is not peculiar to formations labeled *gang,* but is established for group formations of sufficient structure and stability—no matter what their particular activities. This feature will be developed later in this chapter, and more fully in Chapters 7–10.

Hence, the first step in the analysis of group formation and the consequence of membership for the individual should be assessment of those motives and goals of the participating individuals which, under prevailing conditions of the given social setting and neighborhood, are instrumental in bringing them together to interact.

Self-Radius and Goals of Adolescents

Earlier in this chapter, adolescence was characterized as a period of change, physically and socially, from the status of childhood to adulthood. The extensive studies of adolescents in this country document the new problems faced by the individual during the period —new urges and new dilemmas which he cannot ignore, many of which cannot be satisfied or solved in socially acceptable ways until he too is recognized as "adult." The years of seeking solutions may seem very long while they are experienced.

Even if the child has had stable ties with his social world (as a boy or girl, an obedient son or daughter, good or poor student, good buddy on the playground), the adolescent period shakes these links between self and environment. Even if age-grading of social life did not adequately inform him, his changing body with its unaccustomed new feelings would tell him that he was changing, and must change relative to the opposite sex and to many aspects of life important for approaching adult status.

But, in most industrial societies, the developing adolescent faces a period of years during which he is neither child nor adult, neither boy or man, girl or woman, neither wholly dependent nor wholly independent of adult authority—he is betwixt and between. This marginal state of the adolescent is apparently general in western, industrial society, at least in western Europe and the United States. A recent comment on the serious problems of youth in Western Europe concluded: "They arise primarily from the uncertainty of adults regarding the role that young people should be given in the life of the community." (Mays, 1961, 31.)

Until the legal age for work, the adolescent is not entitled to become economically independent, and with the increasing technological development of a society, finds himself even then in demand for only the most unskilled, low-paying jobs until he acquires valued skills. In order to acquire these skills, he has, in effect, to accept his dependency. Individuals who have undergone instability in their ties with others and their environment—whether because of unfortunate personal relationships, persistent "marginalities" of status or group membership, or natural or social catastrophes—know that uncertainty is painful and may become unbearable.

In striving to reestablish ties with their social world in stable fashion, at least for a time, to test and prove themselves as developing males or females, adolescents look for opportunities around them, as does any human being. In societies of rapid change, such as most industrial and many preindustrial societies today, the adolescent may find that the adult generation provides no clear-cut solutions which he can accept. Furthermore, he may find that adults have little sympathy or real understanding of his plight, with their usual counsel to be "good," go to school, and wait for adulthood. Hence, in addition to the "psychological weaning" from beloved adult figures which is deemed desirable and natural during adolescence, there comes a rift between the older and younger generation. The rift is expressed by adolescent offspring of sympathetic and modern parents in such terms as "my parents and teachers are all right, even fine; but after all, they are grownups." Children of parents with more traditional notions may come into open conflict with them.

Thus, the adolescent living in a setting where opportunities for peer contacts are available, either formally or informally, turns more and more to others caught in similar dilemmas—to his age-mates who can really understand him. Meanwhile, through interactions with them, through the dictums of adults at home and school, and through the images built by the mass media of communication, the radii of his self-image are expanding in various respects from their more limited childhood scope. They reach to the future and to the various spheres of activity which loom as more important problems than in childhood and which, for the first time, acquire immediacy. Ordinarily, he becomes much more mobile, physically and psychologically. Adults do not expect him to be supervised as closely as in childhood. Both physical and psychological mobility are epitomized by the youth with a car, with all of the varied adaptations it makes possible.

When a society is complex, with residential centers and school districts segregated in terms of sociocultural, economic and ethnic lines, the developing adolescent in one setting sets his sights for himself and future attainments in terms of very different circumstances than those of another setting. The circumstances may support or thwart him, may open or close doors of opportunity, may widen or restrict the alternatives available to him.

Owing to the increasing interest in this country with equality of opportunity for youth, with utilizing potential talents, and controlling socially unacceptable behaviors, there has been much discussion of the values and goals of adolescents in different settings within society. Lacking, for the most part, adequate empirical evidence, but noting official statistics on the positive relationship between school dropouts, delinquency and socioeconomic level of neighborhood, there has been considerable speculation about what values or goals of youth would account for these figures.

Some writers, characterizing dominant values of public institutions as "middle class," have engaged in controversy over whether all youth, regardless of life circumstances, internalize these values common to the entire society, how much they do, or whether, on the contrary, youth in lower class settings have entirely different sets of values and goals (cf. Cohen, 1955; Miller, 1958; Bordua, 1961). The parties to these controversies are not sufficiently aware of the fruitless nature of the discussion without specifying the problem further and without rounded empirical evidence. It is not possible to state whether all youths set their sights in terms of a common yardstick or whether different yardsticks are used in various settings unless the values in the yardstick can be measured.

As an integral part of our research on behavior in groups, data were obtained in areas differing in socioeconomic level and relative acculturation on the *self-radius* and *goals* of youth residing there. Here it is sufficient to note that our results indicate that the question has to be phrased in terms of "which values" rather than whether "the values" of such and such a class are shared by others.

Our results do indeed indicate goals common to youth in settings of high, middle, and low rank. The greaest unanimity occurs in desires for material possessions: Everyone wants a car, television set, telephone, nice clothing, and comfortable housing in the most attractive parts of their cities. But, in the most significant spheres of activity related to attaining these goals, for instance, education, occupation, income, there are differences between settings—not only in the goals set by youth, but in the criteria by which success-failure is judged and evaluated.

By comparing the *latitudes of acceptance* and levels of goals in various dimensions among different social settings, it becomes possible to establish empirical, quantitative baselines for assessing the behavior and goals of single individuals living in a particular setting. This has been the aim of this aspect of our research, as indicated in Chapter 9, where methods and results of the study of self-radius and goals are reported.

GROUP FORMATION
AND ITS CONSEQUENCES
IN ATTITUDE AND BEHAVIOR

We have referred to group formations without formally spelling out what is formed that may be called a "group." As the designation implies, what is formed has bounded properties. These bounded properties distinguish group members from a mere conglomeration of individuals who just happen to be in one place. In this section, the essential group properties and their consequences in the attitude and behavior of individual members will be briefly summarized. They will be expanded in Chapters 4–7.

When a group is formed, members that belong are delineated from those who are not "in," making allowance for those who may be on the fringes. This is *delineation* of the group from its surroundings. Depending on the importance of the issue at hand, certain topics are topics of conversation only among those who are "in."

On the *organizational* or structural aspect, group members are related to one another with definite role expectations involving status differentiation and task differentiation among them. In more familiar terms, this is the aspect in which leader-follower relations in carrying out joint activities are prominent.

On the *normative* aspect, a code or a set of values (norms) peculiar to the particular formation, in addition to what group members may share in other respects with other people of their community, is an essential product of group formation. The code of the group comes to define and regulate what is acceptable and desirable in the attitude and behaviors of group members. The norms, defining the latitude of acceptable behavior and out-of-bounds behavior that calls for correction and sanctions, are not simply imposed arbitrarily to bring about blind conformity on the part of individual members. The consequential norms pertain to spheres of activity related to motives and goals that were conducive initially to frequent give-and-take (interaction) among members. Norms peculiar to informally organized groups are not impositions from outside, but are products of internal give-and-take which regulate relationships and behaviors of members. Conformity to them is not independent of the reciprocities among members which develop through the rise of organization.

Formation of a group is not brought about for the convenience or benefit of social scientists who wish to study role relations, or conforming and nonconforming behavior, or consequences of conformity or nonconformity. Group members form groups and perpetuate them with their sense of belongingness, sense of solidarity (cohesiveness), sense of responsibility, and sacrifice relative to one another, because they discovered in their initial give-and-take that they had common concerns, shared deprivations, frustrations, or goals. Or they discovered, in time, that they find mutual support in one another's company, that they can attain goals directed by their common needs more effectively if they share secrets and engage in activities in concert.

Once formed, *informally* organized groups, with their bounded demarcation, role pattern defining mutual expectations, and internally binding code cherished by members, become the source of the sense of belongingness, of amounting to something, the sense of mutual obligation and support. Henceforth, the approval or disapproval, blame or praise, the bounds of propriety and impropriety which are to be heeded, are intimately tied to the extent of the importance of the group in the scheme of the individual's life at the given time. In conceptual terms, the attitudes (stands) the individual upholds and cherishes, the rules that he considers binding for regulating his behavior, are those defined by such *reference groups.*

The foregoing broad characterization is an approximation, at this point, of the consequences in the attitude and behavior of the individual of his reference group ties. *Reference group is defined here as the group with which the individual identifies or aspires to belong.* This approximation is deliberately presented in broad strokes without specificity in content, for it is applicable to any age level. In the present context, the relevant implication is that underlying the individual's membership in *informally organized* groups through his own choosing, there is a motivational base in terms of the individual's sense of identity, the stability of this identity, his need for human company and mutual support, his felt need to act in concert with the fellow group members for the effective attainment of his cherished goals.

Because of the feasibility of conceptual analysis and empirical follow-up, we found it convenient to study the motivational base and formation of groups during adolescence, with their unmistakable consequences in the attitudes and behaviors of members.

Group Formation of Adolescents

In highly differentiated and "casually patterned" Western societies in relatively accelerated tempo of transition, the new and old, complementary and conflicting values survive side by side. Especially in such settings, adolescents are confronted with conditions that create serious motivational problems in their transition from childhood to adulthood.

With the onset of the "adolescent spurt," even before then nowadays according to Jessie Bernard (1961), the boy or girl is confronted with the feat of attaining an adult role as man or woman in so many dimensions. The sex role, as male or female, an occupational role, educational attainments, and various social roles are among the examples of the dimensions in which adulthood has to be attained with the attendant tasks, responsibilities, and privileges.

The adolescent, through the example of agemates and those slightly older and through mass media of communication, acquires ideas of the desirable steps and processes in establishing himself as an adult. But parents and other adults have their own ideas as to what these steps should be, in terms of the proprieties as they, in turn, conceive them. In cultures in transition, which are characteristic of our time, there are usually gaps and differences in varying degree between adult notions and adolescent notions as to the timing, steps, and processes involved in the transition to adulthood. Owing to such differences, the usual case is adult-youth conflict in at least some dimensions.

The adolescent is more impatient than the adults who have something to say about it, to prove himself in an adult role, especially under immediate promptings of his newly developing urges, in his cravings to acquire instrumentalities, such as money and a car. As a consequence, the adolescent comes to feel that adults (teachers and parents) are, at least in some respects, incapable of understanding him and are nothing but obstacles to his strivings to establish himself as a grown male (or female) in relations with the opposite sex, in his notions of recreation, in his choice of friends, in pursuing occupational lines, as the case might be. The by-product is his craving for emancipation from adult control.

He discovers that he is not alone in these feelings nor in his plight: His agemates are in the same boat. Hence, they gravitate toward one another to exchange notes and, in time, to seek ways and means to take steps in concert which assert themselves and satisfy their desires. This assertion may lead to associated behaviors that are, for their age, acceptable or unacceptable to parents (e.g., smoking, drinking, regulating their own time schedules, choosing their own friends, seeking access to a car and other instrumentalities, sexual experimentation, drug addiction).

In the course of repeated associations, more stable role expectations among them develop, with the more resourceful being looked up to, with needed mutual support and loyalty for one another, with shared secrets, the relative *secrecy* depending on the seriousness of their plans relative to the adults and other outsiders. The end product is formation of a delineated group with reciprocal role expectations, customs, catchwords, and standards for behavior seen as *proprieties* to be followed in matters important to fellow members.

Proportional to the gap between the adolescent's conceptions of the steps and procedures to be followed and those of adults, the adult-youth conflict, which is conducive to the gravitation of youngsters toward one another, is aggravated. As noted by various sociologists, the classic example in past decades was the second-generation youth of immigrant parents from various national and ethnic groups. The parents conceived the transition in traditional ways of the country of origin and the younger generation in terms of the mode of life to which they were compellingly exposed through examples, success stories, heroes and villains within the reach of their experience. Such almost unabridgable gaps also occur in countries rapidly moving from feudal or colonial to modern commercial and industrial life.

But, whether the gap between older and younger generation is wider or narrower and confined to only a few spheres of activity, there is generality of group formation among adolescents in the form of cliques, clubs, gangs, circles, and so on. They participate in them more actively and frequently than in childhood. And even youths selected as having exceptionally close relationships with their fathers reveal their heightened evaluation of the worth of agemates, compared to father, in appraising their relative performances (Prado, 1958).

Groups, "Gangs," and Their Settings

The kinds of activities engaged in by various adolescent groups are determined by the specific nature of the motives initially conducive to repeated interactions of the members and by the opportunities afforded in the setting for specific kinds of activities, freedom from adult supervision, getting together with agemates, and so on. For example, if the members come together to share sexual exploits and adventures, it makes a great deal of difference whether there is a place to meet, whether cars are available, and how closely adults check on them. Members of groups undergoing economic deprivations may steal to secure money if there are outlets for stolen goods known to them.

Conceptually, from the point of view of the essential properties of groups, the difference between groups described in the literature with different labels (*clique, gang, club*) is not whether they are internally structured and delineated from others nor whether they have a code. The code in a clique (e.g., "a boy and girl may neck at a party with others but may not leave the room together") and the code of a gang may be equally binding in nature. The binding nature of the reciprocal expectations and regulations of behavior in terms of the pattern of role-status relationships (organization) and the norms are proportional to the stability and the solidarity of the group.

All group formations referred to by various names or as different "types" (*gang, clique, club, circle, set*) have the essential properties of group formations in varying degree, namely an organizational structure consisting of differentiated roles and a set of norms (rules or standards) for behavior in activities in which they specialize (whether socially desirable or not).

Conception of all such formations as *groups,* in the sense defined here, brings coherence to their study and to the study of the behavioral consequences for members. It is difficult to gain conceptual coherence when effort is concentrated on "gangs" by those involved in preventive and ameliorative work, while researchers on adolescence concentrate on "cliques," even though there is similar emphasis on the importance of membership for individual members. In brief, group formations referred to as "gangs" and "cliques" may have similar impact on the behavior of the individual member.

Therefore, rather than sticking to descriptive labels, it may be more fruitful to concentrate study on *groups* (taking into account their settings and activities) and on the degree of their stability and solidarity, the strength of the prevailing role patterns, the degree to which the norms and decisions are binding for members in each formation. These variables, which are independent variables relative to member behavior, are not unrelated to the settings in which the groups function.

System-Subsystem (Group) Relationships

Groups do not function in thin air, but in very definite settings of space, physical facilities, instrumentalities, and other groups and institutions. So adequate study of group properties and processes, and their import for member behavior, necessarily involves study of their settings as well. If, as our data show, American youth universally desire cars, getting a car will be a problem—in a setting where members have no cars available, no money to get one, but the desire to go places—perhaps to be solved by illegal means. It will be a problem to members in a more favored setting where there are parents' cars, but no Thunderbird. Their desire for the Thunderbird may result in an unauthorized "joy ride," to the owner's dismay. But getting a car will be no problem at all for youths in a setting where parents can readily buy the car that their son feels is his birthright.

In our opinion, analysis of group formation and functioning relative to the various features of different social settings offers the only promise for an understanding of social behavior as affected by group membership, whether that behavior is socially acceptable or not. In keeping with the gold mine of empirical findings on groups engaging in delinquent activities found in the works of Thrasher (1927) and Clifford Shaw (1930, 1931), our data on social behavior in groups indicate no need for resorting to the intricacies of psychopathology to explain socially unacceptable behaviors among adolescent group members, nor to empirically dubious typologies to account for the variety of group activities. The nature of group formation, its consequences for members, and the setting in which it functions provide a more parsimonious and empirical basis for analysis.

Once a group is formed, the goals of its members—experienced by each with feelings of urgency—and the actions they impel are not isolated events. If the goals can only be realized through unacceptable activities, the knowledge that they are unacceptable need not prevent their performance. But if there are no protective adults to cover for the members in the event of detection, the members will face the wrath of hostile adults, even legal authorities. Thus, the facilities of the physical setting and adult resources combine to create conditions that Thrasher saw as conducive to the heightened solidarity and sense of loyalty among members, which characterize those groups formed in less fortunate circumstances called *gangs*. Indeed, it is generally true that conflict *between* social units results in heightened solidarity within the groups in question (Sherif *et al.*,

1961). The impact of intergroup systems upon an in-group is not peculiar to adolescent gangs, but a general variable affecting all groups and their members.

This is one example of the dynamic interplay of variables in the setting which affects group properties and the degree to which individual behavior is bounded by them—in this case, the impact of intergroup conflict upon the group and the resulting increase in loyalty among members and secrecy relative to outsiders.

Adolescent and Delinquent

The adolescent, like other individuals in other periods of their life cycles (adulthood or old age), engages in behaviors appraised as good or bad, socially desirable or socially undesirable, from the point of view of the standards or values of the appraiser. Underlying psychological principles should be applicable to behavior whether it be labeled with social approval or disapproval from the point of view of the evaluative standards of an outside appraiser. Here our concern is not whether the appraiser's standards are justifiable from the point of view of more invariant standards for the good of human beings. This serious problem is not the immediate concern of this psychological analysis, but will be considered later, especially in Chapters 11 and 12, relative to more concrete action.

As long as socially vital topics like "adolescent culture," "delinquent subculture," or "the delinquent boy" are treated as specific social problems for which practical solutions are urgently needed, they are likely to be regarded as *entities* governed by their own rules and crying for solution in their own right. Until they are analyzed as specific instances of more general problem areas, they cannot be placed in an appropriate frame of reference for adequate investigation. The former is the only way out of the prevailing controversies on these topics with their selective choice of facts to fit into theoretical predilections.

A great deal of confusion still prevails over the conception of the "delinquent," as noted by the currently well-known contributors (Cloward and Ohlin, 1960; Cohen, 1955; Miller, 1958). One reason may be the fact that research on the "delinquent" has been intimately tied (even guided) by immediate concerns to find effective measures to cope with the serious social problem. Consequently, researchers are involved in organizational ties and ideological orientations of agencies and programs; sometimes they are creating and promoting them.

An adequate formulation for theory, and hence for practice, lies in the direction of those (1) who cease to make a sharp break (explicitly or implicitly) between the "delinquent" and "nondelinquent," and (2) who approach their definition of what constitutes a delinquent item of behavior (instead of "the delinquent") in terms of more general problem areas.

The general problem areas of which delinquency problems are parts include at least the following:

1. The nature of goal-directed behavior and behavioral variations under different circumstances in adolescence.
2. Problems of deviation from what is appraised as socially acceptable behavior in given dimensions—a problem setting which strips the label "delinquent" of the special value charge which it has when used as if it were an entity.

Latitudes of Acceptance and Rejection of Behavior

In our research program, groups of adolescents are studied intensively in various cities. Some of these groups would, by usual usage of the term, be labeled "delinquent." Since our concern is accounting for behavior whether it is appraised as socially desirable or as socially undesirable, some of the groups chosen for intensive study engaged in socially acceptable activities and in socially unacceptable forms of behavior as well. Therefore, one of our tasks is to adopt a convenient scheme for distinguishing behavior as socially acceptable, socially unacceptable, or "delinquent."

In every social setting, an item of behavior is appraised as socially acceptable or not in terms of social norms established for behavior in a particular sphere of activity. A *norm* for a given sphere of behavior defines what is expected, desirable, and even the ideal mode of behavior. But the expected mode of behavior is not usually a single action. The norm allows for variations and for alternative actions, within certain bounds. Behavior falling within these bounds is within the "latitude of acceptable behavior." Behaviors in the same sphere of activity which are outside the prevailing latitude of acceptance fall within the latitude of rejection, where again alternatives are graded as to how objectionable they are.

For example, borrowing another person's possessions with his explicit permission and returning them as agreed falls within the latitude of acceptance. Borrowing without his permission is acceptable only if the owner and borrower have a relationship of mutual trust. To borrow from a stranger, even with the intent to return the item, falls within the latitude of rejection; while taking the item with the intent to keep or sell it is a highly objectionable alternative officially labeled "theft."

The *latitude of acceptance* and the *latitude of rejection,* relative to a given sphere of behavior, together constitute the *reference scale* on the basis of which evaluations or appraisals of specific behaviors are made. Every setting has its reference scales for appraisal. Reference scales, and the latitudes of acceptance-rejection within them, may be common to all constituent parts of a society. But it is also true that the relative magnitudes of the latitudes of acceptance-rejection may differ in various settings within a society. There are even matters which are considered very important and appraised in terms of clearly defined reference scales in one setting which are not at all important in others.

It is perfectly feasible to measure the latitudes of acceptance-rejection in different social dimensions and to compare those prevailing in different social groups (cf. Sherif and Hovland, 1961; C. W. Sherif, 1961).

All behaviors falling within latitudes of rejection are not appraised as "delinquent." The appraisal and corrections applied vary according to the importance of the sphere of behavior in question (e. g., respect for property is usually more important than cleanliness), and according to the extent of the deviation from the latitude of acceptance. In customary usage, the more serious deviations committed by adolescents—e. g., stealing, vandalism, rape, inflicting physical injury—are designated as "delinquent," although we have no guarantee from gross statistical evidence of how serious delinquent acts may be.

Delinquent behaviors, such as truancy, destruction of property, and theft, are deviate behaviors falling within the prevailing latitudes of rejection of society at large, whether these behaviors are detected by authorities or not. For social-psychological analysis, "undetected" instances of deviations which do not find their way into official statistics are as significant as those recorded as police or court cases. Owing to differentials in detection and handling delinquent behaviors in different settings and among members of different socioeconomic strata, the definition of the *problem* of delinquent behavior on the basis of official statistics may lead to overgeneralizations and unwarranted notions about the nature of the problem (cf. Perlman, 1959).

The analysis of delinquent behaviors in terms of latitudes of acceptance-rejection prevailing in society or in a given setting of a society is applicable irrespective of the way the particular deviate individual is handled in a given locality if detected—whether he becomes a case for the police and courts, or is handled by a social agency, or is handled privately by adult relatives. (Of course, it makes a great deal of difference to the individual, his friends, and family how the case is handled, and it makes a difference in the statistical records.)

Thus characterized, delinquency should be analyzed in terms of behaviors relative to latitudes of acceptance-rejection. Drawing sharp lines between the character of the individual labeled "delinquent" and the "nondelinquent" is of very little value from a scientific viewpoint. It is probably a rare person who, in youth or adulthood, has never behaved in ways which cannot be brought to the open, because they are within the latitude of rejection for matters concerning use of a car, obligations or duties as a citizen, matters of money, or sexual activities (cf. Perlman, 1959; Porterfield, 1946).

If "delinquent" means anything apart from a label for youthful behavior appraised as within the prevailing latitude of rejection, it is *recurrent* deviate behavior by the same individual, repeatedly committing serious kinds of deviation. Analysis of such cases in terms of recurrent deviation is preferable to study of "delinquent" *vs.* "nondelinquents," which terms are heavily charged with emotional overtones. The tendency, as in any instance of a persistently deviate individual, is to describe the "delinquent" with a string of unfavorable adjectives, which contributes very little either to research or to specifying the antecedents of the behaviors.

Irony of Greater "Sociability" of "Antisocial" Youth

In this book, the neighborhood and its larger settings are taken as the framework for study of group formation and functioning and the ways individual members deal with problem situations related to their significant motives, whether these modes of behavior are acceptable or unacceptable to society at large.

Of course, it is individuals—not groups—who have motives, and individuals who performs acts appraised as desirable and undesirable. If these motives and behaviors are to be analyzed adequately, they must be related to the group processes and settings in which they occur.

We do not suggest that motives and behaviors are determined mechanically by group or setting. Nor do we suggest that the social desirability of behavior is to be appraised in terms of the relative standards of each group or each setting. We do imply that the standards and goals of those appraised are essential data for scientific analysis, hence for prediction of behavior and even for control guided by standards deemed desirable for the good of mankind. And we do suggest that the real dynamics of behavior come through interplay of individual, group, and setting, not merely in deep, hidden wells of the individual considered in isolation.

In contrast, a widely prevalent practice is to describe the characteristics of the individual as though social behavior could be understood in terms of individuals alone, and to assign a label to the individual. One encounters this not only on the part of laymen or practitioners who have to face the uncomfortable facts of adolescent deviations in their daily work, but among investigators of problem cases.

It is a time-honored social practice to label individuals who commit unacceptable or abhorrent acts in ways which place them "beyond the pale." But we cannot seriously pretend that mere labeling increases our understanding of the behavior, or our ability to predict and control it. One form of such *a posteriori* labeling is to assign to the individual some psychopathological label or mechanism which is sufficiently sordid to account for the distaste or horror aroused in the appraiser of the behavior in question. Such accounts are comparable to the explanation of opium by Molière's character, who, in effect, defined opium as a substance with opiate effects.

Indeed, many descriptions of delinquent or antisocial youth lead us to expect morose, morbid misanthropes. On the contrary, there is evidence that a large proportion of "antisocial" youth are "sociable" in interpersonal relations, and participate more frequently than the general run of their peers in social activities (e. g., Attwood, 1933). Any contradiction here is, of course, a dilemma of labels applied in different situations. For example, in a study of "antisocial" students who had withdrawn from Michigan public schools, Dresher (1957) listed a number of characteristics associated with antisocial students, among them being: "They had more out-of-school friends and spent more time with them with greater frequency."

According to Cloward and Ohlin (1960), the estimate, based on Clifford Shaw's study of Cook County statistics years ago, that eighty to ninety percent of court cases of delinquent behavior involve members of adolescent groups, has not been seriously challenged. The dramatic significance of group membership in performing seriously unacceptable acts, like stealing, is revealed in the words of Stanley, the veteran of reformatories studied in Shaw's *Jack Roller:* "I needed someone with me to steal. I was too cowardly to steal alone. A companion made me brave and gave me a sense of security. I couldn't to save my soul steal a dime alone." (Shaw, 1930, p. 86.)

Indeed, there is some indication that prolonged participation in youthful groups which recurrently engage in serious violations of law, hence acquiring for their members labels of "delinquent," "antisocial," "malicious," "irrational," and the like, may be associated with personal characteristics generally deemed desirable in social life. On the basis of the intensive case histories and psychiatrist's reports on the five Martin brothers, all of whom engaged in similar forms of delinquent conduct in the groups to which they belonged, it was found that the brother who participated for the *shortest* period of time was also the brother characterized as "schizoid," while the other brothers were consistently pictured as "sociable," "friendly," and "loyal" (Shaw, 1938, pp. 313, 325).

It is ironic that those personal characteristics ordinarily prized in social life—friendliness, sociability, loyalty—should be associated with longer and more serious participation in activities labeled "antisocial." As Redl (1956) has observed, the seriously disturbed individual seldom belongs to a group whose members engage in seriously deviant acts because other members find that they cannot trust him.

There are, of course, individuals who recurrently engage in unacceptable behaviors without companionship. Such cases are legitimate subjects for research. However, the likelihood is greater that the investigator will achieve generalizations pertinent to the increasing incidence of detected and undetected cases of deviant behavior when he concentrates his study on behaviors by members of groups in different settings. The great bulk of serious violations of prevailing latitudes of acceptance during adolescence are performed by group members.

By the same token, the selection of informally organized groups, to which members belong of their own choosing, is indicated by the statistical fact that the great majority of youth in the country do not participate in adult-sponsored, organized social groups (cf. Horrocks, 1962, p. 283). There is evidence that such formal groups are not so tightly knit, less binding for member behavior than informal associations (Dimmock, 1937, p. 181).

Facts such as those mentioned above led us to study behavior in informally organized groups of adolescents and to our concern that the dynamics of behavior be analyzed within the framework of their functioning in relation to definite social settings.

Groups do not have hands or feet, and cannot steal and run, cannot drive a car, cannot dream, nor desire, nor long for their desire's fulfillment. Only individuals can do these things. But they do not do them without regard to those who count in their eyes, without regard to the actualities of the physical and social environments in which they find themselves, or in which they hope to move in later life.

An adequate social-psychological analysis of individual social behavior must, therefore, relate the behaviors to group-setting-culture-society in terms of empirical findings on each. These empirical findings must be related conceptually for the purposes of understanding and prediction. The research plan and procedures described in the next two chapters represent an effort in this direction.

4 *The gamut of influences shaping behavior*

M ost of the last two chapters has been an orientation to the problems for research and an approach to studying them. Undertaking research involves planning a study design and procedures, collecting data, and assessing these data. But by the time we reach the stage of collecting data, having decided upon a research design and procedures, most of the game is already played. The decisions about what is crucial and what is not, what data are needed and what can be left out, are made in the early stages of research when the problem is approached, explored, and defined for purposes of investigation.

Therefore, clarification of the problem and what is entailed in studying it are the first concern. We have seen that the problem of social behavior in groups is a multifaceted one. In this chapter, we shall present the main outlines of an approach to the study of such multifaceted problems, which provides the rationale for the research strategy adopted. The next chapter gives, in some detail, the actual research design and procedures for collecting data.

We have seen that many of the recurrent behaviors of an adolescent reflect the individual's concerns to establish himself as a person to be counted, as a man or woman, to prove himself in this capacity to people who "count" and to people who doubt him or deny him this role. They reflect his actions to do something to alleviate uncertainty, deprivation, or frustration in some respect, whether these relate to hunger, sexual desires, or desires to belong and prove himself as a person. Frequently, these actions are taken in concert with others in the same predicament. They are "goal-directed" in the sense that they reflect motivational concerns and problems faced in the adolescent period.

The goals that the person feels are desirable and that he feels he must attain are, in no small part, shaped in the course of his give-and-take with others. He seldom sets a goal with complete disregard for what others, with whom he associates, think. He can scarcely help taking into account the range of goals feasible in the circumstances in which he lives.

The conditions and influences that enter into the process of setting identifiable goals by the individual are independent variables for research on social behavior. In psychological research, there is a long and well-ingrained tradition in laboratory experiments that requires specification of the experimental conditions which are among the independent variables. Thus, we take it for granted that an experiment on vision or audition will specify the light or sound frequencies presented and their intensity. We would severely criticize an experiment on learning as a function of drive and reward which did not specify how many hours the organisms were deprived of food, how much and what kind of food they found in the goal box.

When it comes to studying social behavior, however, the same criteria for evaluating research are less frequently applied. The variables related to the setting that contribute to the shaping of behavior may be taken for granted. Or we improvise some notions of our own about the characteristics of the setting. Or we may declare that we are aware of these variables, but the job of studying them is not ours—it belongs to sociology or anthropology. By this logic, we may excuse ourselves from even reading what the social sciences have to say about these variables.

Since the psychologist's study focuses upon the individual and his behavior, it is often thought that he need concern himself only with those conditions and influences within the range of the individual's immediate interpersonal and group relations. In reaching generalizations concerning behavior that will be valid for more than one situation, the student of behavior cannot legitimately overlook the empirical question of whether the immediate conditions in which it occurs are peculiar to a particular setting or whether similar conditions prevail in other settings.

Surely, small groups are not studied for their own sake to secure tidbits of information. They are studied by earnest investigators who wish to contribute substantially to building a science of human relations that is more than an artifact of special research procedures. If their goals are to be brought within sight, the characteristics of the setting, as well as the patterned properties of interaction among members and the unique contributions of individuals, must be integral parts in the plan of study.

The definition of problems for research cannot be dictated by the preferences of the investigator, even if he is an experimentalist. For, even in the laboratory, significant experiments pertinent to an understanding of social behavior are designed by specifying conditions which have relevance to the conditions of interaction in actual social life. For example, group interaction can be studied experimentally if the investigator can see to it that the essential features common to human groups are embodied, at least in prototype form, in the design. If they are not, the experiment should not be designated a study of *group* interaction, but given a more appropriate label.

In sum, the investigation of individual social behavior is necessarily *interdisciplinary,* in the sense that it requires procedures and data ordinarily associated with several academic disciplines (psychology, sociology, anthropology, history, economics, political science, depending upon the particular content area being explored). In the remainder of this chapter, we explore further why this is so and develop an approach to research which provided the rationale of the research in this book.

INTERPERSONAL RELATIONS
IN SMALL GROUPS

The data psychologists collect consist of the behaviors of individuals, whether words or actions. Various procedures are used to obtain such data: for example, experimental methods, interviews, observation, tests, questionnaires, not excluding the free associations of a patient on the couch. The study of social behavior is no exception to this general rule. Social influences, group membership, effects of culture and technology can only be assessed through collecting appropriate behaviors from individuals through some procedures and techniques. Even motivational urges, deep-seated fixations, and psychodynamic complexes are never observed directly. A psychodynamic complex is inferred from the individual's reported associations, his reports of his dreams, slips of the tongue—items of behavior, all of them. So, too, social attitudes, status concerns and aspirations, role expectancies, loyalty, sense of responsibility and solidarity, conformity-nonconformity are never observed directly, but through inferences from specifiable behaviors—words and deeds of the individual.

Therefore, behaviors exhibited by individuals in specifiable relations with others are the principal, concrete source of data for the study of social behavior. Interpersonal relations of any consequence to an individual are reflected in a process of stabilizing reciprocal expectancies toward one another. A close look at the process will be helpful.

When two individuals meet, a part of getting acquainted is placing each other in the schemes of social living. There is an itch to find out where the other person lives, where he goes to school, what his occupation is, what his nationality is, or what the person's religion is (especially if the other person is a member of the opposite sex who appears a likely dating prospect). Even if there is no "getting acquainted," if the other person simply appears regularly in a place where we are, with no clear identification of the reason for his presence, we try to establish in our own minds some place in the scheme of things which would account for his being there.

The process of *placing* other individuals intrudes even into scientific study of behavior. Thus, the "participant observer" installed in a cottage of delinquent boys quickly finds himself labeled a "spy" for authorities, a "newspaperman," or a "writer" of books who will expose them—despite his repeated assurances that what he sees will be kept confidential (e. g., Polsky, 1962, Chapter 7). In our own research, an observer who simply hung around a crowded pool hall to see if he could identify any regular patterns of association among individuals there found to his surprise that he had been placed as a "private eye" by the other players. Overtly, all he had done was to come by himself rather regularly to play pool—accepting invitations from others if offered, otherwise just watching. He had felt sure that the place was so busy and crowded with changing combinations of individuals that his presence would not even be noted by others.

This *placement* of others in some social category certainly plays a part in shaping the process whereby individuals come to have reasonably stable expectancies about one another in interpersonal relationships. A change in our placement of a person is reflected by changes in our expectations of him, even if he tries to treat us in the same way and goes out of his way to appear as the "same old buddy." Thus, if a friend comes into a financial windfall through inheritance or promotion, we *look* for signs that he is "putting on airs." Even if we are relieved that he is not going "snooty," we do not really expect him to remain "the same." Or a fellow worker with whom a man has "kidded" and "horseplayed" is promoted to foreman. He is no longer "one of us." He is now a "management man," a particularly objectionable breed of one, in fact. Even if he has been a nice guy, the relations with his former coworkers cannot remain the same, for by definition, "foremen are management men" (cf. F. Riessman, 1962, p. 28).

Our friend is not simply a "good egg," a splendid story teller, a wonderful outdoor pal: He is also white, Protestant, an Eisenhower Republican, successful lawyer, and prominent citizen of our town. Our girl friend is not merely the most beautiful and sexually desirable person we know, the best dancer, trustworthy confidante of our secret thoughts: She is also the daughter of a respected family, member of such-and-such clubs, president of her school class, a social "catch," and so on. The fact that these individuals *are* our friends means—nine times out of ten—that the categories in which we have placed them, or certain major ones, are acceptable to us. When they are not, we may experience strong ambivalence in our feelings toward them or be caught in severe conflict situations relative to our relationship.

And where do these places we assign to individuals with whom we interact in concrete, immediate situations come from? They come from the existing or developing schemes of organizations, stratifications, and classifications in the setting of which we are parts and the larger society in which these settings are found.

What do the foregoing examples and the countless similar ones tell us about the study of behavior in interpersonal relations? *The process whereby expectations of other individuals are stabilized inevitably involves placement of those individuals in terms of some social scheme or categories.* Therefore, if we want to collect data in the specifiable locus of interaction among individuals, as we should, the larger social setting intrudes into our little microcosm—whether this is a laboratory room, a college dormitory, or a private home. To say that we are not interested in studying the larger setting, to say that that is the job of a sociologist or student of culture, amounts to the investigator saying: "I know that the behavior I am studying is affected by influences which are not immediately apparent to my naked eye and which I cannot control. But I am only interested in what *I* can see here and now in this situation." Perhaps it was a lot of trouble and effort to plan or arrange those conditions. Nevertheless, we would never tolerate such an attitude in a space scientist who decided to concentrate on, say, temperature regulation within a space capsule, without regard to the temperature outside, the speed and altitude of the capsule.

Unfortunately, much of the theory and study of interaction processes in the "dyad," the "triad," in "five-man groups," "communication networks," and "decision-making" is almost as myopic as the above remarks suggest, insofar as it focuses on interaction as an abstract process. Unfortunately, interaction is not "pure process" devoid of content, nor are its participants devoid of persisting attitudes and goals, merely because this assumption fits some convenient model or analytic technique.

There is a widespread assumption that if any influences of the larger setting (its values or organization) are effective in an immediate situation, they will reveal themselves in the words and actions of the individuals in that situation, there and then. Of course, this is the only way they could reveal themselves in a concrete, specifiable setting where the social objects and communications available are carefully controlled by the investigator. But they will not automatically reveal themselves to an observer or data-recording device not set to look for them. Social research and discovery in the enormously complicated process of human interaction is not so automatic. In short, influences of the larger setting will not be revealed in immediate situations if the investigator is not prepared to study them. Without explicit provision to include them, the study of face-to-face situations is incomplete.

The reverse of the coin gives an equally incomplete picture of social behavior. The study of cultural values and shared goals— which is a proper endeavor in itself—is frequently juxtaposed with data on individual behaviors, as though these values and goals were all the data needed to explain the words and deeds of individuals. The explanation of social behavior of individuals in terms of broadly defined cultural values is most readily given to the behavior of individuals whose values differ from our own, as, for example, certain values of lower socioeconomic groups may differ from those of the social scientist interested in problems of delinquency. In the latter case, elaborate theories of behavior have been constructed, based largely on the assumption that culture determined behavior. If this premise is accepted, we have only to compare cultures in order to understand behavior.

The result in many recent accounts of juvenile delinquency, for example, is that that "subculture" of lower socioeconomic groups is either (1) a distorting mirror of the "dominant mores" of society, (2) reaction against these dominant mores recapitulated at the individual level in a "reaction formation," or (3) unique and more or less closed from the rest of society (cf. F. Riessman, 1962, pp. 6–7). This state of affairs is, in our opinion, aptly summarized by H. W. Polsky (1962, p. 27):

We have the anomaly of very few intensive first-hand studies of contemporary deviant youth subcultures and extended sophisticated speculation about them at a distance. Each time a new finding is uncovered, the theory is stretched to make it "fit."

Polsky concludes, as we have above relative to many studies of interaction processes: "One of the chief weaknesses of the studies reviewed is that in each instance an artificial separation was made between the boys' value orientation and their actual social interaction" (p. 28).

Certainly, one of the reasons for the spectacular popularity of small group research today is the opportunity it allows for studying social behavior of individuals interacting in some constellation of interpersonal relations and with reference to values or norms in specifiable locations. Within a small group, the study of interpersonal relations, their patterning, and the value orientations prevalent in them can be related to the behaviors of particular individuals.

The Contexts in Which Small Groups Function

Like other interpersonal reciprocities, the patterns of relationships among individuals and the normative concerns in a small group are not insulated or self-contained systems. Without a picture of modern urban conditions, for example, it is impossible to account for the very existence of many small groups—the clubs, sects, corner cliques, improvement societies, and gangs which flourish in any large metropolis.

Once in existence, most small groups in the highly industrialized societies of today are constantly in contact with other groups—small and large. The harmonious or exacerbating nature of these contacts, the cooperative or competitive relationships, the complementary or conflicting nature of their directions have a decided impact upon the pattern of interpersonal reciprocities and the norms *within* the groups.

The kind of leadership a group requires, the definition of a "good member," the degree of secrecy surrounding its activities, as well as established routines for carrying out activities are decisively affected by the state of relationships with other groups (cf. Sherif and Sherif, 1953, 1956; M. Sherif, 1962). The most consequential intergroup relations are those of irreconcilable conflict for territory, facilities for activities, and social standing or control, or conversely, those of complementarity in these respects.

Without understanding the state of relationships among groups and with established figures in their setting, it is impossible to assess the claims or pretensions of one group or another. For example, we often take for granted that so many hours (6 or 7 or 8) make a "day's work" and that such-and-such an amount is "fair pay" for certain jobs. We forget that behind these claims as to what is a day's work or a fair wage are a long series of disputes, conflicts, bargains, and agreements between different human groupings (cf. Homans, 1950).

Nor can the activities and goals of a group be understood divorced from the sociocultural and organizational context in which the group functions. This context is taken so much for granted by those who are parts of it that it seems much like the earth's atmosphere: One is not even conscious of it until he climbs a mountain or flies too high without an oxygen supply. However, a person's awareness or lack of awareness does not make oxygen intake less essential in human metabolism, as physiologists inform us. Can the investigator of small groups give less attention to the context of the units he studies?

Suppose we are studying a small group and find its members taking automobiles which do not belong to them. One of the first things we need to know is that this action is defined as a deviation from prevailing latitudes of acceptable behavior. It is defined as an inexcusable assault on the property right of others. The traditional next step is to look at the individual boys in an attempt to discover flaws of character or deep-seated "needs" to which stealing is a response. Or a cultural approach would look for the existence of a "subculture" whose norms permit stealing as an acceptable activity. Both approaches to the problem pay little heed to the fact that the boys in question steal cars.

In order to understand why the boys steal *cars* or why the norms of their group do not sanction such behavior, the following information is surely pertinent: the enormous success of the automobile industry in this country; the constant reminders on radio and TV that everyone needs a car and that they are available to anyone with the money to purchase one; the system of streets and highways; the mobility and many activities a boy can have with a car that he cannot have without one; the prestige of driving in a car; even the existence of markets for stolen cars which bring quick cash, no questions asked.

Not infrequently, boys in a "favored" neighborhood take a car to go for a "joy ride"—perhaps with no intent of keeping it. How, apart from an understanding of the "car complex" in American life, can we understand that by the age of 17 to 18 most boys come to feel it is their birthright to have a car—that the world owes them a car? It would seem that the conditions responsible for this attitude are decidedly pertinent to understanding the moves that boys make to get a car—whether these moves involve hard work and saving over a considerable period of time or the dangers involved in stealing. After the general picture of car ownership and use is appreciated, then we are in a position to analyze the more immediate influences from a boy's group or from within himself which direct him toward one path or another to obtain the prized object.

PREVAILING TRADITIONS AND NEEDED ORIENTATION IN RESEARCH DESIGN

It may well be objected that the foregoing discussion sounds as if the student of social behavior has to study *everything* in order to perform significant research, and that this is humanly impossible. There should be some division of labor and responsibility.

Of course there must be, and there is division of labor in human studies: Each of the academic disciplines—psychology, sociology, anthropology, economics, human geography, political science, history—has traditional problem areas pertaining to the various aspects of social systems, their cultures and technologies, their physical resources, and human behavior. For example, sociology's province traditionally includes problems of social control, social organization, and stratification in communities and societies. Economics focuses on systems of production, distribution, and exchange of commodities. The social systems and cultures of non-Western societies are usually left to the anthropologist. Political science is concerned with political parties, power, and the governing of men. Psychology is concerned with the behaviors of individuals.

Clearly the traditional problem areas of the academic disciplines do not constitute entirely different universes of discourse. Nor are the general aims of study different; all aim at the understanding and prediction of human events and behaviors.

The more investigators in any one field have probed the complexities of their problems, the more they have become aware of the need for information, theory, and concepts from other fields of study in order to complete the picture. The need for interdisciplinary sharing and joint efforts is nowhere more urgent than in studying problems of social behavior. As we have already pointed out, the study of social behavior requires *at least* two essential sets of data (omitting for the time being data on physiological functioning):

1. Data on the behaviors being studied.
2. Data on the antecedent and concurrent conditions (correlated stimulus situations) of the behaviors.

Since the antecedent social conditions and those in which social behavior occurs consist of other individuals, groups, large organizations, institutional and community settings, technological and productive schemes, and their cultures, the study of social behavior necessarily involves crossing back and forth across the lines of traditional academic disciplines to learn about the patterned properties of the social environment.

On the other hand, the social scientist studying large organizations or culture patterns or economic systems needs an account of the motivations, expectations, and adaptations of individuals participating in them.

Especially since World War II, interdisciplinary conferences, research projects, and programs of study have increased under labels like "human relations," "culture and personality," "social relations," or "behavioral science." Even the professional schools of medicine and business administration, which once considered their walls inviolable to all but a few, are launching interdisciplinary courses of instruction and research projects. Thus we now find psychologists, sociologists, and anthropologists within their walls as staff members.

Unfortunately, most of the lessons gained thus far from efforts to meet the need for integrating findings from different social science disciplines and psychology are lessons in what *not* to do. With all the good intentions and efforts, the results are usually a patchwork of information, theory, and jargon from each of the fields represented. Or worse yet, a single discipline achieves hegemony and the theories, techniques, and jargon of its representatives dominate the picture, as frequently happens under the label of "behavioral science."

Interdisciplinary efforts have not been a total loss, certainly. But why have they not been more successful? Our answer turns upon a state of affairs which exists today in every one of the social sciences and in psychology. The resolution of this state of affairs points to ways of achieving effective cooperation and efforts (Sherif, 1963).

Variations on Two Themes

If, as we have said, the study of social behavior requires relating data on 1. the behavior and 2. its context (the social stimulus conditions), there should be no divorce between the two in the process of analysis. Yet deep in our intellectual heritage lie philosophical doctrines of individual-group relationships which have resulted, not merely in a division of labor in the study of these two sets of data, but in dichotomizing them as antithetical. From habitual concern with one or the other set of data and intensive work developing procedures to study one or the other, there have arisen not just contrasting "viewpoints," but an elaborated set of concepts and research techniques to deal with each one separately. These "viewpoints" are contrasted in each of the social sciences and psychology as different "approaches," the labels varying from one discipline to another.

Thus, we hear in psychology of the "personality oriented" approach and the "group approach" to problems of prejudice, leadership-followership, and conformity-nonconformity. In sociology, we hear the study of small groups, particularly through experimentation, contrasted with the study of large organizations and power structures. In anthropology, there is a schism between the "culture-personality" approach and the study of social systems and culture. In political science, the dichotomy is discussed as "behavioral" *vs.* "institutional" approaches. There is also an "institutional approach" in economics, which is pitted against "marginal" theory, whose mathematical model rests upon a few extremely simple and doubt-less ethnocentric assumptions about the motivations of "economic man" (Pollis and Koslin, 1962). Each of these "approaches" has a jargon and a set of favored research procedures and techniques.

In general, those approaches which center around the "individual" or "behavior" strongly favor experimental methods, standardized tests, and precise measurement of particular behaviors (e.g., reported perceptions, judgments, decisions, communications, stated opinions). Those labeling themselves as "personality oriented" are partial to "projective" techniques and "depth" interviews.

In general, approaches labeled "group," "culture," or "institutional" are less prone toward experimental methods, tests, and behavior indexes. Their focus of study is upon patterned and recurrent forms of association and modes of behavior from which the properties of social systems, organizations, and their cultural values may be deduced.

Those on the "individual-behavioral" side of the fence are accused of neglecting the central problems of their disciplines (cf. V. O. Key, 1956; D. Truman, 1955; C. Wright Mills, 1959; A. Rose, 1954), and neglect of comparative and longitudinal data. Those on the other side are sometimes viewed as "social determinists," as lagging behind the times in method and procedures, as confirmed cataloguers and classifiers of phenomena and gross statistics.

Controversies over "approach" and methods are reflected in interdisciplinary efforts in various ways. Most frequent, the social scientists and psychologists do their "jobs" with favored procedures and techniques, analyze results, and reach conclusions which seem to have little bearing on each other. Thus we may read an institutional analysis of a social system with little reference to interactions of particular individuals in it, followed by an account of the behaviors of individuals in the social system in terms of intrapsychic conflicts and needs with little reference to the social system. Or large and complex phenomena are stripped of the properties which make them of significance in order that a "behavioral scientist" may perform an experiment to secure data which fit his preferred "model," leaving his bewildered colleagues to wonder what his results have to do with the social organizations and cultural patterns they are studying.

Such disheartening outcomes can be avoided if the traditionally maintained "approaches" which sharply separate social behavior and social institutions and organizations are shed once and for all. The dichotomies, continued through tradition, do not reflect actualities of the problems studied. By eliminating them, the relationships of the social sciences and psychology are seen in fresh perspective.

RESEARCH UNITS AT DIFFERENT LEVELS OF ANALYSIS

If the false dichotomy between individual and group approaches is discarded, it becomes apparent that psychology and the social sciences approach related problems or the same problem areas at *two different levels of analysis.* The psychologist's unit of analysis, whether he is a "social" psychologist or not, is the individual. His concepts, procedures, and techniques are those appropriate to the study of individual behavior (his reported perceptions, judgments, his acquisition of skills, his motives and attitudes, and so on). Anthropologists, sociologists, economists, and political scientists all study different aspects of social systems, organization, institutions, material and nonmaterial culture. Their units of analysis are, therefore, social units, i.e., groups, institutions, shared values or norms, productive and distributive systems, religious forms, language forms, and so on. Of course, all of these things are manmade. They are produced or function through the actions of men, or at least have bearing on the designs of men. But they cannot be studied by adding up the behaviors of so many individual men, even if one had time and resources to do so.

In other words, it is neither feasible nor defensible to reduce all social study to the study of individual behaviors. True, to understand the production of this book, we would need to know something about the behavior of the writers, the editor, the copy editor, and the printers. This is certainly inadequate without some understanding of publishing institutions and the mechanics of distribution and sales. A book is a tangible social and physical product of individual behaviors, materials, and functioning organizations. To reduce this product and the process by which it is produced only to the motives of the writer or the publisher would be regarded as absurd.

To take another example, the distribution of opinions of unrelated individuals on some important social issues (say, 40 percent pro, 50 percent con, and 10 percent undecided) is not identical to the same distribution divided among the members of two well-organized parties upholding pro and con views (Sherif and Koslin, 1960).

Therefore, if research is concerned, as ours is, with the behavior of individuals in groups which function in different settings, it must obtain data on the settings, on the groups, and on the individual behavior. In order to relate these data and to reach generalizations, the two levels of analysis must be incorporated into the study design at its inception, not as an afterthought or appendix. Sound criteria for procedures and techniques cannot be in terms of the personal preferences of the investigator or popularity in professional circles. Sound criteria should be in terms of their appropriateness to the units and level of analysis involved. "Appropriateness" of procedures refers here to their utility in securing data without reducing or otherwise mutilating the crucial properties of the phenomena studied. This means that no single technique is sufficient in itself; a combination of methods and procedures is required.

There are several ways in which procedures for collecting data for more than one level of analysis required by a problem can be included in a single study design. One of them is to survey existing data at each level of analysis (that is, from psychology and the social sciences) and to build a single experimental design which embodies, at least in prototype, essential features abstracted from them. This alternative is feasible only when the problem area has been thoroughly explored.

However, even prior to experimentation, laboratory techniques yielding precise behavioral indicators can be adapted to the study of the actualities of behavior in the field, the results being crosschecked by results obtained by other techniques more traditional in field research.

If social psychology and the social sciences are, as we maintain, attacking the same or related problem areas at two different levels of analysis, there can be no conflict between valid findings on these two levels. For example, if the sociologist reports that groups have distinctive properties (such as organization and values), the psychologist should find, as he has, that individuals behave differently in group situations than when alone—because they are influenced as members by the properties of the group.

Many of the conflicting findings on different levels of analysis stem from a lack of coordinated research focusing clearly on the same problems at different levels. This is one reason why interdisciplinary research should be designed deliberately to provide checks and cross-checks of data obtained (1) at different levels of analysis and (2) by different techniques and procedures on the same level. In this way there need be no conflict between "approaches" or rivalry about the inherent superiority of one or another "method." Then the study of social behavior, of the properties of groups in which it occurs, and of properties of their settings will be complementary. Indeed then, psychology and the social sciences can supplement one another to produce rounded and valid accounts of major problems confronting each.

If utilized in a research design giving due recognition both to the social science level of analysis and to the psychological level of analysis in terms of behaviors of the single individual, the choice of "field methods" or "laboratory methods" will be more than a matter of preference or professional interest. Their utilization in the same study design will provide cross-checkings of the validity of generalizations attained through each.

5 *Research design*
required by the gamut
of influences

O ur task, then, becomes the development of a research design which does encompass the gamut of influences on individual behavior. Of course, this task includes spelling out the operational procedures to be used. With the strategy of focusing upon a critical period of human development and social life, this chapter summarizes such a design for study of adolescent behavior as a function of group membership in different settings. The rationale for the design can be summarized briefly.

Individual behavior, whether directed toward socially desirable or undesirable ends, occurs within the context of ties and reciprocal expectancies between the individual and other individuals. These interpersonal relationships, in turn, characteristically take place within the bounds of groups—not any old groups, but groups whose acceptance or rejection of the individual, whose approval or disapproval of his behavior, whose attribution of the prerogatives of status and prestige, are serious personal concerns for him.

However, small groups are not closed in insulated compartments, especially in highly differentiated societies. They function in particular spatial, physical, and social settings. They use facilities of those settings, whatever they may be. And in these settings, other people and groups carry on the business of living within some social schemes and with reference to some bounds defining what is acceptable (latitude of acceptance) and what is not acceptable or what is deviate (latitude of rejection) among them.

Even in interpersonal contacts, the niches in which individuals place one another reflect the classifications prevailing in their groups and in the larger social schemes for living. And within the bounds of a small, intimate group, the impact of the activities, interests, and values of other groups—small and large—is reflected in the daily concerns of members, their definitions of a "good member," their friendly or hostile stance toward others.

If individual behavior is related to the interpersonal, group, sociocultural, and ecological contexts in which it occurs, then ultimately all of these will have to be articulated with reference to specific sequences of behavior. In order to do so, the gamut of influences and the behaviors need to be studied in a single research design.

Therefore, the design of research will include data collected through procedures and techniques appropriate to different *units* of analysis at two *levels* of analysis:

1. On the psychological level of analysis, the unit of study is the individual; and the data are actions and behavioral indicators of motives, attitudes, expectancies, and appraisals. However, the behaviors in which our research is interested are not unrelated episodes. Patterned *sequences* of behavioral events are studied in terms of consequences for the individual's attitudes, goals, and actions with regard to fellow group members, outsiders, and significant objects and activities within his ken.

2. On the sociological level of analysis, the units of study are groups and their settings. The data pertain to the organization or patterning of status-role relationships and the values or norms of the group, to the features of the neighborhood relevant to group interactions, including its facilities and spatial arrangements, its population and their occupations, educational levels, living standards, and their prevalent latitudes of acceptance-rejection defining the bounds of propriety and aspiration.

It follows that data are obtained through a *combination of methods and techniques* selected by the criterion of appropriateness to the level of analysis and essential properties of the phenomena in question. In this way, the findings at one level of analysis can be crosschecked with those at the other level, and with other results at the same level of analysis. If results are valid, the generalizations at one level of analysis will not contradict, but will supplement, those at another level. If results are reliable, two procedures or techniques applied at the same level should yield congruent data.

THE RESEARCH STRATEGY

The research design to be summarized represents a stage of development in our efforts toward integrating field and laboratory approaches, and the techniques associated with each, in the investigation of behavior in small groups. This aim requires a strategy in a step-wise progression: 1. Start with gaining intimate familiarity with existing findings from studies of small groups and of their sociocultural settings. 2. Formulate hypotheses on this basis for experimental study. 3. Apply techniques to obtain behavioral indicators developed in experimental study to behaviors occurring in the actual interaction situations of the "field" (cf. M. Sherif, 1954).

In the present research, we have attempted to apply in field situations procedures and techniques developed in our earlier experiments on group formation and functioning (Sherif, 1951; Sherif and Sherif, 1953; Sherif et al., 1961). The design includes further experimentation to test hypotheses based on the findings of field methods.

In brief outline form, the operations of the research design are as follows:

I. Selection of ecological settings (living areas or neighborhoods) differentiated as to social rank (high, middle, low) through socioeconomic and cultural measures, and specification of those features of each setting relevant to interaction processes of small groups of adolescent boys functioning within them.

II. Determination of the reference scales for evaluating social objects and behaviors and for setting goals which prevail among adolescent youths in each of the differentiated settings, thus specifying further the normative character of the settings, their common and distinctive values, and establishing a baseline for assessing the relative typicality-atypicality of group members in these respects.

III A. Selection of small groups composed of teen-age boys (13–

18 years old) within each of these settings and intensive study of them over a time period through a combination of techniques, including observation, informal sociometric choices, ratings by regular and other observers, "situational tests," and judgmental indexes adapted from the psychological laboratory.

III B. Experimental testing of hypotheses concerning group formation and behavior of members through study of interactions among unacquainted individuals selected from settings of different rank.

IV. Assessment of the unique personal qualities and skills of individual group members with reference to the activities and properties of their groups and to salient features of the setting—conceiving these personal characteristics as products of reciprocal interaction of the person and his environment(cf. G. Murphy, 1947).

The major hypotheses and the above interrelated aspects of the research are summarized in the remainder of this chapter. The research project, initiated in 1958, has thus far studied a dozen groups in several cities in the Southwest. The continuing research will secure data for certain of the hypotheses which require a statistically sufficient sampling of settings and groups, and will execute the procedures for aspects III B (experimentation) and IV (personality assessment). The procedures and techniques used to collect data for aspects I, II, and III A, above, will be discussed in detail in Chapters 6–10, along with representative data.

From the viewpoint of method, the following have been of greatest concern at every step of the research:

1. To check the *validity* and *reliability* of findings through use of a combination of methods for securing comparable data.

2. To utilize whenever possible the advantages of experimental methods and the precision of behavioral indicators standardized in the laboratory, both in field and experimental conditions.

3. To adapt all techniques of measurement in the study of groups to ongoing activities and interactions, thus avoiding undue interruption, deflecting, and cluttering of these processes with the measurement procedures—which are extraneous to the phenomena studied.

In choice of measurement techniques, we have been guided by the criterion of *appropriateness,* that is, the utility of a technique to yield data at the level of analysis in question without mutilating or dissolving the essential properties of the problem and associated events. Whenever appropriate, procedures and techniques available in prior research literature were used. For example, in characterizing a neighborhood, we consulted sociologists and surveyed their research reports (e.g., Firey, 1947; Hawley, 1950; Schmid, 1937, 1944; Shevky and Bell, 1955; Talbert, 1956). Likewise, in studying interaction in small groups, we used techniques available, such as rating methods, checks on observer reliability through statistical comparisons, and sociometric choices (adapted to informal conversation between observer and group member).

On the other hand, the methods of observation were considerably altered from those traditional in anthropology (where the interview of key informants is the characteristic method) or sociology (where the observer seeks to become a participant in the social group or system studied). The detailed account of methods of observation is given in the next chapter. The exact procedures to be followed by observers are presented in the Appendix, pp. 331–360.

We found, as the research progressed, that in many problems of interest to us, there were no established or adequate measurement units. In these instances, we were guided by the phenomena observed and tried out indicators appropriate to them. A number of the measurements mentioned in the next section were developed in this manner.

MAJOR WORKING HYPOTHESES

In contemporary psychology and social science, the term *hypothesis* has been given a somewhat elevated position. There even seems to be the attitude that one should not do research unless the data test some hypothesis. In fact, if an hypothesis is not "testable"— that is, if there are no existing operations and measures of the events being predicted—it is suggested that one really should not state it seriously (as though the existing state of research were a permanent affair).

The most opprobrious term that can be attached to an hypothesis these days is that it is *obvious*—an astounding state of affairs when one recalls that the hypothesis of evolution was "obvious" to a good many biologists before Darwin. Newton's hunches, and ultimately his principles, did not start with repudiation of the obvious, such as the fact that apples fall to the ground. In the early stages of development of a science—certainly the present state of psychology and the social sciences—the great challenge is the search for a system of relationships to handle the obvious facts. Of course, once the seemingly obvious hypotheses are established, we have to proceed to derive hypotheses which may not be at all obvious and follow to whatever unexpected discoveries they may lead.

The deceptive thing about all this hue and cry about hypotheses is that everyone has them—whether he does research or not—and that in many cases an elegant statement by the researcher does not represent the hypothesis with which he started research at all. "Hypothesis" is a more dignified word for "hunch." Whether a hunch is testable depends in part on how explicit it can be made, and in part on whether one has the available techniques to *measure* the conditions and the events which are predicated as somehow related, or has the ingenuity to develop such procedures and techniques. When hunches are not supported by the data, there have been instances in which a researcher writes hypotheses which predict what *did* happen.

Our working hunches or hypotheses were formulated on the basis of extensive surveys of sociological and psychological literature (reported in M. Sherif and Cantril, 1947; M. Sherif, 1948; Sherif and Sherif, 1953, 1956; Sherif *et al.,* 1961). Therefore, many of them have much in common with hypotheses advanced by other investigators of small groups (e.g., Bales, 1950; Bass, 1960; Hare, 1962; Hare, Borgatta, and Bales, 1955; Homans, 1950; Kelley and Thibaut, 1954; Riecken and Homans, 1954; Stogdill, 1959), and with investigators of community and behavioral correlates (e.g., Faris and Dunham, 1939; Shaw and McKay, 1942; Hollingshead, 1949; Tryon, 1955).

The hypotheses were formulated before our present research was undertaken (Sherif 1959; Sherif, 1960; Sherif and Sherif, 1960). We have specified the measurements by which they are to be evaluated. Our initial hunches when undertaking this research follow, the ways of measuring the variables being italicized:

A. When two or more individuals experience motives (interests, frustrations, aspirations) as common, they will tend to enter into repeated interactions, *as measured by frequency and regularity of association over a time span.*

A1. The kinds of motivations conducive to interaction among individuals vary according to prominent features and facilities of their settings. Specific features and facilities of the settings are indicated by *census, municipal,* and *survey data.* Kinds of motivations are inferred (a) from *life history material* and (b) from the *kinds of activities characteristically engaged in by group members in interaction and communication.*

A2. The content of interactions among members will reflect concerns (motivational problems and goals) prevalent in the setting in which the individuals interact. Concerns prevalent in the setting are inferred from *indicators of the physical and social facilities of the setting* and *indicators of the reference scales and goals prevalent in the setting* (see Chapter 9). Content or focus of interactions is assessed through *communications among individual members* (discussions and conversations), especially when problem situations arise, and ways and means of handling them are under discussion. (It is essential that such *analysis of content and duration* of communication be performed upon conversations and discussions relative to problem situations which are important to the members, hence which occur spontaneously and are recorded without awareness of the observed.)

A3. The greater the importance (motivational relevance) of the group to individual members, the greater the personal efforts exerted by members to associate with the group.

Importance of the group is inferred from (a) *the length of time members have associated,* and (b) *the duration, regularity,* and *variety of activities engaged in.* Personal efforts to associate are measured through indexes appropriate to the groups, e.g., (a) *distances covered on foot in order to be together when members do not have other means of transportation,* (b) *extent to which members maintain contact with one another's whereabouts and activities when not physically face to face,* either through personal intermediaries or telephone calls to key persons.

A4. The greater the importance to an individual member of a natural group under study, relative to other groups and affiliations (family, school, church, formal clubs, etc.), the more binding for him are (a) participation in activities initiated by the group, and (b) regulation of his attitudes and actions in terms of the latitudes of acceptance-rejection of the group in specific dimensions. By "binding for him" is meant the experience of feeling that participation and regulation of his behavior is a necessity. The measure of such social control through inner promptings is *initiative taken by the individual without external sanctions or threat of sanctions from other members.*

The relative importance of a group to an individual can be inferred from (a) *the proportion of his time he spends or wants to spend with group members* and (b) *his own ranking of the importance of the group to him relative to other affiliations.*

The significance of participation in group activities and regulating behavior in terms of the group's latitude of acceptance are measured by (a) *the individual's behavior in choice situations where group activities or norms diverge from or conflict with those of his other affiliations and personal relationships;* and (b) *his consistency in participating in terms of the group norms without overt moves toward sanctions by its members.*

B. Relationships among individuals interacting with motives experienced as common are stabilized over a period of time into more or less differentiated status and role positions, the pattern of which constitutes a group organization.

Status differentiation is based on *observed frequency of effective initiative displayed by individual members, expectancies for per-*

formance of skills important in the group, independent ratings in problem situations, and sociometric choices in these dimensions.

B1. The relative degree of solidarity of a group *as measured over a time period* is proportional to the importance of belongingness to individual members.

The importance of belongingness is measured (see above, A3) by longevity, duration, regularity, and variety of activities. Indicators of relative solidarity are:

(a) *Similarity of behavior of other members when the leader is present or absent,* with greater similarity indicating greater solidarity.

(b) *Resistance and secretiveness relative to outsiders in discussing group membership and activities.* A secrecy index is based on reactions of members to outsiders in different situations, e.g., physical withdrawal of members from the situation or abrupt change of the direction of conversation when an outsider enters into the situation.

(c) *Exclusiveness of members in situations involving nonmembers.*

(d) *Degree of coordination of role performances when facing situations of mild stress,* as for example competition with another group.

B2. To the extent that a group organization or structure is stable, the status relations of members will be reflected in a consistent *pattern of communication* in matters of consequence to the group. Specifically, the higher the status of a group member, the greater the *frequency of suggestions concerning group activities which are addressed or relayed to him for his reaction.*

C. Group products, notably a set of norms regulating behavior in matters of consequence to the group, are stabilized in the interaction process.

Norms are measured by (a) *Regularity and frequency of actions and practices,* (b) *Praise or rewards to individual members for adherence to such practices,* (c) *Correctives for behavior deviating from the range defined as acceptable by the group norms.*

C1. Latitudes for acceptable behavior and for achievement in specified activities vary within the range of reference scales for evaluation prevailing in the sociocultural setting in which the group functions. Underlying this prediction is the hypothesis that reference scales for evaluation will differ significantly in different settings, when the range of objects or population characteristics in those settings differ.

Prevailing reference scales in the setting are *measured independently by schedules administered to representative samples of adolescents in the settings studied* (see Chapter 9).

C2. The relative diversity among different groups in the same setting with respect to norms and reference scales varies as a function of the rate of transition of that setting. The degree of similarity between the norms and reference scales of different groups functioning in a given area is expected to be greater in more stable areas.

C3. The following hypothesis relates to the relative size of the latitudes for acceptable behavior which define conformity and deviation in the group: The latitude of acceptable behavior defined by the norms of a group related to matters affecting the existence and perpetuation of the group will be narrower (permit fewer alternatives) than the latitudes defined by norms regulating behavior for matters of less significance.

The limit of the latitude of acceptable behavior is defined as *the point at which variation in behavior is reacted to as deviation by the members*. Norms relating to the existence of a group include those regulating activities bearing on the motives which brought members together. Matters affecting the perpetuation of a group include members' actions relative to each other and outsiders.

C4. Degree of consensus among members in adherence to particular norms of a group varies with the importance of belongingness to its members and thus is closely associated with the relative solidarity of the group. (*For independent measures of solidarity, see B1 above.*)

Importance of the group is inferred as already noted in A3. Measures of degree of consensus are (a) *Relative frequency of cases of deviation from norms,* (b) *The extent of participation by group members in applying correctives for deviation,* (c) *The severity of correctives.*

C5. The content of group norms for behavior toward other groups will vary as a function of features of the setting and specified functional relationships between the groups in the past and present, but will not be significantly associated with variations in in-group characteristics (e.g., type of organizational structure, norms regulating in-group relations).

This hypothesis pertains to relations between groups selected for intensive study and *other groups* in the setting, namely, their intergroup relationships. Among the features of the setting to be considered are the *rank position of the setting relative to others, stratification within the setting, relative coordination of various groupings in the setting by adults* (family, school, church, social agencies), *specific rivalries or cooperative encounters between the groups in question in the past.*

D. Intergroup relations of any consequence for the activities and goals of a group will have discernible impact upon the group, specifically in the following respects:

D1. Competitive evaluations relative to another group in the setting will accelerate the formation of a group organization. In other words, the *rate* of group formation (as measured by *the relative stability of the pattern of status-role positions*) will be speeded by *competitive comparisons* between the groups by their members.

D2. Opposition to, or restriction of, the group's activities and goals by outsiders (e.g., authority figures or other groups) will increase solidarity within the group. (The impact of other groups upon in-group solidarity is one of the best articulated observations in small group studies, coming from the earliest empirical studies. Cf. F. Thrasher, 1928.)

D3. Proportional to the discrepancy between latitudes of acceptable behavior prevailing in the setting or in larger society, and the activities of the group, its membership will be exclusively defined and secrecy observed in matters pertaining to membership and activities.

D4. Encounters with other groups in the execution of consequential activities will result in changes in the patterning of status within the group in the direction of increasing the effectiveness of the group in handling problems of intergroup relations.

If the encounters are cooperative and friendly, the resulting changes in status will involve enhanced positions for members showing appropriate skills. If the encounters are hostile, the positions of members skilled in conflict will be enhanced, unless sure defeat is anticipated by the members (cf. Sherif and Sherif, 1953, pp. 252–266; Sherif *et al.*, 1961, pp. 126–128).

SPECIFIC RESEARCH STEPS AND PROCEDURES

In the context of the present chapter, it remains for us to translate the methodological concerns and tests of hypotheses into operational form. Because of the scope of the research, this is done in the following pages in modified outline form. Further specification will be made in the chapter pertaining to each aspect of the design.

I. Study of Differentiated Settings in Which Groups Function
   A. In each city included in the study, three areas are chosen differentiated as "low," "middle," or "high" in social rank. The most feasible composite indexes for this purpose at present are those developed by Shevky and Bell (1955). Considerable generality for their indexes has been reported for cities in various regions of the country (Van Arsdol, Camilleri, and Schmid, 1958). Even without a composite index, it is feasible to rank neighborhoods on the basis of consistent level and pattern of their various features.
      1. The measures are available in U.S. Census Tract Statistics.

2. Various measures permit specification of the relative homogeneity-heterogeneity of the areas and rate of transition.

B. In addition to census statistics, available statistics from municipal and other local sources are collected to specify other salient features of the areas, e.g., additional population characteristics, delinquency cases, local welfare cases, participation in social agency programs, school attendance and dropouts, etc.

C. The physical character of the area and its facilities (housing, recreational, transportation, educational, etc.) are surveyed and mapped out, so that group interaction can be studied with reference to these.

D. If necessary, block surveys of residents in the area are conducted. Such a block survey was carried out, for example, in San Antonio for every tenth house in the areas studied, particularly to check on the relative acculturation of the Spanish-speaking residents.

II. Study of the Reference Scales for Evaluating Social Objects, Behavior, and Goals of Adolescents in Each Setting

This aspect of the research is specifically designed to link the socio-cultural and ecological measures into a social-psychological analysis of the patterned behaviors of group members. Mere specification of those aspects of the setting available in census and local statistics leaves crucial questions for social-psychological research. For example: "Do individuals living in differentiated areas actually perceive themselves and their neighborhoods as the ecological measures might lead one to expect? Are persisting attitudes, interests, and goals similar or do they differ significantly in different settings? How representative of the adolescents in a given area are the behaviors and goals of particular individuals interacting in small groups which are selected for study?"

If the physical arrangements of the neighborhood and the behaviors of its residents vary over a period of time within definable ranges, and if these affect the pursuit of one's interests, then different neighborhoods may be expected to play a part in creating different pictures of one's plight or one's fortune, as the case may be.

On the other hand, in a modern society where mass communication is the rule and where physical movement out of one's neighborhood and city is so greatly eased by modern means of travel, we may also expect that individuals' evaluations and goals would be similar in certain respects in all settings of that society. Here the question is, "How similar are they and with respect to what spheres of living?"

A questionnaire technique was used to answer such questions. It was administered to adolescents—that portion of the population whose reactions are most pertinent to the behavior of other adolescents living in the same area. The self-reference and dimensional character of the items suggested the title "Self-Radius and Goals Schedule" for the form.

A. The Self-Radius and Goals Schedule was administered in high schools serving the high, middle, and low rank areas selected for study. It was presented as a "Public Opinion Survey for Teen-agers" with anonymity of responses assured. Samples of around one hundred students were secured in each school from required classes throughout the day to assure representativeness.

B. Through analysis of data secured in different settings, we can assess in what ways the evaluations and goals of adolescents living in areas of different social rank are similar, and in what ways they differ. Furthermore, these data provide a basis for assessing how representative the values and goals of the small groups studied in each setting are relative to other adolescents in the same setting. The data pertain to the following:

1. acceptance-rejection of behaviors evaluated as socially desirable and undesirable by adults;

2. conceptions of the acceptable ranges for achievement and goals in various social spheres (e.g., financial, material, educational, occupational);

3. extent of harmony or conflict perceived with parental and school authorities;

4. established stands (attitudes) toward various out-groups.

III. Intensive Study of Groups

IIIA. Study of Natural Groups in the Field

In order to permit statistical comparisons required by the hypotheses, our target is successive replication of procedures in the study of natural groups. The procedures for a single group require about 5–7 months.

The attempt has been to select one group in each of three urban areas or neighborhoods (low, middle, and high in rank). One observer is assigned exclusively to a single group for the period of its study; and he must be familiar with the area and must fit *into* the area, in the sense of resemblance in speech and appearance to the people living there. The problems associated with availability of observers suited for study in a setting have limited the representativeness of our data so far, particularly in studying groups in high rank areas—which are very mobile and have many private facilities in which to associate.

The research during the last four years has furnished realistic leads as well as correctives as to the choice of appropriate methods of data collection. From these experiences, it is clear that it is possible to observe a group with the consent and cooperation of authorities in the area and without group members becoming aware that their actions are of research interest. Specific details of procedures are given in the next chapter. The general procedures are as follows:

A. Observation of the selected area and possible gathering points for informal groups of teen-age boys. Initially, observation is "from a distance," without contact between observer and members.

B. Selection of a group for study in each area on the basis of observed frequency and regularity of association at specified locations, prior to contact with the group.

C. Establishing contact with the group thus selected through pretexts which bring group members to the observer.

D. Direct observation of group activities and interactions by the observer. Since continuous rating of interaction and communication is not possible under the field conditions of this aspect, two methods are used to minimize uncontrolled, selective bias in observation:

  1. The observer's tasks are focused on different aspects of the interaction process in successive phases in accordance

with instructions and categories prepared on the basis of pilot research. The successive phases of observation are in the following order:

   a. Group organization: status positions and member roles in different situations and activities.

   b. Group products: common practices, verbalizations, behavioral indications of expected or ideal practices, specific instances of shared goals, rewards and penalties for deviant behavior, as well as areas of behavior not normatively regulated in the group.

   c. Detailed study of interactions and member behavior in a variety of situations.

2. A combination of techniques to obtain data is used for each of the major hypotheses, in addition to observations and ratings by the observer:

   a. Status ratings by independent raters who have not previously observed or been informed about the group.

   b. Sociometric choices obtained in informal interviews.

   c. "Situational tests" observed by independent raters.

   d. Recorded time samples of communication among members to be analyzed for content and other characteristics.

   e. Judgment techniques adapted from the psychological laboratory and presented as situations and tasks which interest and appear natural to group members. The social perceptions and judgments thus obtained provide indexes to be compared with observational findings and with similar indexes obtained in the experimental aspect of the research.

   f. "Natural history" material on the group obtained from all available sources.

   g. Life history material on individual members obtained upon completion of the observation.

IIIB. Experimental Study of Group Formation and Functioning Among Previously Unacquainted Individuals in Controlled, Yet Naturalistic Conditions

  A. In the experimental aspect of the research, subjects will be adolescent boys from the different sociocultural settings studied in the research. They will meet requirements of personal stability (as determined by psychologists), physical well-being (as determined by physicians), and have written permission from parents to participate. Parents and other responsible adults will be informed of the research nature of the undertaking.

1. At any one time, all subjects in the experiment will be from the same sociocultural background, namely, one of the settings studied in this research. Thus, by successive replications, comparisons between groups experimentally produced among individuals from settings of high, middle, and low social rank will be possible.

2. Subjects will be selected through observation of potential subjects in their neighborhoods, homes, and schools; interviews of parents, teachers, and youth; and the necessary physical and psychological tests. (Selection procedures in our previous experiments on group relations required approximately 300 hours of observation and interviewing.)

3. At any one time, from sixteen to twenty-four boys will take part in the experimental procedures, divided into two or three groups.

B. The experimental site will be a summer camp available for purposes of the research and staffed by research personnel with both research and camping experience.

C. Control over conditions of interaction will be established, as in previous group experiments, through extensive and detailed planning in advance of the spatial arrangements of facilities and objects so that subjects are faced with compelling problem situations. The focus of the problem situations, which prompt subjects to *initiate* projects rather than to accept projects imposed on them, is to be determined on the basis of the preoccupations and interests discovered through the Self-Radius and Goals Schedule. Staff, observers, and other experimental personnel will be integrated into the situation with traditional positions of a summer camp staff. Detailed accounts of the methods in our earlier experimental studies are given in Sherif and Sherif, 1953, 1956; Sherif *et al.*, 1961.

D. The major working hypotheses stated in this chapter concerning group formation are to be tested in the experiments. In addition, more specific predictions will be examined pertaining to variables affecting (1) the rate of group formation, (2) the relative "steepness" or "flatness" of the resulting status organization, (3) relative solidarity, and (4) the formation of group norms.

A detailed outline of the experimental plan and the major hypotheses will be distributed to colleagues interested in this area before the experiment, as was done prior to the previous group experiments (see Sherif *et. al.*, 1961, Chapter 2).

Whenever possible, the techniques for data collection in the experiment will be the same in the experimental and field aspects of the research to permit quantitative comparisons in the two research settings. Time samples of continuous interaction for content analysis will be secured through concealed transistor tape recorders, and photographic records will be made with telephoto lenses. With the exception of the data on "natural history" of the group, which in this experimental aspect becomes the *topic of investigation,* all of the techniques used in the intensive study of natural groups are appropriate for experimental study as well. In fact, the techniques for status rating and securing judgmental indexes were originally developed in experimental settings.

IV. Study of Contribution of Unique Personal Characteristics of Individual Members

In this research undertaken to further understanding of social behavior, whether socially acceptable or objectionable, generalizations have to be based on the actual behaviors of individuals. A group or a neighborhood cannot feel, cannot aspire or behave; only the individual can do these things.

The hypotheses stated earlier in this chapter concerning group formation, role-status relations, solidarity, norm consensus, conformity-nonconformity, involve predictions about the behaviors of individual members. Why, then, such concern over characteristics of the setting and reference scales prevailing in it which define what is acceptable and objectionable to its inhabitants?

The explicit inclusion of the characteristics of the neighborhood and its inhabitants in the study plan was predicated on a generalization based on experimental study of psychological processes. The cardinal principle, to be heeded in studying any kind of human behavior (social or not), is that an item of behavior is not determined by the characteristics of a single stimulus or task presented to the individual. In order to understand even a fairly simple response, the context of the stimulus and the situation have to be specified.

For example, responses to an inkblot may be misinterpreted without consideration of the conditions of the situation in which the test is given (cf. Sarason, 1954), and so may responses to an intelligence test (cf. Riessman, 1962). Emotional facial expressions are very likely to be misinterpreted without knowledge of the position of the body or the context in which they occur. These are all examples of the well-known principle that a part-process is significantly affected by the pattern or system of which it is a part.

Applied to the problem of studying social behavior as a function of group membership, it becomes clear that a group (the immediate context of behavior) is part of a specifiable setting constituting its natural habitat. The goals the individuals set for themselves, their feelings of acceptance or rejection by others, their desires to be appreciated are not independent of appraisals of the goals available and treatment by others in the environs.

In other words, the setting and its available facilities and goals are among the independent variables which cannot be ignored. In experimentation, ignoring independent variables which affect behavior would be regarded as inexcusable in any psychological laboratory. We cannot be more lax in studying behavior in small groups.

In our study of small groups, one invariant finding was some patterning of the status relationships among individuals, which affected their behavior in predictable ways, depending on relative position and role expectancies of the person. But knowledge of these patterns does not help appreciably in explaining why particular individuals come to occupy given positions.

From Cecil Gibb's extensive survey of leadership (1954), we can safely conclude that the characteristics which lead the individual to various niches and levels of the status structure vary with the major tasks, activities, problems, and goals of a group. The skills and unique characteristics with which an individual comes to an inter-action situation, however, are shaped through complex interactions of his psychological make-up and his experiences in particular circumstances.

In addition to his skills, each individual differs with respect to his degree of intensity and level of activity. Interaction processes from which group organizations develop require of the individuals continuing regulation of their efforts and intensity relative to others. Some individuals habitually aim too high—pitching their bids for respect, prestige or influence at too far-distant a target. Others tend to aim low, putting forth less effort and falling short. A level of effort and initiative "just right" for the task and the situation—shooting neither over nor short of the mark—is achieved by relatively few.

To explore such problems, a battery of psychological tests was administered to each of the individual boys before they took part in an experiment on group formation in 1949 (Sherif and Sherif, 1953).

In the experimental aspect of the present research, we propose to include the assessment of personal characteristics and skills of the individual, relative to his past history and to the main properties of the experimental conditions.

If we take seriously the principle that part-processes are influenced by the system of which they are parts, the study of variations in personal characteristics has to be *preceded* by specification of the milieu and specific interaction situations in which the individual's behavior is a part-process. By meticulously following this *sequence* of operations, study of the distinctive and unique contributions of particular individuals may acquire a sounder basis than attempts at assessment in the abstract have yet been able to build.

PART III

Behavior in interaction, self-image, and setting

6 Studying behavior in groups: methods of selection and procedures

Within the research design in the last chapter, the focus of interest is on patterned sequences of behavior in small groups functioning in their natural habitats. We are concerned with the consequences of membership in groups to which individuals belong *of their own choosing,* and any characteristics of interaction in those groups which lead to such consequences. Therefore, we cannot ignore the spatial and sociocultural frameworks within which the individuals actually behave and interact. In fact, specification of the sociocultural setting and neighborhood is the logical and necessary first step in actual research operations.

In presenting the findings of a multifaceted investigation such as this, there is decided advantage in looking first at the groups and member behavior. In this way, we can be more specific about the domain of discourse, and the interplay between individual behavior, group, and setting can be made more explicit. Accordingly, in this chapter we shall describe in some detail how groups were selected for study and how they were studied. In Chapters 7 and 8, we turn directly to a review of data on behavior in groups obtained thus far in the research. In Chapters 9 and 10, these and further findings on individual behavior and group activities and properties will be related to their neighborhoods and sociocultural settings in more detail.

THE DOMAIN
OF GROUPS STUDIED

Groups of six to a dozen or more boys, from 13 to 18 years of age, have been studied for periods of time ranging from five to seven months or longer. These groups were all "natural" formations, in the sense that they had evolved from the individual members' own choices of association, rather than from adult initiative and programming. Such informal patterns of association, developing through initiative of the participants, are particularly significant during the adolescent period, for reasons noted in Chapter 3.

The groups were chosen for study on the basis of regularly observed interactions among the same individuals at specified locations. In other words, we looked for *regular* and *recurrent interactions,* leaving the issue of whether these associations were patterned and whether the participants shared any values or traditions as a question to be investigated. Our hypotheses predicted that clusters chosen on the basis of frequency of association would be patterned, but patterning was not the initial criterion of selection.

After the area or neighborhood of study was specified (high, middle, or low in social rank), the search began for recurrent associations among adolescent boys within that area. An observer assigned to the task began watching any or all locations where boys might congregate: for example, empty lots, drugstores, drive-in restaurants, pool halls, school and church grounds, parks, and recreation centers. During this phase of the study, he was instructed never to approach boys of this age directly and never to *question* them if they should approach him.

When he had observed a regular association of the same boys on several successive periods of observation—possibly at different times of day, in different activities, and at different locations in the neighborhood—it became the focus of his observation. This method of selection involved several calculated risks. In the mobile and changing scene of a modern city, the observer might witness coincidental associations of boys on two or more occasions. Or, after gathering at certain spots several times, some boys might not congregate again at these same locations for weeks because of changing weather or new interests.

It would have been much easier to have selected formally organized youth clubs or activity groups for study. Our more difficult method, however, insured that the associations were the kind developed through the initiative and choices of the individuals involved.

The criterion of observed frequency of interaction meant that the groups selected gathered frequently in public locations, as contrasted with exclusive contact in one another's homes. This limitation on the kind of groups studied can be turned to an advantage in investigating the interplay of individual, group, and their setting. "Visible" groups both contribute to the character of their neighborhoods and are, like others, affected by it.

The problem of how "representative" visible groups are will be tackled in Chapters 9 and 10 by comparing the values and goals of group members studied with those of representative samples of youth in their neighborhoods. Continuing research in the project is intended to provide more adequate sampling of groups and neighborhoods. So far, the research has led us to the hunch that the problem of how representative the "visible" group is of its neighborhood does not have the same answer in neighborhoods of high, middle, and low rank.

The next section takes up problems of research procedures and methods which are universally important in studying human groups and behavior of members. These are the problems which led to the development of the methods for study used in the present research.

METHODS IN STUDYING
THE HUMAN INDIVIDUAL

Even the physical sciences have become aware that the procedures and instruments used to study a phenomenon may affect the phenomenon itself (cf. N. Wiener, 1961). In the social sciences and psychology, the seriousness of the problem is magnified many times because human beings not only act and react, but think about their actions and reactions. The sentient individual usually tries his best to behave in ways he considers appropriate to the situation, in ways he thinks he is *expected* to behave by those who count for him— including his friends, his employer, his cronies, and even a researcher whose profession he holds in high esteem.

There was a period after World War II when investigators of small groups and social influences collected data on group communications by tape recorder and through one-way screens as though the foregoing problems did not exist. They assured themselves and others that "people get used to the microphone after a few minutes and forget they are being observed."

People may lose their initial awareness of a piece of equipment or even of a live observer busily recording their words and deeds. But does reduction of initial self-awareness mean that they are behaving without regard to the very significant fact that they are being studied? It does not.

In recent years, there has been growing concern among researchers over the highly special character of social situations where one participant wears the halo of "scientific investigator" and the others the yoke of "subject." Thus, there has been both theoretical analysis and research into the "social psychology of psychological experiments" (e.g., Hofstätter, 1957; Riecken, 1958; Orne, 1959, 1961; McGuigan, 1961; Rosenthal, 1961). Exactly the same problems inhere in field studies relying on *direct* observation and interviews, as we shall see.

The critical feature of the research situation—as a social situation —is that the individual has allowed himself to become an object of investigation and that he is aware of being so. This overriding fact is indicated by his willingness to engage in tasks and discussions on topics which would seem nonsensical to him in any other setting, his concern to turn in a creditable performance, his questions about his behavior ("Did I do well?"), his wish to "see through" the procedures, and even his desire to contribute data which confirm the research hypotheses (cf. Orne, 1961). It is this fact that accounts for his unwitting sensitivity to signs in the situation which point to certain behaviors rather than others (cf. Rosenthal, 1961). As McGuigan (1961) indicates, automation of research procedures for data collection cannot vitiate this overriding fact. Many years ago, Dashiell (1930, 1935) demonstrated that the mere knowledge that one is participating in an experiment at the same time as others can produce behavioral effects ordinarily found in face-to-face competition. Even though each subject performed in a room *alone,* the sight of other individuals going to other cubicles made him sensitive to the fact that his performance would be compared with theirs.

In experiments on group formation and intergroup relations in 1949, 1953, and 1954 (Sherif and Sherif, 1956), we sought to eliminate the "investigator-subject" relationship which gives most research situations a distinctive, even unique, character. The "subjects" were not informed that they were subjects in an experiment, but came to the scene as campers in a summer camp. Their words and deeds were never recorded in their view, nor were they informed of the arrangements of facilities and tasks prepared as part of the experimental conditions.

In the present research on groups in field situations, the same problems were considered and the same solution adopted. When people are carrying on the business of living, the fact of being observed is even more serious than in the laboratory—which is, after all, a special sort of place set apart from one's "real life."

In real life, groups develop among individuals whose emotional and motivational promptings (as well as sheer proximity at work or play) lead them into interaction with one another. In the course of their interactions, they become bound to one another through awareness of common problems, of being in the same boat, of mutual sympathy and understanding, of "belonging" together. Such groups do not form or maintain themselves for the whims of the researcher who wants to study them.

Most "participant observers" in field settings (neighborhood, factory, club) find this out. They are apt to receive protests against their presence and procedures which "invade our privacy" (cf. Polsky, 1962, Chapter 7). Observers who do not try to "participate," but merely record frequencies of interaction, encounter similar protests when they try to get within earshot to record the content of those interactions (cf. Miller, 1954).

Therefore, in the present research, the individuals who were observed did not know that they were being studied. All methods of data collection were adapted to insure that they did not.

The fact that individuals were not behaving as "subjects" does not eliminate the importance of the observer's *presence* to them as another individual. But it does insure that the situations in which observer and group members interact are not perceived by them in terms of the highly special character of a "research situation"—with all that means concerning one's personal worth, "normality," and the protection of one's "secrets" (especially if these secrets concern socially unacceptable behaviors).

"Investigator Bias"

In research in field situations, the problem of "investigator bias" is even more aggravated than in laboratory research. Here we refer not to deliberate dishonesty, but to the all-too-human tendency to search for facts from the constant flow of interaction which support one's cherished hunches. In a sense, this problem is less serious than those of "subject-awareness," because, in the long run, science is not a one-shot, all-or-nothing affair. The scientific observer who specifies his methods and procedures leaves the way open for correction by others with different hunches.

Nevertheless, the problem of *selectivity* in observation cannot be avoided by the conscientious investigator. In the present research, we have met this problem by using a *combination of methods* to obtain data (see Chapter 5), and by the use of independent observers who were not informed about the problem or the nature of the group under study. If the results of several independent procedures are congruent, we have an operational basis for claims to the validity and reliability of findings.

Perhaps the best control for observer bias in our research has been the search for invariant properties of group interaction and their behavioral consequences. When different observers of groups functioning in locations hundreds of miles apart and at times over a period of several years report similar behavioral events time after time, we may reasonably expect that their reports reflect recurring and significant processes.

OBSERVERS AND
SELECTION OF GROUPS

The decision to eliminate the "investigator-subject" relationship and the resulting "awareness of being studied" meant that an observer had to be able to enter and move about a study area without attracting attention as a mysterious outsider. Consequently, the primary qualification of an observer was his "fit" into a neighborhood, in terms of the dominant characteristics of its population.

If the population of an area was predominantly white, native-stock American, on the one hand, or, on the other, Spanish-speaking American of Mexican descent, the observer represented those classifications in appearance and speech. As often as possible, the observer had had experience living or working in neighborhoods of the type he entered for study. This was particularly important in low rank neighborhoods with Spanish-speaking residents, since the dialect spoken is well-nigh unintelligible to other Spanish speakers, including native Mexicans. Even among English-speaking youngsters, however, an observer had to be sufficiently informed on youthful lingo to keep from sounding like a "square" to them.

In many instances, observers adapted their behavior to local customs as the study went along. Thus, one observer found himself gaining greater acceptance when he altered his "table manners" to conform with those of group members, who usually ate without knives or forks. Another found that "gunning" the motor of his car when starting brought him in closer touch with the "drag racing" buffs he was observing. A third found that he was expected to share a cigarette with others present.

Observers were all young male adults from about five to ten years older than the individuals they studied. Most were students at the time of the research; a few were working in allied fields, for which the problems and tasks of observation were pertinent. Each was instructed by the senior author in periodic personal conferences and by prepared written instructions before and during the entire period of observation. In each city, professional colleages served as on-the-spot supervisors, as the authors have gratefully acknowledged in the Preface. The revised and expanded sets of instructions to the observers are presented in the Appendix, pp. 331–360.

While "good fit" with the neighborhood was an essential qualification of an observer, definite limitations upon this "fit" were necessary. Observers were somewhat older than the youths studied. This age gap was necessary in part because the tasks of observing required a higher educational level than those of the adolescent boys studied. In addition, however, the age differential was regarded as essential to avoid the observer becoming too closely identified, psychologically, with "his" group, and to preclude his involvement in their activities as a "member" competing for "standing" in the eyes of others. This possibility assumed more than methodological significance in those groups which did engage in socially unacceptable ("delinquent") behaviors. An observer who came to feel himself as *one* of a group which engaged in activities illegal for the adolescent age (e.g., drinking) or in general (e.g., theft) might not have been able to heed the unequivocal instruction to all observers not to engage in illegal activities (even though they might learn about them before or after they occurred).

Whenever necessary, authority figures in a neighborhood (e.g., police, recreation or welfare officials, businessmen) were informed of the purpose of the observer's presence in the neighborhood, both to protect the observer from any possible suspicion or rumors from adults and to assure their cooperation in establishing appropriate conditions of study, which invariably has been given generously.

Methods of Selection

During the course of the research, procedures for selecting and observing groups have been developed, tried out, and elaborated. The information on procedures given throughout this chapter summarizes the detailed written instructions developed on this basis for observers and discussed with them at length.

The method for obtaining data about a group for potential study was the observer's concrete reports on the frequency of *interaction* among the same boys in specific locations in the neighborhood he was to concentrate upon. Direct questioning of the youths themselves, even of their names, was specifically forbidden at this point. Any information that came to the observer *without* direct inquiry was utilized, of course (e.g., an adult commenting, "Those kids are always hanging around here"). The selection of a group, however, hinged on the observer's reports on *frequency of association* in interaction episodes he had witnessed.

The observer was instructed to go about getting information on recurrent interaction episodes as follows:

Choose one or several locales in the area as the initial base of operations: for example, a park, soda fountain, empty lot, playground, "hangout," agency, or recreation center. Observe the interactions among boys between the ages of 13 and 18 years.

Investigate these locales at different times of the day, but regularly. While it is important to have several possible bases of observation, these should be within the area agreed upon for study. Do not move your base too frequently. By returning regularly at different times to a location where you have observed boys interacting, the probability is increased that the same boys will be observed again. Once a recurrent association is spotted in one place, it should be followed to other locations.

All observations at this phase of study are from "outside" or "at a distance." Your behavior should not attract the special attention of individuals you may eventually select for study. Until a particular cluster has been singled out for study, appear to be interested in the activities of others, as well, before you get close to the group more likely to be selected. If individuals approach you, you should respond, but not question them about each other or their activities.

When a number of boys, 13–18 years old, have been observed interacting together during at least four observation periods within approximately two weeks, this cluster is a potential group for study.

Interaction includes arriving or departing together, conversing, playing, or "taking sides" with each other.

While *frequency of association* is the main criterion for selection, any *unsolicited* evidence of "sticking together," mutual secrecy, exclusiveness from others, or other manifestations of being part of a group should be carefully recorded in terms of *behavioral events* which you observed. These observations should be specific, not in the form of an "impression" on your part.

The aim of the selection procedure is to locate a pattern of regular association among at least six or seven individuals, possibly with a "fringe" of less frequent interaction with other boys.

METHODS OF OBSERVATION

Observation is a basic procedure for data collection in most of the social sciences, even in experimentation. Too frequently it is regarded as an art whose success depends upon unique skills of the observer. There is no question that the experiences and interests of some individuals equip them better for observation than those of others, and that we know very little about what makes a person a "good observer." For example, we know very little about the experiences and skills which enable the "good observer" to see behavioral events in terms of sequences of actions, reactions, and interactions of all of the participants, instead of perceiving and evaluating them solely in terms of how they affected *him*.

Nevertheless, we can and have learned about *conditions* and *procedures* for observation which are optimal for any observer in order to collect relevant and significant data about behavior in groups as it actually occurs. The primary condition of observation, from which all others in this research stem, is that at no time should the individuals being observed be aware that they are *subjects* of study or that the observer is their *investigator*. As we have seen, the knowledge that one is being observed, even while performing a simple task, does influence behavior.

If we are interested in behavior in groups as it occurs in actual life and in the variables which affect it, the "investigator-subject relationship" is extraneous. So too are any procedures or techniques for data collection which clutter and interrupt the natural course of give-and-take among the individuals studied.

The interaction process as it occurs in a natural way among individuals who "count" to each other is essential data to explain the behaviors of a single participant. Lacking such data, a competent social worker characterized one of the boys we studied as "not only *anti*social, but completely *a*social." She had observed and interviewed him at a recreation center whose adult personnel was a special target for members of the boy's group. They took particular delight in outrageous behavior in the presence of these adults. This "asocial" boy happened to be the recognized leader of the group, and frequently displayed a strong sense of responsibility, loyalty, and protectiveness toward its members. Conversely, we have observed numerous instances in which "Sunday best" manners were adopted for the benefit of an adult "investigator" or a teacher. After this display of sweet reasonableness, the adult would be unable to understand how the boy could participate in some of the activities of his group.

In order that individuals not be aware of being "studied," observers were instructed *never* to take notes or write down observations in the boys' presence. If a specific situation called for writing something (for example, keeping score, making a list, taking "minutes") he could utilize the opportunity to jot down other symbols without being detected. As a general rule, however, observers were instructed to write all observations *as soon as possible* after leaving the group. Adherence to this rule was strongly emphasized, to minimize omissions and commissions of forgetting.

The foregoing procedural precaution necessarily resulted in loss of many details of the interaction process from the observer's reports. This sacrifice was made deliberately. It was our conviction that recurrent events in different groups reported by different observers, cross-checked through independent techniques for data collection, would provide more relevant data in the long run than detailed accounts or records of single interaction episodes under artificial conditions.

The loss of data from the observers' reports was reduced by another method: While it is clearly impossible for an observer to recall everything that happened, even immediately after the event, he has a much better opportunity of good recall if he focuses *on only one aspect* of the interaction process at a time.

Accordingly, the observation of a group was divided into successive phases, the observer being instructed on the *focus* of each forthcoming observation phase. The first of these, as we have seen, was simply *frequency of interaction* observed from a distance. Successive phases of observation then focused on 1. status differentiations among the individuals (organization), 2. normative or evaluative behaviors, including reactions to deviation, and 3. specification of each member's behavior relative to the group's organization and norms. Data on relations with other peer groups and with adult authorities in the setting were obtained throughout these phases, usually being so striking that they were not difficult to recall. Only when the phases of observation were complete did the observer begin to interview the boys themselves and other people in the neighborhood to reconstruct a "natural history" of the group, using public records, private reports, and case history materials.

The Observer's Role

The condition that the observer never appear to the group members as an "investigator" of their behavior required that some credible pretext for his presence be established and that he develop his own role in the interaction situations in harmony with this pretext. The pretext and the role further had to be such that the observer's presence would appear natural, while interfering as little as possible with the ordinary flow of interaction among members. In brief, the aim was for the observer to gain admittance and eventually to be welcomed into group discussions and activities as a participant *without* becoming an adult leader or a member competing for attention and prestige with others.

Such a role is not as difficult to establish as it may sound, nor is it an unusual relationship, as we found in the course of the research. Most of the groups we studied had contacts with one or more young adults toward whom they turned for advice, special skills, or small favors. Many times these outside contact were with older brothers, relatives of members, friendly neighbors, or recreation workers who took an interest in them.

The observers were told to try to develop pretexts for being around which made them appear "harmless" in the boys' eyes and which could be developed into "big brother" relationships through doing small favors and helping out when asked. The observer was *not* to give unsolicited advice or push himself into their affairs to "help."

Since neighborhoods, observers, and groups differed, the pretexts used varied also. The desired consequence of a pretext was always the same, however: to bring the boys *to the observer,* instead of the observer intruding upon the boys. One rather well-padded observer began working out at a play area in a poor neighborhood with a brand new ball. When, as he had hoped, the boys asked him to let them play with the ball too, he told them he would be working out fairly regularly in an attempt to lose weight. Another in a well-to-do neighborhood became a devotee of the charcoal-broiled hamburgers at a drive-in restaurant and of folk music at a popular "beatnik" coffee house patronized regularly by the boys he observed. The youths came to him out of admiration for his new and expensive car, whereupon he obliged by letting some of them drive it, by driving past the homes of girls they wanted to impress, and so on.

A more common pretext at parks or recreational facilities was to tell the boys (after they came to investigate the observer's sports equipment or car, or ask him to fill in on a team) that he was receiving school credit for experience in some recreation or sports activities. He was required to have actual experience with boys their age so that *eventually, in the future,* he would be prepared to have a job working with youth. This pretext required the cooperation and active sympathy of officials in the park or recreation area. It was essential that they understood his role and reinforced the fact that he had *no authority* in that location over the boys or anyone else. Observers using this pretext were also cautioned to demonstrate to adult authorities that their function in the research in no way implied an evaluation of the authorities' program or agency, as indeed it did not.

Establishing Rapport with the Group

Observers were instructed from the beginning to report any efforts they made toward gaining entry to and establishing rapport with the group. Any behavioral evidence of *resistance, suspicion, secrecy,* and *deliberately misleading statements* on the part of members was noted, as well as any evidence of acceptance by the group. The criterion for judging acceptance by the group was that the more the observer was welcomed by members at places and in activities they considered as exclusively group affairs, the more he had succeeded in establishing good rapport.

One of the major findings of the research is that every observer reported evidence of curiosity, suspicion, or mistrust from group members during the initial period of the study, before his role was clearly established by his own consistent behavior. The degree of such suspicion, its manifestations, and duration differed. Its significance in the present context is that even with a clear and acceptable reason (pretext) for the observer's presence, the boys required specific demonstration of his helpful and harmless intent through his own behavior before accepting him into their circle.

In other words, we found that some degree of "privacy" and of secrecy is characteristic of groups to which individuals belong of their own choosing. In general, the degree and extent of such secrecy in the dozen groups studied have varied with the frequency with which the members engaged in activities which would have been appraised as socially unacceptable by adults if they had known about them. In view of these invariant findings of "secrecy," one wonders at the validity of pronouncements about the character of relationships and interaction in youth groups or gangs from those who have viewed them only from outside the bounds of the group's privacy, or only through interviews and "tests" of individual members.

Signs of the reduction of secrecy and increased rapport with the group included such dramatic incidents as members telling the observer their real names after cooperating in a hoax of pseudonyms. Many boys came to trust their observer to the point of telling him about escapades that they would not have revealed to their parents or authorities. A few even asked the observer to join in such activities (which he was instructed not to do), promising him protection and their testimony of his innocence if they were caught.

The observer was instructed to gain acceptance and develop good rapport in the following ways:

1. To insure by word and deed that group members are aware of his lack of authority in the situations where they were together.
2. To appear in word and deed as a "bigger brother" who is interested in them, wishes them well, and may be helpful on occasions.
3. To avoid any signs of dislike or disapproval of any member, on the one hand, or signs of "favoritism," on the other.
4. To avoid suggesting or initiating activities for the group *unless* such activities are deliberated planned as a part of the research design.
5. To be helpful in activities initiated by group members without display of skills which put the observer in a rivalry situation for status with group members.

On the basis of experience, we found that the greatest difficulty for the young adults who served as observers was to temper their efforts to be helpful, their efforts to be accepted, and their cautiousness in following instructions in a way that all three could be accomplished. Therefore, it was emphasized that too aggressive attempts to be accepted might be seen as "meddling," and too effective help or skills be viewed by high-status members as a "challenge" to their positions. On the other hand, complete passivity could be interpreted as indifference or disapproval, and lack of skills would result in loss of interest by the boys. For example, when members started an activity, such as a game, the observer was to show interest in it and sufficient skill to appear a "regular" guy, without competing or "stealing the show" from group members.

Reports on Observation Periods

The observers' written reports on every period of observation, their ratings of member behavior, and their subsequent reports on interviews and pertinent public records after the observation period provide the basic data on behavior in groups in natural field conditions. Through the course of the research, the information to be included in these reports has been specified in standard form. Description of the reports will indicate what kind of data were obtained.

The regularity and frequency of observation periods with a group has been emphasized, with three periods a week regarded as the minimum goal. In the event that the observer could not locate the group, he was to report the circumstances and his efforts.

Study of the dozen groups so far has varied in thoroughness and completeness. The length of each observation period has varied with the length of time the members stayed together, as well as the availability and persistence of the observers. Nevertheless, the *smallest* total of hours for collection of data on a group reviewed in this book is one hundred hours—no small sample of behavior.

The form of observation reports as developed in the study includes the following:

1. Date and exact hours of observation.
2. A rough diagram or map of the places where observations were made, to be located within the neighborhood studied or outside it, as the case may be.
3. Description of and approximate number of persons (including nonmembers) present at the start of each observation.
4. Changes in the participants and the circumstances of these changes (arrivals and departures).
5. Activities or topics of discussion throughout the observation period in sequence.
6. Description and details on behavioral events relevant to the focus of the phase of the study at the time (e.g., status differentiation) in terms of specific words and actions of the participating individuals, designated by name or symbol (before observer learns names).
7. Separately indented comments, giving the observer's impressions, evaluations, or "hunches," labeled as such, or his comparison of an observation with an event or action previously reported.

8. A separate report on efforts made by the observer to gain acceptance and the results of these efforts, including the observer's estimate of the comparative degree of his acceptance with members of various standing in the group.

In addition, the observers' reports contain the description and outcomes of procedures planned for each successive phase of observation, for example, his ratings of relative standing in the group, behaviors in special "test" situations, and others to be specified later.

Observers were cautioned that the purpose of the study was scientific, and that the data and the identity of individuals were to be treated as confidential, out of respect for individual rights to privacy. In other words, there has been no public access to individual identities for any reason whatever. All names used to refer to individual boys or their groups in this book are pseudonyms.

REFERENCE NOTATION
FOR THE GROUPS

The sheer volume of data on a dozen different groups and their neighborhoods requires that our review of it in the chapters to follow be highly condensed. Specific details of some groups and individual behavior will be included as illustrations to make the general findings concrete.

In referring to the groups, an index or cataloguing system will both aid the reader and save space. Accordingly the following notation will be used in identifying the sources of the data:

1. *Cities:* At present, the cities in which observations have been made can be conveniently characterized in terms of the cultural backgrounds of the populations. In a city like Oklahoma City, the great majority of the population is white, English-speaking, of Midwestern background, with statistical minorities of English-speaking Negroes, Spanish-speaking whites, and American Indians. San Antonio and El Paso, Texas, on the other hand, have substantial bicultural populations, that is, bilingual residents of Mexican descent. Cities will be classified as follows:

    A. Dominant (Southwest) American.

    B. Bicultural.

    2. *Areas or Neighborhoods Within Cities:* Neighborhoods can be ranked in terms of their sociocultural and economic status, as discussed in Chapter 9. Therefore, neighborhoods are designated as:

    I. High rank.

    II. Middle rank.

    III. Low rank.

The population of a neighborhood can be further classified as comparatively homogeneous or heterogeneous in ethnic or cultural composition. Thus, neighborhoods are also classified as:

    S. Segregated, whether exclusively white, Negro, or Spanish-speaking.

    M. Mixed or heterogeneous.

    3. *Groups:* No classificatory scheme for the small groups themselves is proposed here. Instead, they are simply assigned numbers. These numbers will be followed by a letter, however, to indicate the cultural or ethnic background of the members as follows:

    a. Members are white and English-speaking.

    b. Members are bilingual (Spanish and English).

    c. Backgrounds of members are heterogeneous, that is, the group is "mixed" in terms of cultural background.

Thus, reference to a group as A IIs 2a means it was in (A) a city typical of the dominant Southwest setting, (II) a middle rank neighborhood which is (s) residentially segregated, and (a) is composed of members who are white, English-speaking Americans. Reference to a group as B IIIm 9b means that a group was in a bicultural city (B), low rank neighborhood (III) whose residents are mixed (m) or heterogeneous in cultural background (e.g., Negro and Spanish-speaking) and its members are (b) bilingual (Spanish and English).

With these tools in hand, we proceed in the next chapter to review findings concerning the groups and their members.

7 Patterns of interpersonal relations within group structures

What were the boys doing when observed? What drew them together and brought them back time and again? Was give-and-take among them in discussions and activities haphazard and casual, or were there regularities and patterns to their interaction?

In this chapter our findings on group activities and interaction are reviewed with emphasis on behaviors and events recurring in all of the groups studied. We shall also refer to differences among them, which will be further elaborated in the following chapters.

GROUP ACTIVITIES

What people do and what they talk about when they get together regularly from their own choice can tell us a great deal about them. Too frequently, accounts of behavior start with a single dramatic episode and work backward, painting a motivational backdrop in hues which complement its drama. If the episode is socially approved and desirable, the colors selected highlight its admirable features. If the episode is socially undesirable and injurious to others, the backdrop is swirled with the grays and greens of hidden complexes and reaction formations waiting to uncoil.

The range and variety of activities engaged in by the youths observed in our research provide a factual background for their more dramatic actions. Much of the time in every group was spent just "hanging around" together—talking and joking. All but two of the groups spent a large portion of their time and energies participating in, discussing, or attending athletic events and games. The two exceptions were both in low rank neighborhoods.

Automobiles were a regular preoccupation in every group—one way or another. Whether they owned cars or not, these American boys discussed, compared, and admired cars. Those who did not own a car knew what kind they wanted, and frequently faced problems of having access to one—in order to go some place or to take out a girl. Those who did have cars spent amazing lengths of time in and around them with their pals—many times driving to "look around" or to be seen by others.

Girls, and specifically sexual activities, were recurring topics of discussion, planning, and reminiscing. The rules to this game varied considerably in different neighborhoods. For groups in middle and upper rank neighborhoods, an important accompaniment of being together was looking for chances to be with girls and insuring that at least all of the inner circle got dates for important social events. One group whose members had cars regularly "integrated" their girl friends in most of their activities. In the others, having a "steady" girl friend was disruptive of the member's participation in the group, hence usually of his standing as well.

A considerable portion of time in every group was consumed by rehashing past events and planning for games, parties, and projects in the future. Thus, despite the apparent aimlessness of much of the "hanging around," constructive activity was often in progress. It concerned a party planned after the school prom, plans for the evening, arrangements and strategy for a game the next afternoon, a scheme for avoiding trouble with a neighboring gang, or for "controlling" street life at the city's annual fiesta.

Adults figured in conversations and plans as means to needed resources (cars, money, athletic equipment), as figures whose authorization was needed ("If I can get out . . . ," "If the recreation director will let us back in the Center . . ."); as obstacles to be overcome or circumvented ("Tell her we're going to study . . . ," "If you tell them the truth, they say you're lying. If you lie they let you go. . . ."); and occasionally in terms of devoted obligations ("My brother-in-law started roughing her [mother] up and I'm going to give it to him"; "My brother gets away with murder—he doesn't even give Mom his paycheck like I do").

In short, the activities and conversations engaged in by the boys show that they came together for a wide variety of reasons—even those boys whose joint activities were chiefly athletic. The range of activities with agemates widens in adolescence in comparison to that of earlier childhood, and the significance of adults—even highly valued parents—declines as the determinant of decisions, and as bearers of greater skill and wisdom (cf. Prado, 1958; Rosen, 1955; Seidler and Ravity, 1955). There is the urge to *belong* with one's fellows, to *count* in their day-to-day scheme of things, and to do things with them without adult initiation or interference.

As we shall see in the next chapter, the *particular* activities around which interaction centers and the particular concerns of the members do color the character of a group. But the general finding—over and above variations from group to group—was the positive preoccupation with pleasure of each other's company, with problems of having some *place* with one's peers apart from adults, with relationships with adult authorities, relationships with the opposite sex, and the appurtenances of being an adult male (including a car). Much of the constructive discussion and planning in every group centered around these concerns.

However, another striking finding was that in every group the observer found, and confirmed, that members engaged in behavior not only socially unacceptable to adult authority, but violating the law. The most common of these was drinking alcoholic beverages, which is illegal at this age. One group in a middle rank neighborhood, whose members were not reported to drink and who came together chiefly to play athletic games, regularly acquired cigarettes from the corner grocery by purchasing a nickel candy bar from the son of the owner (a fellow member), who then put a package of cigarettes in the bag.

Members of the group in the highest socioeconomic level studied —sons of prominent business and professional men—regularly drank alcoholic beverages, sometimes engaged in illicit sexual activities, and held a mixed swimming party at a motel by forging the registration. The party involved not only illegal drinking but property destruction, which the boys paid for themselves—all without parents or legal authorities detecting these activities.

In a middle rank neighborhood, the observer verified the fact that members had accumulated hundreds of dollars' worth of fines for traffic violations (a fact which they both worried and bragged about), had habitually been truant before the legal age of school dropout, and that they had been repeatedly reprimanded for noisy, objectionable, and destructive behavior in public places. Only one of these boys had been in legal difficulties, except over the traffic fines.

The most dramatic instance of property destruction in a lower rank neighborhood—breaking the windows in a whole side of a high school the year previous to the study—was performed by group members in retribution against a teacher who had "kicked out" one of their members. The culprits were not detected by the police.

In the low rank neighborhoods studied, the boys were under police surveillance frequently. A number of them had been in detention and reform institutions—for theft or crimes of violence (knifings or shootings), the latter invariably growing out of conflict with rival groups. Minor theft was common even among those boys who had never tangled with the law, except to be stopped and searched when they left their neighborhoods. The list of other undetected legal violations by members in low rank neighborhoods included drinking, carrying illegal weapons, smoking marijuana, and "paint-solvent sniffing" (a variant of glue sniffing).

The boys in low rank neighborhoods, on the average, spent much longer periods of time together than those in more fortunate circumstances. Even holding school attendance constant—by comparing boys who had dropped out of school or those who attended school in middle and low rank neighborhoods—the sheer amount of time spent with fellow members in low rank areas was disproportionately greater—for reasons to be discussed in later chapters. (Youths in middle rank areas who dropped out of school or completed high school were not only under greater pressure from their families to get jobs, but were aided by them in finding jobs—a resource not usually available to parents in low rank areas. Boys in low rank areas who attended school had fewer school and neighborhood recreational activities apart from their groups.)

Thus, the rather dramatic list of illegal activities engaged in by the groups we studied in lower rank neighborhoods needs to be considered relative to the amount of time and the variety of other activities the boys engaged in together. From this viewpoint, it appears that activities unacceptable to society at large and the law in particular occupied a fraction of their time together not appreciably greater than that of the neighborhood athletic team which regularly executed its little plot for stealing cigarettes from the father of one of its members.

Therefore, we have been unable to find empirical support for those theories which paint a picture of hidden and twisted motives to account for antisocial acts by members of adolescent groups. In fact, a youth caught in intense and prolonged intrapsychic conflicts, on the one hand, or unable to distinguish between what his fellows regarded as "right" and "wrong" ("weak superego"), could have lasted scarcely a week as a member of any of the groups studied.

The motivational components contributing toward entrance into a group and toward behaviors as a member—for good or for evil— are properly viewed within the context of interaction with others and its significance for the individual. Our confidence in this conclusion is strengthened by Polsky's report of his study of cottage life among institutionalized "delinquent" boys—many of whom had had severely disturbed lives. Polsky concluded that the "impact of the boys' own structured relations" in their day-to-day contacts was a fundamental source of the emergence and continuation of undesirable social behavior, and inquired why this context of behavior is so "understressed" in theory. His answer was that "Those theoreticians more removed from the boys' actual scenes of operation are in contact with the derivatives of the boys' social practice—their attitudes and values—rather than the impact of their actual interpersonal relations." Yet in actual contact, the observer finds that much of their emotional life is centered about the problem of position in a group. "This raises in sharp relief the extent to which previous investigators have penetrated the social structure . . . and have understood its crucial role . . ." Polsky, 1962, p. 173).

All this is not to say that the problems faced by youth in different neighborhoods were the same, for they were not, as we shall see in later chapters. It is to say that they all came together in positive efforts to deal with motivational urges faced in common with others, and that their moves to do something about them were, above all, *regulated* relative to their ties with each other. It is this *regulation* of behavior which concerns us in the remainder of this chapter.

PATTERNING OF INTERACTION IN GROUPS

The hypotheses of our research predicted that associations singled out for study solely on the basis of *frequency of interaction* would have the essential earmarks of groups: namely, some organization of the individuals according to different status-role positions; common traditions or customs, common conceptions of what is acceptable and what is objectionable (norms); and a demarcation of who is "in" from who is "outside." These properties have been identified in each of the dozen groups studied.

The methods for identifying group structure or organization, group norms, and delineation of the group from "out-groups" hinge upon the fact that the behaviors of individual members are *regulated* with reference to these group properties.

Interaction among the individuals is hardly haphazard or casual. It exhibits patterned regularities of varying stability and duration. The patterns change from time to time as members come or go, and with marked changes in the interests of the members.

There is nothing mysterious about the patterned properties of group interaction. They are inferred from the behaviors of individuals, not discretely considered, but relative to one another. Let us make them very concrete through experimental findings on the *formation* of groups among unacquainted individuals who came together with common interests and problems.

The Formation of Group Structure

In three experiments conducted at summer camps, unacquainted boys interacted in activities of common appeal to them for periods of several weeks (Sherif and Sherif, 1953; Sherif, White, and Harvey, 1955; Sherif et al., 1961). During this time, observers regularly made ratings of each boy's standing relative to others in terms of *effective initiative*. "Effective initiative" refers to suggestions, actions, or decisions which were taken up and actually followed by other individuals, including actions involving the reward and punishment of others which were supported by other individuals. Thus, while sheer brute force or bullying which went unsupported or was rejected by others is not effective initiative, the dimension of behavior rated was indicative of the *power* or *control* exerted by the individuals.

The observer's ratings from one day to the next were compared, and at first very little agreement was found. Over a period of time, however, his ratings began to exhibit regularities. Usually, the extreme positions, those individuals who displayed most and least effective initiative, stabilized first. Subsequently, individuals occupying intermediate ranks were rated more consistently.

When the observer had ranked the individuals in a group consistently three times (i.e., the ratings were significantly correlated), an independent observer who was not regularly with the group made ratings on the same dimension. At about the same time, individual members were questioned informally as to whom they liked to be with best (popularity), who usually got things started, and who usually got things done in their groups. Then the observer's ratings were compared with those of the independent observer and with the sociometric choices made by the individual members themselves.

From these comparisons, it is possible to construct in schematic form the process of formation of a group structure, with the understanding that the specific forms of the pattern will vary from group to group. Figure 7.1 presents such a scheme, based on composite findings, to trace stabilization of structure in two groups whose organizations differ in pattern.

In the uppermost two cells of the figure, the individuals are represented by circles, arranged haphazardly, to show that upon their initial encounter an observer could not assign status positions to them in any reliable way. From one activity to another, different individuals took the lead, and some contributed in one activity, but not another.

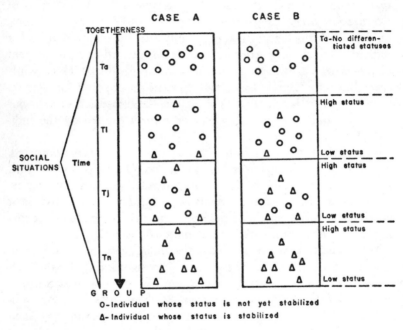

FIGURE 7.1. Formation of status structure in two groups from initial encounter of individuals (time *a*, at top) to stabilization (time *n*, at bottom). Adapted from Sherif and Sherif, 1956.

Looking downward in the figure over time (*t*), we see that the *top and bottom positions emerge clearly first,* as represented by the location of triangles at the highest and lowest ranks. Over a period of time, one individual started to coordinate various activities and showed his ability to start lines of action which worked, smoothing out difficulties, and encouraging participation by others. Others lagged behind, making fewer suggestions or engaging in activities which disrupted the efforts. But, as the figure shows, the behaviors of other individuals did not become patterned as quickly (see the circles in the middle).

At intermediate ranks, there was jockeying for position, competition for attention, and considerable fluctuations in the observer's ratings for a longer period. When, as in the lowest two drawings, the observer was able to rate the individuals in a consistent fashion from day to day, we found that his ratings were highly correlated both with those of an independent observer and with the sociometric choices of members themselves made in terms of effective initiative.

The position occupied by a given individual, once stabilized, was closely related to the *expectations* other members had of him. For example, members appraised the performance of high status members as considerably better than it was, but tended to depreciate the performance of low status members (Sherif, White, and Harvey, 1955).

Structure of Interpersonal Relations in Natural Groups

School, recreation, and community officials are prone, when questioned about informal groups of adolescents in their institutions, to say, "We have no cliques or gangs here." Probably this reaction comes from the assumption that informal groups of adolescents mean "trouble," and from the widely prevalent practice of meeting such trouble by breaking up the groups or dismissing the members from the institution.

Our findings show, on the contrary, that behaviors among adolescents who associate with some regularity of their own choice are invariably patterned or structured in some degree. Thus, behaviors in informal associations—whether socially acceptable or unacceptable —involve mutual expectations sufficiently stable to be measured and sufficiently clear-cut that *changes* can be assessed. The stability and clarity of these role relationships among different adolescents do vary. So does the degree to which the patterning of roles is interlocked and "closed"—ranging from very tightly knit structures, such as those often called "gangs," to more fluctuating and open-ended patterns *polarized only when the individuals engage in certain activities.*

Among the youth involved in associations with agemates of their own choosing, problems of *conformity* or *nonconformity* to certain practices and to achievement levels in various activities (sports, school, recreation) arise from the expectations that others in these structures have for their behavior. These are the people whose opinions *count* for them. These are the people whose appraisals of their achievements and their failures bring great satisfaction or distress. Psychologically, the informal structure of agemates is the major reference group for its members—the locus of their emotional involvements and their concrete daily concerns.

Because the informal group is the seat of problems of conformity-nonconformity for adolescents, the most salient dimension of their role relationships is the *power dimension,* having to do with control and coordination in the group and the capacity to *sanction* behaviors.

Of course, it is perfectly feasible to study several other dimensions, such as physical skill, attractiveness, social prominence, standing in various activities. While our study has chiefly concerned social power in the group, measured primarily in terms of *effective initiative* in various activities, we shall also refer to *popularity*—that is, how frequently a person is *liked* by his peers—and to relevant skills.

In terms of popularity, skill, physical attractiveness, or frequency of participation, it is possible for members of a group to be fairly similar. Thus the structure of a group in terms of these attributes may be rather undifferentiated: Arrangements of members in terms of the degree to which they exhibit them may look flat. On the other hand, effective initiative or power is necessarily differentiated in any group. If one person's suggestion is accepted, those of other members are dropped for the time. Thus, arrangements of individuals according to their effective initiative or control over others in various activities are *hierarchical* in form. Unless a group engages with equal frequency in different activities wherein different members assume control, one individual is bound to emerge as exhibiting greater power than others, at least for the time. Other members will be rated after him in various steps.

Methods for Study of Structure

After an observer had made contact with a group and gained sufficient rapport to be present during its activities, as described in the last chapter, he was instructed on the focus for Phase 2 of his observations, namely, the structure or organization of roles and statuses as observed in the interaction of members. Through personal conferences and assigned readings (e.g., Sherif and Sherif, 1956, Chapters 5 and 6), the observer was instructed on the *dimension* of interest (effective initiative).

During this phase, the observer was to make special note in his reports of who made suggestions, to whom remarks were addressed, how suggestions made by different individuals were received, what decisions were reached, how they were agreed upon, and what actions were taken as a result. These observations were to be made in as many different kinds of activity as possible.

In particular, the observer was to record the sequence and duration of decision processes when the members faced a problem situation: for example, trying to decide what to do, making plans for some event, or attempting to meet some external challenge. *Effectiveness* of suggestions and decisions was to be assessed in terms of the immediate situation and also in terms of subsequent events.

At the end of each observation period, the observer recorded a ranking or ordering of the *individuals present* in terms of *status* or *effective initiative*. He was cautioned *to relate these rankings closely to the records of interaction process in his reports,* and to support them with specific comparisons of behavior, since ratings unsupported by behavioral evidence are of doubtful value in scientific study. When the group engaged in several activities during an observation period, the observer was told to give greater weight to activities engaged in more frequently and appraised as more important by the members.

The actual operations for status ratings were as follows:

To denote an individual, a circle with his name or symbol was used until the observer had behavioral evidence that he was a member of the group. Subsequently, a triangle was used, their relative positions on the page denoting the observer's rankings. The symbols were arranged with the highest position at the top and the lowest at the bottom. If the observer could not, at the time, differentiate between the positions of two or more individuals, he placed their symbols horizontally at the level signifying their rank.

During the early observations of this phase, observers almost invariably felt very uncertain of their ratings. They included these uncertainties in their reports, noting specific events which made them uncertain and led them to order the individuals in the way they did.

Any evidence of *change in an individual's position* was also emphasized, and the direction of the change (up or down) was noted by affixing an arrow to the triangular symbol of that member.

When an observer's ratings of the two highest and two lowest status positions in a group agreed for three successive observation periods, independent checks were made on his ratings.

Ratings by an Independent Observer.   In order that an independent observer could rate the group, the observer had to have established sufficient rapport that he knew the group's plans or could (for the first time) suggest an activity in which all members would be present, establishing some reasonable pretext for the independent rater to be present. The activity suitable for the independent rating was specified as one involving the entire membership (exclusive of hangers-on or fringe members), which presented them with some problem in planning and execution, and which was representative of their usual activities. In order to insure that members attend, the observer was told to volunteer some "treat" for the occasion, such as a meal after the event or refreshments during it.

The independent observers, like the observer, were selected to "fit" the group in appearance and language. They were not informed about the individual members of the group or its activities before observing. The independent rater was simply told to watch everything that happened during the occasion and to pay particular attention to who made suggestions, how the others received them, who agreed or disagreed, what decisions were made and by whom, who was the butt of criticism, or who the recipient of praise. He was told he would be asked to rank the individuals in these terms after the event, using descriptions of them if he could not recall names.

Most of the independent rating situations were athletic competitions which the group had scheduled or the observer had volunteered to arrange in response to their expressed interest in matches. In some of these, the independent rater came as the referee or scorekeeper. On one such test situation, the observer avoided this role for the independent rater because he had observed that members of the group habitually blamed the referees for any losses, so vehemently that the independent rater could not have joined the group after the game for the meal at a drive-in restaurant promised by the observer. Therefore, he earlier let the boys see him playing pool with the independent rater, then brought him along as a friend.

In other groups, especially those which did not engage in sports, the independent rating situation involved plans for a party or actual execution of the arrangements for a picnic, which the members very much wanted to have. The latter situation provided an entire day of observation for the rater, during which the boys planned, purchased, cooked, and ate a picnic feast.

After the event, the independent rater ranked the boys by himself, and his ratings were compared with those of the regular observer.

Sociometric Choices.   When the observer had established sufficient rapport with a group that the members would talk to him without suspicion and he could have conversations with individuals apart from the others in a natural way, he secured the sociometric choices of each individual in casual and informal conversation. Frequently, this operation was the most difficult of the observer's tasks.

One observer who successfully accomplished it did so by driving the members to their homes after athletic games, dropping the members off each time in different order so that he would have a chance to converse alone with the last boy remaining. He eventually talked to all of them in this way.

In one case, early in the research, the attempts to secure sociometric choices in one group were counted as utter failure. Although the boys responded, they mentioned the names of only the youngest members of the group who had never been under police surveillance.

The group was in a low rank neighborhood. The observer had been making progress in gaining rapport, and had been asked by top status members to drive them to a dance contest. They did not hide the fact from him that several, including the leader, had been institutionalized for theft and other misdemeanors. However, as the observer began to secure sociometric choices, four of the members came under close watch of the police in connection with the injury of a boy in a neighboring area of the city. This event led to renewed suspicion of the observer and other outsiders, and doubtless to their "nonsense" replies to his questions (for example, saying they liked best to be around a neighborhood boy about 12 years old). Shortly afterward, these four boys left the city to avoid police questioning.

On the basis of this experience, we were able to take precautions that the external situation and observer rapport both be optimal before sociometric choices were attempted. The observer was told to frame the questions in the language and slang of the members, to convey the following meanings:

1. Who are the fellows you like to hang around with best or that you like best?

2. (For middle and low status members only.) Who would you like to hang around with if accepted by them as an equal, or if you were sure they would like you as you like them?

3. Who are the fellows who usually suggest and organize activities, and see that they are carried out? or Who are the fellows who get your plans and activities started and see that things get done:

    (a) In general or over-all?

    (b) In fights with others?

    (c) In other activities such as parties, going to movies, or something just to have fun?

Before the individual mentioned any names, the observer asked, for each question, for a first choice ("Whom do you like best?" "Who does this most?"). He then asked for three more choices, noting all others that were volunteered. At the conclusion of the conversation, he immediately left to write down the choices.

The responses to these questions permitted several comparisons: Relative frequency with which an individual was chosen could be compared with the observer's ratings; popularity (frequency of choice as *liked*) could be compared with effective initiative in general and in fights or social affairs, as well as the observer's rankings.

Patterns of Interaction

If the observer's rankings of status are highly and significantly correlated with those of an independent rater, we may say that both are reliably observing structure along the same dimension—namely, effective initiative in group interaction. If their rankings are, in turn, highly correlated with the relative frequencies with which individuals are chosen by their fellow members as the ones who get things started and see that they are carried out, we have not only reliable but valid evidence for structure. The claim for validity here rests on agreement between observation from *outside* the group and members' appraisals from *within* the group.

The correlations (Spearman rank order, corrected for ties) between observers' and independent raters' rankings range from .816 to .982, the median being .88. The lowest of these is statistically significant at less than .05 level, and all the others at less than .01 (for the appropriate degrees of freedom). Thus, we may say that our observers have detected structure reliably.

Likewise, the observers' ratings agree closely with the members' own appraisals of status, supporting their validity. The lowest correlation was .875 ($p. < .01$), and the highest was .90.

Therefore, the conclusion is warranted that frequent associations in which adolescents interact of their own choosing *are* patterned or structured. This finding runs counter to the verbal statements of some individual members, who stated in response to direct questioning by an outsider: "Oh, we don't have a leader. We are just a bunch of friends. Everyone is alike." It also runs against the pronouncements of some adult observers, who have announced that adolescent associations are not structured systems—are not *groups*—but only loose aggregations focalized about prominent individuals. Of course, the findings above do not in themselves tell us how differentiated or tightly knit the structures were. We shall turn to findings bearing on this later.

Status Structure and
Interpersonal Preference (Liking)

When we compare the relationship between the observer's ratings and the relative frequencies with which the members are chosen as preferred companions (Question 1), we find that the relationships (correlations) are both lower and more variable from group to group. (The same statement holds if we consider the correlations between popularity and the group members' choices of the most effective and responsible members, which are closely correlated with the observer's ratings, as we have seen.) Now the range of obtained correlations is from .637 to .84, the former not statistically significant ($p. > .05$) and the latter significant ($p. < .01$) for the respective degrees of freedom.

The lowest correlation (.637) was for a group (B IIm 1b) which regularly played games after school hours. It was the group in which athletic skill and age were most closely related to status, as rated either by the observer or by members' choices. Its members were among the least secretive, and the most informal with their observer. Rapport was very good when friendship choices were obtained. This group was distinctive in other ways. When the leader left town for a week on a visit, the other members did not get together as a group, although they did associate in pairs and threesomes. It was, in short, a cluster of buddies rather loosely knit around a highly skillful and clever coordinator (leader) of athletic activities.

The general finding of a significant relationship between status and popularity might be expected. After all, these were associations by the members' own choice and many of the classical problems of sociometry (e.g., Moreno, 1935) were already solved by a sifting process, whereby the more irreconcilable interpersonal frictions had been honed away by exclusion and dropouts.

Nevertheless, our findings show that status (or power) in the groups and popularity are distinguishable dimensions, as have a number of other studies (cf. Hare, 1962). They further suggest that the relationship between status and popularity varies considerably in different groups.

At present, let us look at a single group (B IIIs 8b) which is about average with respect to the correlation between observer rating and independent rater (Spearman rho = .87), between observer rating and member choices on effective initiative (Spearman rho = .89), and status and popularity (rho = .84).

This group is suitable for present purposes since it did not engage in athletic activities, where differences in skill are often prominent. Furthermore, age (within the limits of 15 and 19 years) was not a primary determinant of status, as indicated by the fact that two of the high status members were among the youngest and that one of the leader's older brothers was ranked near the bottom status level.

In Figure 7.2, the observer's mean rankings of the members over a period of three months when all members were present (vertical axis) are plotted against the rank order of frequencies with which each member was chosen as a fellow who gets things started and accomplished (Question 3a). The straight line indicates perfect agreement between these measures.

Figure 7.3 plots the observer's mean ratings against the rank total sociometric choices for four questions (excluding Question 2). The deviation from perfect agreement is reduced, in comparison with Figure 7.2. The combination of sociometric choices for the four questions (three of them on status) permits greater differentiation of the lower and upper ranks, where now agreement is perfect.

Finally, Figure 7.4 shows us that the widest discrepancies of all occur when the observer's rankings are plotted against rank in popularity. In fact, they agree exactly only for the lowest status position (upper right).

The acknowledged leader of the group is fourth in popularity. His two "lieutenants" (tied at the second status rank) are first and seventh in popularity. Well might this be so, for the most preferred companion provided his backyard for get-togethers, while number seven in popularity was the fellow to be counted upon to support the leader's preferences in any disagreement—not always a popular role.

In short, as Turk (1960) found in an institutional setting, popularity or frequency of interpersonal liking is less "consensual" than

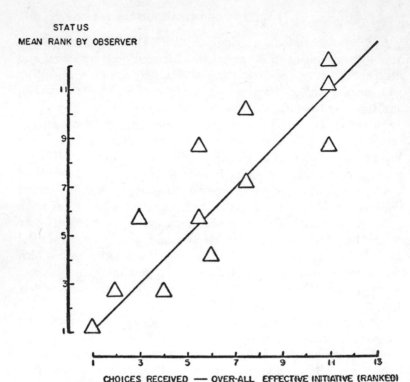

FIGURE 7.2   Agreement between two measures of rank. Mean of observer's rankings of status (vertical) and rank according to number of choices received from other members on over-all effective initiative (Question 3a) in Group B IIIs 8b (horizontal).

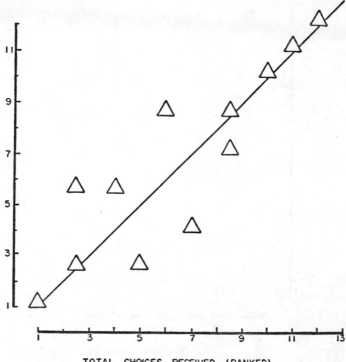

STATUS
MEAN RANK BY OBSERVER

TOTAL CHOICES RECEIVED (RANKED)

FIGURE 7.3. Agreement between observer's rankings of status and ranks according to total choices received from other members in Group IIIs 8b. Mean of observer's rankings (vertical) over three-month period and rank of individual by total number of choices received on four sociometric questions, three of them on effective initiative (Questions 1, 3a, 3b, 3c).

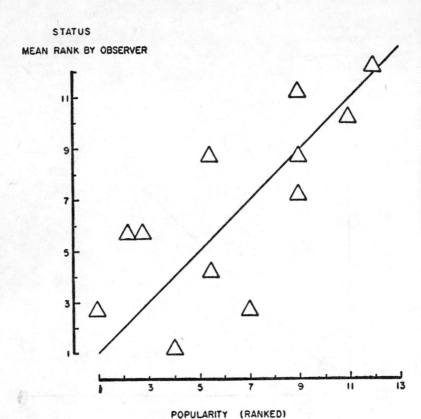

FIGURE 7.4. Relationship between rank in status and popularity in Group IIIs 8b. Mean of observer's rankings (vertical) and rank according to number of choices received from other members as liked.

member recognition of status. Yet, psychologically, it is certainly significant whether an individual is liked by his fellows, as well as whether he carries weight in their activities and joint decisions.

The imperfect correlation between status and interpersonal preferences, and its variation from group to group, suggested to us a two-dimensional analysis of group structure: status, represented as a vertical dimension, and interpersonal liking, represented as a horizontal dimension. In Figure 7.5 a, b, and c, three groups are represented in such bivariate analysis. On the vertical axis, the observer's mean ranking for each individual is shown when all members were present, and on the horizontal dimension the number of times each was chosen as preferred (liked) by other members. Deliberately, we present groups from similar neighborhoods (low rank) in the same city (B). It was not possible with this restriction to have groups with equal numbers of members.

Thus represented, the structures of these three groups, which function in similar circumstances and were composed of boys from similar sociocultural backgrounds, do differ. Status and popularity coincide most closely in Group 6b (Figure 7.5a). Group 7b (Figure 7.5b) is notable for the proportion of its members chosen as liked by half or more of the membership. Group 8b (Figure 7.5c) has three high status members exceeding the leader in popularity and a noticeable gap between members above and below the fifth rank in both status and popularity. To some extent, this gap reflects *psychological distance* between the lower and upper levels. When lower status members were asked whom they would like to be around if accepted as equals, three of them who had not mentioned the leader as a preferred companion *now* mentioned him. (He was mentioned by every other member as the one most frequently taking initiative and carrying things through.)

Changes in Status Structure

Since structure is a property of the interaction of individuals, it changes as members come and go, as the individuals succeed or fail in meeting the expectations of others, and as the members' interests change markedly.

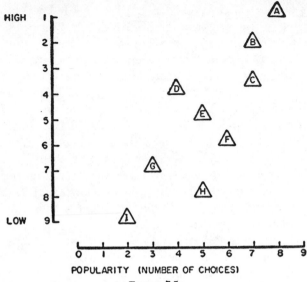

STATUS
MEAN RANK

FIGURE 7.5a

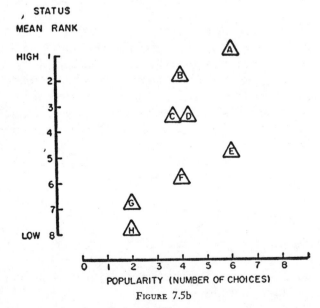

, STATUS
MEAN RANK

FIGURE 7.5b

146

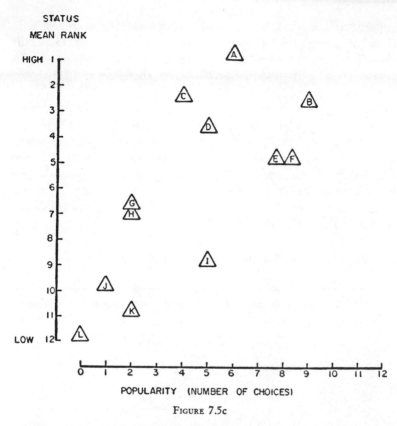

FIGURE 7.5c

FIGURES 7.5 a, b, c. Two-dimensional analysis of group structure. Observer's mean rankings of status (vertical) and popularity (horizontal) according to *number* of choices received from other members as liked in Group B IIIs 6b (Figure 7.5a), Group B IIIs 7b (Figure 7.5b), and Group B IIIs 8b (Figure 7.5c).

Particularly in the groups of middle and high rank neighborhoods, comings and goings of members were not infrequent. Generally these additions and eliminations occurred in the lower status ranks. These groups were in some degree open at the lower end for changing "fringe" membership or temporary hangers-on.

However, when a member entered or left the group at higher status levels, the structure was more significantly affected. This can be illustrated by events in two groups in the same city (A) which gained and lost members during the observations. The first Group (A IIIs 12a) of six boys in a low rank neighborhood received a new member after the observer's ratings had become stable. The means of his rankings of the six boys over seven observation periods are shown in the left column of Table 7.1.

TABLE 7.1 OBSERVER'S RANKING OF MEMBER STATUS
(GROUP A IIIs 12A)

Members	Mean Rating 7 Periods	X-first Meeting	X-second Meeting	X-third Meeting
A	1.1	2	1	1
X	Not present	2	2	2
B	2.0	2	3	4
C	2.8	4	4	3
D	4.3	5	5	5
E	6.3	7	6	6
F	6.6	6	7	7

The new member, labeled X in Table 7.1, was known to the others when he first appeared on the scene some three months after observations began. He was a lively, personable fellow, and unlike any others, he had access to a car (1952 Chevrolet). The advent of X, who knew member C better than the others, affected the status structure for the next three periods, as indicated in the three right columns of Table 7.1, after which it stabilized again. In short, X's appearance at first made it difficult to distinguish between the positions of A, B, and X; then X displaced B in second rank, and eventually raised the standing of his closest acquaintance—C. The relative standing of those *below* C did not change.

A more complex series of changes occurred in a group (A IIs 11a) in a middle rank neighborhood of the same city. Over a period of four months, a former member returned to this group from another city and a high status member gradually withdrew from it. The latter's withdrawal was initiated in the first instance by pressure from his parents. They felt the group was not a good influence, moved him to a relative's home across the city, and insisted that he get a job. Even though he travelled miles across the city to meet with the group, the time limitations imposed by his job, and especially the other members' growing conclusion that he had changed, finally resulted in his continuing absence. These events are reflected in the observer's ratings shown in Table 7.2. Each column shows the mean

TABLE 7.2. OBSERVER'S MEAN RANKINGS OF GROUP (A IIs 11A) IN BLOCKS OF OBSERVATIONS OVER THREE MONTHS

Members	Period			
	I	II	III	IV
A	1	1	1.1	1.0
Y	2.5	2.5	5.0	—
B	4.4	2.8	1.9	2.0
C	3.3	4.5	3.5	3.3
D	4.7	4.8	3.9	3.6
X	—	5.3	6.0	5.0
Number of Observations	8	10	10	7

ranking for blocks of seven to ten observation periods, as indicated. The new arrival is designated X, the departing member by Y. Individual B acquired a part-time job in the second period and bought a car (1937 Plymouth), which he subsequently traded for a 1955 Chevrolet—events reflected in his steady rise in status.

In two groups studied, the leader was absent for considerable periods near the end of observations. These groups were followed up a year after observations were concluded to see what effect the leader's departure had had.

When the leader of a group in a low rank neighborhood (Group B IIIs 3b) got a job, the members remained loyal to him, wished aloud he were around more, and actually deferred decisions on their plans until he was present to give his word. The group seemed on the verge of disintegrating when observations stopped. A follow-up a year later contacted ten of the former fifteen members. Four of them continued to associate regularly, but four others were members of other groups and a fifth was preoccupied with a girl whom he planned to marry. Still, the leader kept contact with the remnants of its membership.

The leader's absence in another group in a similar neighborhood (Group B IIs 6b), occurring after the conclusion of observations under quite different circumstances, resulted in the group's disintegration during the subsequent year. In this case, the leader was detected by the police in a nearby small town in the act of car theft, not with members of his own group, but with a friend of his brother's. It was a spur-of-the-moment act on their part, undertaken while they waited for the brother who had taken them with him on the serious business of stealing tires for his automobile. When they learned of the incident, members of the group felt that their leader had been very foolish to take such a risk when on a dangerous mission anyway. They stuck by him during the trial, but drifted away and apart during his incarceration. When he was released, he got a job and reported that the old group was not as it used to be. The number of get-togethers had become infrequent and unsatisfactory.

Changes in Structure with Changed Activities. Group B IIIs 7b (see Figure 7.5b) underwent a marked change in structure during a period of one month after they had broached to their observer the idea of engaging in athletic competition with other teams.

The group met in a neighborhood noted in former years for its "toughness." Following a killing a few years previously, parents and social workers in the area had been fostering interests in sports. The boys were interested in sports when the observer met them. But they were not and did not want to be in any organized program, and had no one to help them improve their skills. (Three of the boys were still in school, and one of these was a good enough athlete, in the observer's opinion, to have made the school team. He told the observer, however, that he preferred the company of his buddies, who would not like it if he took time away from them; and he felt that he was not good enough to make the school team anyway.)

The observer agreed to help them, and found his training and coaching suggestions rigorously translated into action by the leader— a "tough" boy who had inherited a mantle of aggressive strength from an older brother. The members followed his orders as if they were law. His younger brother was also a member, similarly reputed for "toughness." In the weeks preceding the end of December, 1961, the group practiced and trained. The first drawing in Figure 7.6 shows the observer's mean rankings of the members, which at this point were fairly stable. The younger brother of the leader (A) is designated as D.

The actual game activities (basketball), planning and putting strategies into effect, and substituting the right players at the right time called for skills other than toughness and bravery. The leader was not as good a player nor as effective in team decisions as others. As a result, other boys started to come to the foreground. The resulting fluidity in group structure is represented in the second drawing of Figure 7.6, showing the observer's average ratings over a period of twenty days after the first block. Arrows indicate the direction of movement he predicted at this time.

By the first of the next month, the group had stabilized again with a new and acknowledged leader (C), with member F's status higher, and the erstwhile leader's younger brother (D) considerably lower. (See bottom drawing in Figure 7.6.) It is noteworthy that these changes occurred without fighting or interpersonal conflict within the group. They were actually supported by the former leader for the good of the group, which had considerable success in basketball contests. On three different occasions, the erstwhile leader volunteered to withdraw from play when he felt he was not playing well enough. Once he said he felt ill, but the observer noted that he "recovered" quickly.

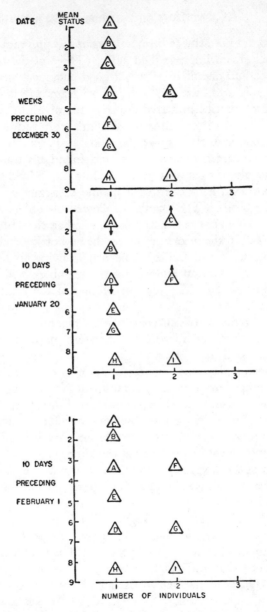

FIGURE 7.6. Changes in status structure with alteration of the group's main activities during a month. Observer's mean ranking of individual's status (vertical) and number of individuals occupying each rank (horizontal) at specified periods of time.

ORDER IN THE STABILIZATION
OF POSITIONS

It will be recalled that in experimental studies of group formation, the leader and bottom positions stabilize earlier in the group's development than intermediate positions (see Figure 7.1). In the previous section, several examples were given of the leader's withdrawal from the group and its effects on the structure. The effects are, as we learned, much more extensive than additions or subtractions of members at the bottom status level.

The ratings of the observers in the present research reveal that, invariably, the first individuals to be rated consistently in terms of effective initiative are those at the top of the structure—the leader and those of adjacent high status—with bottom positions emerging next.

These facts, taken together, suggest that the extreme positions, and especially the superior one, polarize the organization of role and status in a group—both for the members themselves as a structure forms and in the perception of an existing structure by an observer trying to appraise it. If this be the case, we may be dealing with a general phenomenon of human judgment found in laboratory experiments with various physical dimensions (e.g., weights, tones, length of lines). The phenomenon is called "end anchoring," referring to the tendency of the individual to identify the extreme stimuli (weights, frequencies, lengths) in a series presented to him, and to judge others relative to them. Thus, judgments of extreme items become accurate more quickly than others, and are made readily and with greater confidence (cf. Volkmann, 1951; Sherif and Hovland, 1961, Chapters 2 and 3).

De Soto and Bosley (1962) have recently reported a similar phenomenon in a learning experiment. Subjects were required to learn the college class (freshman, sophomore, junior, senior) affixed to a series of names of unknown students. Both in terms of numbers of errors and number of trials to perfect recall, learning was faster for the lowest (freshman) and highest (senior) classifications, suggesting an end-anchoring effect in the identification of position in a social structure.

As a *social* structure, a group is, to a greater degree than physical dimensions, affected by the superior (high-status) extreme. That is, the leader position tends to exert a greater anchoring effect than bottom positions, both in promoting group formation and in the perception of an observer.

If the leader position serves as a primary anchor and the bottom positions as a secondary end anchor in assessment of group structure, this should be revealed in successive ratings by the observers. One possible measure of the effects is the variability of their rankings of different individuals over a period of time. The ranks should be *least* variable at the high status, followed by the lowest positions, with greater variability in between.

Since we are dealing with ranks, the average discrepancy between an individual's rank on successive observation periods provides a direct and concrete indication of the relative variation in the observer's ratings over a time period. In order to make the necessary comparisons, we selected observation periods from the beginning to the end of an observer's experience with a group when most or all members were present. The results are presented for five groups of different size in Table 7.3.

In Table 7.3, an average change of zero means that the observer did not change his ranking of the individual at all during the block of observation periods. A mean change of .5 for a block of eight observation periods indicates that the observer changed his rating of an individual on the average of half a position for each of the eight periods. Such an average could result from changing the individual's rank by one position for four periods, or by changing it by two positions for two observation periods. A mean change of 1.0 indicates an average shift of one status rank from one period to the next. Thus the mean change indicates the observer's clarity or confusion in rating the individual, rather than deviations from his mean rating of that individual (which yield very similar quantities, however).

The blocks of observaton periods included in this analysis were selected in part simply because the most members were present at these periods. However, periods were eliminated in which the observer noted that *changes* were occurring in the group structure and

TABLE 7.3. MEAN CHANGES IN RANKS* ASSIGNED BY OBSERVER TO
INDIVIDUAL MEMBERS OF DIFFERENT STATUS (MEAN RATING) IN
GROUPS OF DIFFERENT SIZE

Individual's Mean Rating	Group Code				
	A IIs 11a	A IIIs 12a	A IIs 10a	B IIIs 6b	B IIIs 8b
1	0	.1	.1	0	0
2	.6	0	.2	.2	
					$\left\{\begin{array}{l}.5^a\\1.2\end{array}\right.$
3	.5	1.0			
			$\left\{\begin{array}{l}.7\\.7\end{array}\right.$	$\left\{\begin{array}{l}.9\\1.0\end{array}\right.$	
4	.3	.5			1.2
5	.2	.3	.4	1.3	
					$\left\{\begin{array}{l}.6\\1.3\end{array}\right.$
6		.3		.3	
			$\left\{\begin{array}{l}.4\\1.5\end{array}\right.$		
7		.3		.5	.8
8			0	.1	
					$\left\{\begin{array}{l}.8\\1.5\end{array}\right.$
9				0	
10					.8
11					.3
12					.6
Number of Observations	8	7	6	9	8

* Rounded to nearest .1.
a Braces indicate tied ranks.

gave his evidence of this. In other words, the data in the table represent as nearly as possible the observers' status rankings after the identity of members was known and at times when there was no striking evidence of structural change in progress. In this sense, they represent facts about the observers' judgments more than reflections of changed interaction, although the latter can never be held constant.

The data in the table clearly support the notion that the leader position serves as the major anchor in the observer's judgments of status. Not only does he single out the leader position first, he is also more consistent in ranking that individual over extended observation periods.

The trend of the mean changes in each group from high to low status positions also tells us that the bottom position in the group frequently serves as a secondary end anchor. In Groups 12a and 8b, the variations in rating the bottom positions are attributable almost entirely to the presence of "hangers-on" or fringe members at various periods who affected the rating of these individuals. Although it may seem an artifact that discrepancies in ranking bottom positions in these groups occur because other fringe members were present, it is a fact that a number of the groups were constantly in a state of flux at the lower end of the structure. The comings and goings of occasional associates were a regular feature of several groups which must be reckoned with as a fact, not an artifact.

By tracing the observer's ratings over successive weeks, we gain some understanding of the process of appraising a status structure. Such a comparison is possible only for a relatively small group. The members of large groups simply did not gather with one hundred percent attendance as frequently, even though varying combinations of the members spent the major part of almost every day together.

Figure 7.7 presents the average changes in the observer's ratings of a small group over three months of observations, totaling twenty-five periods in which members were all present, divided into four successive blocks of time. During the first and last block, five members are included in the analysis. The second and third blocks contain ratings of six members.

Starting with the first block of observations, we see that the observer singled out the leader first and ranked him as leader with no change. The greatest confusion in ranks occurred just below the leader position. In the second block, the general level of changes is lower. The observer has reduced the variability of judgment in the second and third positions, but there is more confusion in the ranks

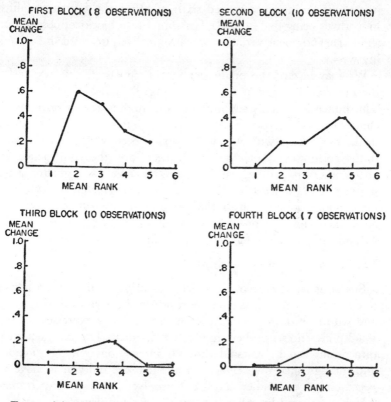

FIGURE 7.7. Variations in an observer's rankings of individual members over successive periods of time—an illustration of end-anchoring and stabilization of a reference scale in social judgment. Mean of differences between observer's successive ranks assigned to individual (vertical) and mean rank he assigned to given individuals for specified period.

The member at rank 6 in the second block of observation periods (upper right) rejoined the group during this period after an absence. The member in rank 2 during blocks 1 and 2 left the group in block 4 (lower right). During the third block of observations (lower left), the member in rank 2 acquired a car and was tied with the leader for one observation period.

just above the newly acquired sixth member, the fourth and fifth individuals being tied in rank. The subsequent blocks of observation show that judgment variation was progressively reduced in succeeding weeks.

We may hazard the prediction that a similar process occurs for the member of a group during prolonged interaction with others. This hunch is partially supported by our finding that in sociometric choices by members according to effective initiative, no ties occurred in the frequencies with which the person occupying the uppermost status position was mentioned. Furthermore, the coincidence between observers' rankings and sociometric choices was greater at the upper and lower levels of the structure. The greater clarity of the upper and lower positions in the group to members is striking when all of their choices (for effective initiative in three spheres of activity and for general preference) are combined, as in Figure 7.3.

Leader-Follower Relationships

Status, as we have seen, is an hierarchical power dimension having to do with initiative and effective conduct of activities in the group, and with control in *decision* processes. Popularity expresses the personal preferences of others for each individual. The fact that these dimensions can be assessed through interactions among members and through their own choices means that the individuals have *expectations* of each other and are themselves focuses of expectations which are shared by others and stable in some degree. We emphasize that the extent to which role expectations in a group are shared and stable is a matter of *degree*, not an all-or-none affair.

The power dimension (status) has been stressed because it is highly predictive of what the members of a group ordinarily will do when faced with a problem situation involving their interests. In addition, the individual's rank in the status structure colors not only his treatment by others, but also his conception of himself.

Earlier, we referred to the boy who preferred occupying a rather low status in his group to trying out for the school team. The boy also felt that he was not good enough to make the school team—a judgment not shared by the observer and independent rater who watched him perform. The observer noted that the boy's conception of his own ability could hardly be conceivable apart from his treatment by high status members, who made a sport of insulting him despite his obvious contributions to their victories. When he played well, they called him by his nickname, "Lalo"; but at the slightest error on his part, they called him "Lattow," which was the name of a Negro athlete at the school he attended. By this name, these Spanish-American boys not only made note of his dark skin, but berated him for the fact that he still went to school, and outside of his district—to a more prestigeful school than any they had attended before they dropped out. In their view, if he had to go to school, he certainly should go to Whittier or Tech, instead of McClellan High. At fifteen, he was the youngest "regular" member of the group. The observer wondered how long going to school and being a group member could be continued side by side.

In short, the power dimension colors interaction processes and member roles in them. But neither it, nor popularity, are the only attributes contributing to the expectations among members. The role relationships among leaders and followers express expectations concerning attributes and qualities highly valued by members and also the particular skills, personal characteristics, and contributions (or lack of them) that each member brings to group interaction.

Some of the qualities and skills requisite for standing in the group are closely related to the motivations which brought members together and to their significant activities. In middle and high rank neighborhoods, accessibility to a car is almost a "must" for a leader, and a great help to any member, in maintaining the respect of others. So is the capacity to "operate" smoothly with one's peers and adults. Manliness is prized alike in all adolescent groups, and success with the opposite sex is a great boon in achieving prestige. Athletic skill is highly valued in all groups that play games. In low rank neighborhoods, "toughness" is a general requisite of standing in a peer group. But the leader need not have the best car, be the smoothest operator, the biggest lady-killer, nor the toughest, as the case may be. In fact, usually he is not.

The leader position is the top rank in the status structure, but the leadership role involves the shared expectations of other members for a particular individual occupying that position. These expectations vary markedly in terms of the kinds of activities the group engages in and the qualities which count in their scheme of things. Invariably, however, they involve the supposition that what the leader approves of, what he suggests himself, or what he decides will be accomplished, will work out well. When his initiations to action and his decisions lead to failure in interteam competition, or result in social gatherings which bore and distress members, or get his fellow members into unnecessary trouble with authorities (parents, police, school)—then his word ceases to be effective. A new leader takes the initiative or the membership drifts away to other centers of interest, as we have seen in several of the groups studied.

It is necessary to understand this condition of effective leadership in natural groups of adolescents in order to analyze the roles of the various "followers." *Too frequently, the leader-follower relations are viewed as simple "dominance-submission," with the result that the followers' roles and their ties to the group are completely misunderstood.* Correction of the prevailing idea that group organization reflects simple dominance-submission among members does not mean that physical or verbal aggression plays no part in leader-follower relations. Verbal insults designed to keep members in their place were found in every group.

In some groups in low rank neighborhoods, a very good idea of the status structure could be gained by simply counting the number of insults traded and designating who was the butt of them. Likewise, physical aggressiveness sometimes had a lot to do with attaining leadership. Yet the leader did not have to use physical aggression to maintain his power. Even those followers who were better fighters and tougher refrained from challenging him. Why? The very question implies that the role relationships and ties of members to each other have not been duly considered.

Take the case of a boy in an exclusive neighborhood who was a member of one group studied (Group A Is 9a). He was in the lower status ranks of that group and was the object of "riding" by others for his "stodginess" in not drinking, smoking, and the like. This boy was president of the student council in the school they all attended, and no social isolate. He could have had other friends. The facts are that he not only kept associating with this group—which represented the exclusive fast set—but served a definite function in it. On occasions when trouble might arise from overindulgence or other "off-limits" behavior by members, he could be counted upon to see that they got home. His standing in school, in turn, lent prestige to the group in respects other than "fastness." His role in the group was secure, membership desirable, and the teasing which kept him in his place recognized qualities that he himself accepted as true.

The relatively minor role played by sheer physical force or its threat in group functioning can be seen time and again in the way leaders succeeded in influencing the course of group actions. Frequently the other members appealed for his opinion. Or when he gave it, the bickering and discussion of alternative plans died down. Thus, in planning a party, members were haggling over contributions in money and actions. The leader had kept fairly quiet through this, but had found out just what resources were available. His announcement of how much each member would contribute and his assistance in certain borrowing arrangements and matters of timing simply set the course of action and eliminated further discussion.

In another closely knit group (B IIIs 7b) the observer noted that in some matters the leader *did not even verbalize decisions, but just acted*. When the boys went to a game and someone said, "Where shall we sit?" he simply gestured to the far corner, started to walk, and was followed with no complaints that they were passing many available and better seats. This apparently arbitrary decision actually avoided possible friction with other groups by physical separation.

One important reason that exclusive preoccupation with dominance-submission inadequately characterizes the role structure of the group is the many-sided character of the expectations shared by members. Within the framework of the status structure, there is a very considerable range of possibilities for the roles of "good members," taking into account the particular skills, qualities, and characteristics of each individual. In this sense, accommodation of individual differences is "built into" leader-follower relations in an informal group. The full range of expectations for a member, based on his past behaviors, is essential to understanding his particular role in the group and the extent to which he willingly fulfills the obligations of membership. This can be seen by considering the roles of individuals occupying tied ranks in status and popularity.

For example, in Group B IIIs 7b (Figure 7.5b), members C and D are tied in status and popularity, but members had very different expectations of these boys. One was very tough, aggressive, and eager for a fight. Other members admired his fighting skills (he was first in choices of a fighting companion), but were wary that he would get them into unnecessary trouble. On numerous occasions, when they detected signs of his mounting aggressiveness, they cooperated in calming him down and suggesting alternatives which would circumvent needless conflict. The other boy occupying the same rank was characterized by the observer as "mild-mannered," though he hastened to add that this characterization held only for the context of other members of this group, since the boy's manner would have seemed that of a thug in the observer's own neighborhood. At any rate, this boy was not considered tough, but very skilled in sports and a "mainstay" both for team play and other activities. A very similar contrast in roles is found in Group B IIIs 8b (Figure 7.5c), where members E and F were tied for second rank in popularity and fourth in status. F was first choice of his fellows in fights, and E was the genial embodiment of the member who could always be counted on to pitch in and help in any group activity.

Likewise, the discrepancies occasionally found between status and popularity are largely attributable to expectations specific to the member and based on his past interactions with others. Member E in Figure 7.5b was chosen as liked by as many boys as the leader, but his status was markedly lower. He had associated with the group for several years and was considerad an excellent athlete and pleasant buddy. However, he had been exceedingly unreliable in attendance, partly because he had a steady girl friend. When the group began to engage in athletic competitions in earnest during the observation, the members made positive efforts to insure his attendance. Leadership changed hands, and the new leader was more "functional" in his approach to substitutions in play, so that this good athlete got to be in the game more than previously. His amiable person glowed under the circumstances, but he was not accorded a commensurate voice in planning and decision-making. After all, the other members knew of his erstwhile unreliability and could not yet count on his continued "steadiness."

Thus, an understanding of leader-follower relations in such adolescent groups as these, whether they be called "cliques" or "gangs" or "our set," is woefully inadequate without considering the range of expectations they encompass. If it were a simple matter of "compliance to external pressures" or submission to superior physical aggression, the role of follower would be exceedingly difficult to understand. The fact is that in the vast majority of group activities observed, the individual members willingly and without overt pressures regulated their behavior in terms of the shared expectations and other norms of the group.

In other words, *social controls* are not confined to external pressures, but include the internalization of shared expectations and other norms which regulate the behavior of members. Belonging was important to the individual, and belonging in some fairly clear-cut relation with other members, even if this relation involved unfavorable comparison of certain of his characteristics. In fact, he often accepted the evaluations by other members of his own strengths and weaknesses, whether this involved exaggeration in positive or unfavorable directions. Through repeated and prolonged interaction with his fellows, he came to think of himself as "one of them," to feel it important that he live up to their best expectations of him, and to take into account their evaluations of his weaknesses. Even if, as happened in several groups, he was trying his best to raise his standing or make his voice the deciding one, he was careful to do so in ways which would not bring disapproval from other members.

The patterned webs of interpersonal ties among individual members, translated day after day into concrete action situations in significant activities, are basic to sustaining the individual member's conception of himself. Thus, they are basic to understanding his conformity or nonconformity to the group's values and to his conceptions of what is the "right" and "wrong" thing to do. Much of the talk about adolescent morality and conscience has been divorced from these real and significant centers of the adolescent's activity and existence. Much can be gained by relating his actual behaviors to the currents of interaction in the social schemes that really *count* for him—the groups of peers to whom, psychologically, he relates himself—namely, his reference groups.

8 Acceptable and unacceptable behavior defined by group norms

During the adolescent period—the transition betwixt and between childhood and adulthood—agemates in general and one's own associates in particular become major reference groups for the individual. Being in the same boat, they appear more capable of understanding him. They are the ones whose opinions *matter* and whose actions *count*. The "inner voice" which prompts and regulates his social actions is likely to tell him what *they* will think.

When a youth interacts with others of his own choosing in patterned relationships of the kind analyzed in the last chapter, he takes part in developing its "customs," its "traditions" (however temporary), and in stabilizing common evaluations of other people, objects, and events which members regard as "our slant on things." No matter how lowly his standing, he can, with some justice, feel that this "slant" is more nearly his own doing than the values and moral precepts taught in family, school, or church. It becomes his own view of things: "What I *am* relative to others," "What is acceptable to *me*," "What is a good life, and what I *want*," "What I should do and should not do."

In short, when the individual shares in the formation of group practices and norms, or assimilates them as his own, they are reflected in his attitudinal reactions—his stands *for* some things and *against* others, his preferences, likes, and dislikes. Therefore, *psychologically*, the central problem of conformity-nonconformity, of adolescent morality and "conscience," is the problem of attitude formation and change,[1] especially of those attitudes relating his conception of self to other persons, objects, groups, and institutions.

This chapter illustrates norm-regulated behaviors in the groups of adolescent boys. Through these findings, we are in a better position to answer the initial and fundamental question to be raised in any discussion of conformity: "Conformity to *what*—what standard, value, or norm?" (Cf. M. Sherif, 1961).

As soon as we become concerned about the *sources* of the norms and *why* the individual conforms to them, the gamut of influences from the group, the neighborhood, and larger society have to be brought into the picture. In the mobile stream of modern urban society, individuals are not confined to the bounds of their group membership, nor are their groups insulated from outside influences.

In this chapter, we shall see examples of circumstances in which conforming behavior occurs in ongoing interactions of small groups. Even within these bounds, the standards are frequently not indigenous—in the sense of arising uniquely within the group. But once they are group concerns, the webs of influences commanding attention to the standards are enormously strengthened. In the next chapter, we shall look directly at the settings of groups and their prevailing reference scales for evaluation, with the aim of better understanding the sources of group norms and the personal and group conditions which intertwine as the background for conformity-nonconformity.

NORMATIVE REGULATION OF BEHAVIOR

The last chapter reported findings in the patterns of interaction in a dozen groups of adolescent boys who came together regularly at their own choosing with common interests and problems of being adolescents in their particular settings. We found that such recur-

[1] Some sociologists use the term *sentiment*, in line with William McDougall's formulation of the concept, instead of *attitude*. The concept of *attitude*, however, is associated with a considerable research literature, and has been an empirically based concept in both sociology and psychology, at least since W. I. Thomas' pioneering work.

rent associations *are* patterned. Individual behavior of members is regulated with reference to mutual expectations of one another's behavior. These mutual expectations—reflected in behavioral regularities—are sufficiently stable over a given period of time to be measured reliably. The role relationships composing the structure incorporate as a salient dimension a gradient of *power*—defined by the relative effectiveness of individual members in initiating or otherwise controlling the course of activities in the group, including notably the capacity to invoke sanctions (rewards and punishments) supported by other members.

As members interact in joint activities with appeal value to them, they develop common practices, common evaluations, and shared tastes in addition to those which brought them together. They develop nicknames for members, frequently epitomizing their roles in the group ("Chief," "Fox," "Old Shoe," "Ears"). Sometimes they adopt a name for the group. They arrive at common definitions of what is good and desirable, how a "good" member *should* and *should not* treat his fellows and outsiders.

Generically, all such products of interaction may be called the "norms" of the group. The standardized practices and evaluations which are called norms need not, however, be identical with typical or statistically average behavior in the group. They often embody conceptions of *expected* behavior, of the goals or ideals for a "good member." This "ethical" or "moralistic" feature of norms can be detected in criticisms of behavior or performance in the group, in praise of successful group or individual effort, and in the outrage which greets instances of deviation.

For individuals who take a social unit as their reference group, the norms of that social unit are the standards by which behavior is to be appraised. They are the *referents* of his conformity or nonconformity. Much of the unsavory reputation of "conformity" in current popular literature reflects the tendency of the writers to condemn conformity itself, rather than examining *what* is conformed to and *why* individuals conform to certain values rather than others. Conformity and nonconformity are, by definition, behaviors relative to some standards, which standards may be assessed as good or evil. Divorced from these referents, however, conformity or nonconformity cannot possibly be appraised in itself. The terms become meaningless.

In this chapter, therefore, we ask *what* group members were conforming to when their behaviors exhibited regularities and similarities, or when they reacted to cases of deviation. Our hypotheses predicted normative regulation of behavior in matters of consequence to the group, such as the motives which brought members together, their most important activities, and matters affecting the identity and maintenance of the group. It was also predicted that the latitudes for acceptable behavior—that range of actions not subject to criticism or sanction—would be more constricted in such matters. Conversely, the correctives applied for deviations in such spheres would be more severe and the degree of consensus among members in applying them would be greater.

Procedures

Observers were instructed at this *third phase of their observations* to concentrate on recording any and all regularities in the words or actions of group members, as well as external signs of membership, such as dress, insignia, decoration. They were told to note the relative *frequencies* of similar behaviors and expressed evaluations of individual actions, group performance, and of persons and objects outside of the group. In particular, they were to note exceptions to the common practices—who followed them and who did not, who agreed and who did not. Instances of praise, blame, punishment were to be noted, the members who initiated, supported, concurred, or objected being specified.

Further material related to member attitudes, self-conceptions, present and future goals was obtained after observations were completed. In interviews with members, the observer could find out more about their membership, stated attitudes, and expressed goals. These were in many cases supplemented by interviews with parents and teachers, and records of schools, social agencies, and police. With these and observational data, let us examine the group practices and products for which the latitude of acceptance was most restricted and reaction to deviation most severe.

Insignia of Group Membership

All but four of the twelve groups had names by which members referred to themselves. Three of the four which lacked names functioned in areas of middle or high rank; and none of them regularly engaged in interteam sports competitions, although they did play games among themselves. However, most members of a group (A Is 9a) in a high rank area had belonged to a secret fraternity, officially abolished by school authorities but continuing to function "underground." All but one of the members had been forbidden by parents to continue fraternity membership. They all regretted this and often expressed the wish that they could rejoin. In a sense, even these boys had an identity as former "Alpha Beta Deltas."

The groups which had a name in use for a considerable time were either 1. groups whose explicit purpose was athletic competition and/or 2. groups in areas of the city where conflicts among adolescent groups were relatively frequent. They were *not* all identified by police as "delinquent."

The role of intergroup conflict in sharpening the identity of a group and in its adoption of a name is strikingly apparent in Group B IIIs 8b: The name "Los Apaches" was adopted by this group in the middle 1950s before the present membership was adolescent. Before that time, there were several groups within the area. These groups were friendly toward one another, and would get together when attacked from the outside. The oldest brothers of the present leader were members when it adopted the name "Los Apaches." In fact, one of the leader's older brothers is referred to as "El Apache."

Interestingly enough, this colorful and bellicose designation, in which members took great pride, was not even entirely an in-group product. Here, in the observer's words, is how it was acquired: "During a fight with the Lakeside [gang], in which a member of the Lakeside was fatally wounded, a member shouted the words 'Los Apaches' as they were chased by policemen. The next day, the local newspapers gave an account of how a gang by the name of 'Los Apaches' had defeated the Lakeside. The name Los Apaches stuck with the group thenceforth—present-day members take interest in reading the newspaper in search of articles regarding Los Apaches."

Insignia of membership, like names, were associated with intergroup rivalry. The fraternity boys of Group A Is 9a had put away their pins, but they still felt it was the best fraternity—even far superior to college fraternities. When the boys in Group B IIIs 7b acquired basketball shirts, there was great excitement and serious consideration to the matter of selecting insignia. The observer wrote that there was no discussion about which member should have what numeral. When the box of shirts arrived, the three top status members stepped forward, the leader sorting through the shirts first to pick his numeral, then the others following in order of status to select theirs from those remaining.

Tattoos were common insignia of group membership in low rank neighborhoods with Spanish-speaking population. The location of the tattoo (e.g., between the thumb and forefinger) and the pattern (e.g., a cross between quotation marks) were distinctive to the group. A former member of Los Apaches who is now a settled and employed member of the neighborhood told the observer that he now regretted having a tattoo, but that at the time it seemed the thing to do and he would have been considered "chicken" if he hadn't had one.

Such insignia of membership (tattoos, articles of clothing) made the question of whether one was or was not a group member a clearcut matter. In at least one group (B IIIs 8b), the practice of fighting as a test of entry into the group was also employed on occasion.

However, the most general criterion of membership in all groups was simply whether other members accepted a boy when he hung around with them, and how frequently he was included in their plans. As we shall see, if he violated norms in matters of consequence to the group, such a general criterion made it relatively simple to exclude him.

The lack of tangible insignia of membership at times made particular individuals uncertain of their standing. A fraternity member had a badge, but the hanger-on in a high rank group who lacked a car and money had occasion to wonder if mere tolerance of his presence meant he was "in" or not. Similarly, in a low rank area, members of Group IIIs 6b discussed whether or not a member had belonged to a group formerly existing in their neighborhood. The boy said that he had; the others disagreed, two of them on the basis of their own association with the group.

In summary, the data on insignia of membership support the generalization that the sharpness of the delineation between those who are "in" and those who are not is to a significant degree a function of intergroup rivalry. Tangible signs of membership serve to make the distinction formal. Members of groups which had tangible insignia of membership were also much more exclusive in their contacts, habitually avoiding, ignoring, or expelling outsiders who ventured with unaggressive intent into their circle.

Clothing and Possessions

Among the narrowest ranges of individual variation permitted in the groups was the latitude of acceptable clothing. The norms for dress and hair style in these groups were not, on the whole, distinctive to the groups, but were highly differentiated between groups in different areas. Because of this and because apparel may appear to be a relatively inconsequential matter to males, it might appear that clothing and hair style were not related to group membership.

Apparel and hair style are closely related to important motives which brought the boys together, and the norms governing them did become group affairs. The fact that they vary with rank of the area in the city is simply one example of the norms of a setting becoming the norms for a group within it. There is ample evidence that appearance was a matter of definite concern to these boys, as a symbol of being a maturing male and of being counted as a group member. Members of a group in a high rank area (A Is 9a) wore the "Ivy League" styles of college students uniformly. Those in a neighboring area characterized by lower income and greater urbanization, but attending or graduated from the same school (A IIs 10a), wore blue jeans pushed down to the hips, no belt, and "flat-top" haircuts with rather long sideburns. The greatest difference from these styles was found in the low rank areas in cities with large Spanish-speak-

ing population and in the areas with the poorest and least acculturated population.

The norm for dress in the low rank, less acculturated areas (e.g.,
Groups B IIIs 2b and B IIIs 8b) on occasions when the members
went out socially was a dark suit, with pegged trousers, vest, and
expensive shoes ($25 to $30). The shoes were a matter of particular
interest and desire. In fact, on three occasions, the observer of Group
8b reported that members had beaten up men to rob them of their
shoes. The observer of Group 2b found frequent discussions of expensive brands of clothing, especially shoes. For a time, it was fashionable to remove the heels from the shoes, whether purchased or
otherwise acquired.

Concerns over conformity to acceptable modes of personal appearance are revealed in several reported instances of deviation. In Group
A IIs 10a, one member wore his hair in a very long, full style with
much hair dressing. His father and the recreational director of the
youth center where the group congregated repeatedly told, urged,
and ordered him to have it cut. His fellow members told him that
no girl would have anything to do with him if he did not change the
style, then began to insult him about it deliberately. Following a
particularly humiliating instance of hazing, the boy went to have his
haircut. Upon his return, he was greeted like a hero and praised
warmly for the style he had chosen (a flat-top like the others).

A member of Group B IIIs 8b badly needed a new suit for a social
event and, having no money for one, was overjoyed when the observer offered to lend him one. However, when he saw that the suit
was gray, not black, he thanked the observer and went away without it. He wore his old suit, even though the observer's gray one was
much better and would have fit him.

Similarly, the "required" possessions and their treatment differed
in areas of different rank, but this made the regulation of property
use no less a group concern. In a high rank area, a member of
Group 9a worked after school in a movie theater with the explicit
aim of getting a car of the same model and year as that belonging
to a high status member of his group.

When the boys in the high rank neighborhood planned a party,
everyone was expected to chip in money equally. (Liquor, which

was harder to come by, even with an illegal identification card and money, was shared, but the donor expected payment.) One member with less spending money than others tried on several occasions to get the members to gamble with him for cash. The members liked the game, but let him know their annoyance for trying to get *their* money in no uncertain terms. They began to give him the "cold shoulder" when he appeared.

Individuals in groups with few cars available (A IIs 10a, A IIs 11a, B IIIm 1b) gained enormously in standing by acquiring a car. Other members *expected* transportation from them as a matter of course.

Members of groups in middle and high rank areas would share cigarettes from a package, but not the same cigarette, nor a drink from the same bottle. Group B IIIm 1b lived in a mixed ethnic neighborhood, somewhat more prosperous than several other low rank neighborhoods, and its members all attended school. They once discussed their disdain for sharing a cigarette. The leader told of his great embarrassment on being stopped when on a date by a schoolmate who asked him for his cigarette butt.

In the other low rank areas, where money and possessions are scarcer, a cigarette was routinely shared by passing it around, as were drinks and other consumables. In planning a party, every member was expected to contribute what he had, but was not usually excluded if he had nothing. On the contrary, the member who had more, especially if he were leader, contributed more. On several occasions, leaders in Groups B IIIs 3b, 5b, and 8b were observed to contribute or lend all of their cash to a common endeavor, even though they themselves needed new clothing.

Common Practices in Important Activities

As the activities regularly engaged in by the groups varied, so did the areas in which behavior of members was normatively regulated. Those groups which engaged frequently in athletic activities had certain distinctive customs over and above the formal rules of the game (e.g., "no foul shots permitted," "no back-court rules," "never criticize a fellow member's performance while in competition; save it").

In playing among themselves, fouling by a member usually brought forth strong reprimands from other members. However, leaders of athletically inclined groups (Groups A IIs 11a, B IIIm 1b, B IIIs 7b) were frequently observed to foul rather flagrantly in play with other members without being reprimanded.

For example, Roberto, the skillful athlete and leader of Group 1b, played very roughly against others in his own group—using elbows and hands in illegal ways. Yet, in competition with another team, he was the model of good sportsmanship. A boy in his group with lower standing reacted to in-group and intergroup competition in almost an opposite way. He was not overly rough in play with his fellow members, especially if he was playing against Roberto. But when the group was pitted against another team, he became very aggressive physically and verbally. In fact, in planning the line-up for one match, Roberto kept the boy dangling with the threat that he could not even go with them because "you're too rough and you'll give us a bad reputation." At the last minute, Roberto gave in and the boy went along, chastised but with hurt feelings. Not one member pointed out to Roberto that he behaved in a similar fashion in in-group play. Instead, they urged the boy to "reforrm" so he could go with them.

Fouling was considered all right in intergroup competition if one could get away with it. In instances in which members were scolded or removed from the game by leaders for fouling, it was because the referee caught them.

The most elaborate and most strictly enforced common practices concerned activities which would have been punished by adults if detected. The member of a high rank group, drinking beer in a public place (where drinking was forbidden), was, for the time, screened from view by his fellows, standing casually but strategically to cover him. In a low rank area, the beer at a picnic was routinely covered with leaves and escape routes planned in the event of detection. Those groups whose members drank and hung around recreation centers (A IIs 10a, 11a, A IIIs 12a; B IIIs 2b, 6b) had customary modes and places for drinking which made their detection by the adult personnel less likely.

Groups which engaged in petty thievery often did so as a group. For example, the observer of Group B IIIs 7b was startled to find, after he had treated the whole group to cold drinks at a service station, that they had each managed to acquire at least one more bottle to drink after leaving. On a later occasion, he asked them not to repeat this performance while with him—to no avail. Getting more than paid for was a matter for ingenuity, and was considered a group joke.

In several groups (B IIIs 2b, 3b, 6b, 8b), stealing was not the incidental activity that it was in others. It was regarded as an acceptable and necessary means of getting needed possessions, or, more usually, cash.

Members of the aforementioned groups frequently engaged in theft when they were broke, usually selling articles other than clothing, and often using the money for group entertainment and treats. Such theft seldom involved more than two or three group members at a time. However, *its group reference is shown by the facts that other members were told about these events—with no fear of betrayal—and frequently enjoyed the benefits of the loot.* In these groups, theft was a permissible activity, its successful execution bringing admiration and praise from others.

In two of the groups whose members stole (B IIIs 2b, 6b), some of the boys had jobs paying about $20 or $30 a week. But they seldom had cash from their wages, which were turned over to their parents. This procedure was taken for granted by some of them as a necessity. But one boy, whose father was habitually unemployed, took the rent money he had been entrusted to pay and spent it on a big blowout for his group pals. He was found out, of course, but he said he would have done the same thing again, and his fellow members did not blame him. He stayed with one of them for several days afterward.

The fact that thefts of money, typewriters, tires, and the like involved only two or three members at a time reflects the boys' awareness that theft is a dangerous business in which too many members should not be involved at any one time. Without the element of sure legal prosecution, but with reference to agemate and adult reaction, participation in sexual adventure also usually involved only two or three boys at a time. A rape case occurred after observations were completed in Group A IIIs 12a involving three group members. Boys in Group A Is 9a would consult each other about a girl's reputation; but actual encounters with a "loose" girl were usually alone or with one male companion. This precaution reflected the boys' efforts to protect their reputation among the "nice" girls whom they wanted to date for school functions and private parties.

Girls frequently accompanied or attended the activities of Group A IIs 10a and A IIs 11a, but the members lucky enough to attract a girl aimed at solitary dates. In low rank areas, girls and group activities were more typically separate, except for dances, even though a few members of several groups (B IIIs 2b, 6b, 8b) were married. Taking a girl out in Group B IIIs 2b involved consultations of at least two members, unless she was the one somewhat older woman in the neighborhood whom they all felt free to visit.

It was taken for granted in all groups that fellow members would not trespass on another's right to a girl, while he held that right, whether it included sexual relations or not. In any area, however, a girl known as promiscuous was fair play.

Bragging about sexual activities and information was proof of "manliness" in all of these adolescent groups. It is notable that in Groups A Is 9a, IIs 10a, IIa 11a, B IIIs 2b, 3b, 6b, and 8b, the leaders were all considered successful with girls. The younger, late-maturing, or simply unattractive boy was considered not as manly. However, the conception of manliness in the groups composed of Spanish-speaking boys was coupled with the notion that a good group member must also *show* that he was not at the mercy of the whims of a woman. This concern doubtless reflects a cultural difference, at least in degree. While members of "Anglo" groups bragged of their "control" over girls, they were not constrained by other members for bringing girls into their group's activities, nor for having a date in preference to a group function.

The one instance of attempted fighting observed in a high rank area occurred when a nonmember had the audacity to visit a girl when she had a date with the leader. As noted in relating this incident in Chapter 1, the leader was angry at the boy, not the girl. He proceeded to round up his friends, go to the offender's home, and shout challenges from the lawn. It will be recalled that fighting was prevented by the intervention of the offending boy's astonished father. Nevertheless, Sterling (the leader) was admired by his fellows for "standing up for his rights" with the girl. This, too, is manliness.

The extended conversations about drinking and drunkenness were evidently also related to concepts of adult manliness. Members of Group A IIs 11a (who were 16–19 years old) often engaged in feigned drunkenness, with or *without* alcohol, to the mutual hilarity of all. In fact, interest in having, acquiring, and consuming alcohol was so frequent that it must be considered a valued substance common to these American boys. (The boys in Group B IIIm 1b were the only exceptions.)

To some investigators, this interest in drinking and drunkenness would be indicative of "retreat." However, both the actual circumstances of drinking and the bragging about drunken episodes point to their essentially social nature, tied to the role relationships of youth conceiving of themselves as near-adult males. The same generalization applies to observed instances of marijuana smoking and solvent sniffing. These practices were carried on by some but not all of the membership of some groups, at times when others drank beer and smoked tobacco, and in their presence. These observations, in our opinion, are difficult to reconcile with the classification of drug *usage* as a "retreatist" type of activity, even though the end result of the activity is assuredly a detachment from reality. Addiction, on the other hand, seems to reduce group affiliations sharply, as several authors have found (e.g., Yablonsky, 1962).

More specific evidence of social area and group differences in common attitudes toward male adulthood, toward other groups and institutions is included in the next chapter. Here, however, we turn to the sphere in which group norms were narrowest of all and group sanctions most severe for the deviate—matters of loyalty to the group.

Norms for Loyalty to the Group

Negative sanctions applied to a member whose behavior varies beyond the bounds of acceptability are among the clearest evidence for the existence of group norms. In the foregoing illustrations, such sanctions were seen in the form of urgings, hazing, insulting, or cold-shouldering the offender. However, the observers' reports reveal that sanctions more severe than these "psychological" punishments were decidedly infrequent, confirming the findings of earlier investigators.

The bulk of conforming behavior reported by observers occurred *without external pressure* in the form of sanctions or threat of sanctions. On the other hand, the only severe sanctions observed were applied to members who evidenced disloyalty to the group in the presence of outsiders.

In one rather large group of fifteen boys (B IIIs 3b), the leader discussed with his most trusted associates the need to "weed out" certain individuals whom he suspected of talking to the police about group activities. Even when not police but only parents were involved, members knew that the worst thing they could do would be to talk with outsiders about their covert activities. Members of Group B IIIm 1b, who were not under police watch and explicitly distinguished themselves as different from the "tough gangs" in bordering areas, discussed at length the low character of a boy in the neighborhood (a nonmember) who had had the nerve to squeal to one of their fathers about their habit of smuggling cigarettes from his grocery store.

A boy in Group B IIIs 2b stole a typewriter with the companionship of two fellow members, and gave the police their names when he was caught. He was given a jail sentence. Although his companions were not, the entire membership agreed that a good beating awaited him when he was released.

A member of Group B IIIs 7b made the mistake of running away from his fellows when they were jumped by members of a hostile gang. The fact that the adversaries had knives, and that fright was an understandable reaction, carried no weight at all with group members. The boy was finally completely ostracized by the group.

Members even succeeded in turning the girls in the neighborhood against him. The observer had some contacts with the boy afterward and reported that he was severely depressed, even despondent.

The "proper" way to act in a dangerous situation was formulated by the leader of Group B IIIs 8b: "If you have to run, run like mad, but if one of your boys is caught by the opposition, then you have to stop and help him. If you don't, you're a punk."

When the observer of a group in a middle rank area of City A was riding with one of its members, they passed the car of another member. Through the window, a challenge to a drag race was hurled. Within a few blocks, the other car jumped the curb, smashing into a light post. The car in which the observer rode stopped. The driver rushed over to the other car to consult the accident victims, assuring the observer not to worry but to stay there. After a quick discussion, he came back and drove away, saying that the others were not hurt and had agreed that the policeman shortly to arrive would go easier if they were not present, since it would immediately involve the group in charges of drag racing on a main street. The code of loyalty had been observed and the decision made in terms of group maintenance.

VARYING LATITUDES OF ACCEPTANCE, DEVIATION, AND LEADERSHIP

The foregoing discussion of normative regulation of behavior illustrates a pattern of findings supporting the following generalizations, to be examined in further research:

The latitude of acceptable behaviors, defined by the norms of a group, varies according to the importance of the activity to the members. In matters incidental to the main activities of a group and to the motives bringing members together, considerable variation in behavior occurs without concerted measures by other members to alter it. Especially in matters affecting the identity and maintenance of the group, such as loyalty in the face of outside threat, the latitude of acceptability is restricted and its bounds are clear. In such matters, deviation from the latitude of acceptance calls forth stronger and more consensual sanctions, usually severe punishment or expulsion from the group.

Corresponding to the variations in the latitudes of acceptance in activities of different import to the group, the latitudes of acceptance for members of different standing in the group vary. In matters related to the maintenance of group activities and of loyalty, the leader is expected to be the exemplar. He is expected to contribute more, in the form of money, possessions, or effort, to insuring the essentials for the activities the members enjoy most together. Especially in relationships with outsiders, which is one of the principal leadership functions, the latitude of acceptance is very narrow for the leader.

Thus, the leader of one of the most tightly knit groups (B IIIs 8b) was chastised by his fellows for being so foolish as to carry a weapon with him under the seat of a car, for which he was picked up by the police. Unlike other members, the leader endangers the identity and maintenance of the entire group by such behavior. As noted in the last chapter, behavior which endangered other members was the cause of one leader's downfall. In the description of Group B IIIs 7b in Chapter 1, we mentioned the continuing concern of members over their former leader, who inclined easily to fights with other groups. Their adventurous spirits were now fired with athletic competition, and they saw fights as potentially endangering their chances of playing, as well as getting them into serious difficulties with police.

In activities less significant to the group and *within* its bounds, however, the leader is frequently permitted much more deviation by other members. For example, he can commit fouls in games which would not be tolerated from others, and even strike another member for infractions of rules recognized by others.

These generalizations about latitude of acceptance and leader behavior are in line with the observations of other investigators of small groups (e.g., Homans, 1950). The concept *latitude of acceptance* is amenable to dimensional analysis of the observed phenomena, and to specification of the point at which deviations will be reacted to negatively by concerted actions of the members. In these terms, the generalizations may be summarized:

The more significant the activity for the identity and continued maintenance of the group and its central interests, the narrower the range of acceptable behaviors for all members, the latitude for the leader being narrowest. Conversely, the more incidental the activity to the foregoing concerns of the group, the broader the range of individual variation without the arousal of sanctions, the latitude for the leader being greatest.

Finally, our findings give striking testimony to the relative unimportance of coercion and pressure from other members in the normative regulation of behavior during the usual run of things in these adolescent groups. In terms of frequency, the bulk of observed conforming behavior occurred without punishment or threat of punishment. Conformity occurred, then, largely through the internal regulation of behavior by the individuals, for whom the group norms had become their own attitudes, expectations and ideals.

ADOLESCENT REFERENCE GROUPS AND ADOLESCENT CONSCIENCE

In recent years, the concept of "reference group" has shown its usefulness as a tool for distinguishing the individual's psychological relatedness to groups, on the one hand, and the other groups in which he moves and acts in daily life. Those groups in which he wants to be counted as an individual, which include the individuals whose opinions make a difference for him, whose standards and goals are *his,* are his reference groups (Sherif and Cantril, 1947; Sherif, 1948; Sherif and Sherif, 1953, 1956). Quite evidently, a person can and does have more than one reference group, especially in modern urban life. An adolescent, for example, usually has a family and perhaps school and church groups, as well as groups of peers of which he considers himself a part.

The puzzle in the growing contemporary literature on adolescent conformity, adolescent morality, and adolescent conscience seems to be why adolescents frequently do not reflect the moral values and prescriptions to which they have been exposed in the family, church, or at least in the schools which they have attended for over half a dozen years before reaching adolescence. Aside from traditional conceptions of morality and conscience in religious dogmas, the source of this puzzle lies largely in the predominance of Freudian psychoanalytic conceptions of development and of conscience. In the Freudian conception, the significant events in psychological development occur in childhood, well before adolescence is attained. Socialization is accomplished through acceptance of the prescriptions of society regulating one's instinctive impulses, particularly the prohibitions and dictums of parents. These societal prescriptions, especially those of his family, become his conscience, and he feels guilty when he violates them—hence the self-regulating character of moral behavior.

As Sears (1960) pointed out recently, this classic conception of conscience is almost wholly a negative one—applicable to problems of "resistance to temptation" and "guilt" but not at all to those "positive qualities which become ideals to be attained in their own right" (p. 96). Sears notes that the Freudian conception of conscience was developed to deal with severely disturbed individuals who "resist temptation too little or too much, and who are in trouble one way or another with their feelings of guilt" (p. 96).

If discussions of adolescent morality and conscience are to square with the facts, two lines of factual evidence have to be considered in addition to the obvious fact that life is not wholly made up of avoiding temptation or feeling guilty.

First, there is ample evidence, contrary to Freudian notions, that psychological development continues throughout life and that, in particular, the adolescent period is characteristically a period of change (cf. Sherif and Cantril, 1947, Chapters 8 and 9; Ausubel, 1954; Horrocks, 1962).

Second, the individual's standards of right and wrong behavior are not derived simply from representatives of adult society (parents, teachers, church, mass media of communication), and even these are filtered, reinforced, or contradicted in interactions among those of his peers who count for him. Thus, "conscience" is not a set of prescriptions divorced from his continuing psychological development. It is the warp and woof of his very conception of himself in relation to others who *count* in his eyes, woven in the course of interactions with them—whether the source of its values is parents, school, church, mass media or peers (Sherif, 1962).

This is the feasible explanation for the fact that an individual may know perfectly well what his parents, teachers, and preacher say is right and wrong, *and yet violate this without feelings of guilt if his fellows do not condemn him.* The term "conscience" ceases to be useful as a *psychological* concept when applied only to those prescriptions which adult and legal authority uphold. It becomes psychologically meaningful when used to refer to those standards which the individual *does* uphold and relative to which he *does* experience remorse when he violates them. Such standards are those of his reference groups, whether these be his family, his school, his church, a tightly knit group of his peers, or the charmed world of television and motion picture celebrities.

By specifying the source of the values which actually do regulate the individual's behavior, in terms of his reference groups, it becomes operationally possible to specify why his behaviors are in harmony with the prescriptions of adult society or some part of it, on the one hand, or why his behavior is "immoral," using adult prescriptions as a standard. Such specification of *source* will show us that conscience is a typically human product, even though the particular behaviors which arouse pangs of conscience differ considerably. The boy who defies major values of society without regrets may feel profound guilt if he betrays fellow members of his group.

As we noted in an earlier chapter, it has been found that boys who engage in socially undesirable activities are frequently more sociable, and more responsible and loyal to their fellows, than others. Indeed, our research indicates that in "delinquent" activities as well as in "nondelinquent" activities, those boys who contributed most were those with greatest social and other skills in their groups. This is in harmony with Ruth E. Hartley's study (1957) on acceptance of the values of a new reference group. "Ease in interpersonal contacts" and "acceptant" response tendencies were significantly related to loyalty, pride, and desire to belong to a reference group, while negative personal qualities ("sense of victimization," "cynicism," and "lack of self-confidence") were not.

The adolescent period in modern industrial societies is, as we have seen, marked by shifts in the relative importance of family, school, and other adult groups, on the one hand, and agemates, on the other. W. M. Prado (1958) demonstrated this shift for boys between 8 and 11 years old and in adolescence. He deliberately selected boys who *preferred* their fathers and who felt that their fathers understood them. Then he had each boy with his father and his best friend (agemate) take part in a simple game in which the outcome was not self-evident to the subjects, but which he could score objectively. He asked the boy to estimate the performance of his father and his best friend.

The outcome was that twenty of the twenty-five children appraised their fathers' performances as superior to their friends', but nineteen out of the twenty-five adolescents judged their friends' performances to be superior. (The average sizes of these differences were statistically significant.) In sixteen cases, the adolescents judged their friends' performances as better than their fathers', when in fact the father had done equally well or better (as measured by the experimenter). Thus even adolescents who love their fathers and prefer them tend to overvalue the achievements of friends, which is not the case among younger children.

The shift in the significance of agemate reference groups in adolescence is accompanied by spending more time with peers, engaging in more activities with them, and turning more and more toward their evaluations of one's own qualities and behavior. Pleasure and satisfaction of engaging in desired activities apart from adults, a sense of being someone with a clear-cut place in some scheme of things, interactions in activities reflecting that scheme, contribute to the adolescent's willing participation with others and his willing regulation of his own behavior within the group's shared expectations for member behavior and other norms of the group. For the time, the peer group is his most important reference group. Its values or norms are the ones that count for him. The character of these norms and their relationship to the neighborhoods in which groups function is the major concern of the next chapter.

9 *Self-radius and goals*
of members relative to
sociocultural indexes

The findings reviewed in the last two chapters were chiefly on behaviors within the bounds of immediate group activities. However, the individual adolescent's behavior cannot be accounted for solely in terms of *contemporary* face-to-face interactions with his fellows. His attitudes toward himself and others have both a history and a future. His self-system or ego incorporates conceptions of what is necessary for a "good life" now and in adulthood, what one must do and become to be successful, where he sets his sights, and his estimates of the probabilities of hitting the target. These attitudes toward achievement and failure, toward other persons and institutions, toward work and leisure trace the radius of the individual's conception of himself in these respects. The self-radius, in turn, defines the limits within which he sets his personal goals.

Does growing up in sociocultural settings of low, middle, or high rank within society affect the child's self-radius and goals? In what respects does the larger society, as conveyed through mass communications and other institutions, produce similarities among adolescents who have grown up in different situations? In order to answer such questions, the design of this research included collection of data on the differentiated settings in which the individuals have developed and study of the reference scales for evaluation which prevail in each. As emphasized in Chapter 5, individual behavior and individual personalities are properly assessed within the framework of the milieu of which the individual is a part, the value scales of its residents, and the specific interaction processes to which he contributes. Having discussed interaction processes in some detail, we turn now to the physical and normative settings in which they occurred.

The first step is to examine the physical and sociocultural features of the different settings. The section on neighborhoods in this chapter is a highly condensed summary of the ecological and sociocultural data most pertinent to the concerns of adolescents living in the different neighborhoods. A sociological study of these neighborhoods could quite properly devote more space to the detailed description of their physical facilities and the characteristics of their populations.

However, the physical and demographic characteristics of the neighborhoods are only part of the picture which the individual adolescent faces from day to day. A prominent part of his environment is the actions of other individuals in his own and other neighborhoods which reveal to him their evaluations of what is good, necessary, proper, and desirable in various spheres of living. The evaluations of other adolescents are particularly salient to him at this stage of development. The second major section in this chapter summarizes the findings on the self-radius and goals of representative adolescents in different areas of the cities. These findings are useful for the investigator in still another way. The prevailing evaluations and goals of adolescents in a setting are a meaningful basis for appraising those of particular individuals in small groups with respect to how typical or atypical they may be.

The next chapter concerns the interplay of influences from the social setting and in the lives of individual members which affect the relative importance of the group to its members, and hence the degree of solidarity and consensus which they are able to achieve.

PHYSICAL AND SOCIOCULTURAL SETTINGS OF THE GROUPS[1]

The groups of boys studied in this research lived in three large cities in the southwestern states. The northernmost of these, designated as A in our code for the groups, had a predominantly native-

[1] Unless otherwise specified, demographic data in this section are taken from the *U.S. Censuses of Population and Housing*, 1960.

born white Protestant population of over 500,000 in 1960. The cities designated as B in the group code are located to the south and west, and differ notably from A in having substantial populations of bilingual residents of Mexican origin or ancestry.

Since most of the groups of Spanish-speaking boys were studied in the larger of these cities, data on the prevailing attitudes and goals of Spanish-speaking youth were obtained in that city (as reported later in this chapter). For purposes of comparison, therefore, the ecological data in this section pertain to the same city. This city had a population of almost 588,000 in 1960, 41.4 percent of whom had Spanish surnames. Less than half of these Spanish-speaking persons were of "foreign stock" (i.e., one or both parents born outside of the United States).

Altogether, 49.99 percent of City B's population was classified in the census as "nonwhite" or as belonging to ethnic and national groups from Latin American or southern, central, and eastern Europe (that is, to groups traditionally accorded low status in the country). Approximately 7 percent were Negro. In contrast, only 14.2 percent of the residents of City A were classified as nonwhite or from these countries, this proportion including the 11.6 percent classified as Negro.

As a dramatic corollary of these population differences, the median reported income of families in City A was $5601 and that in B was $4691. For families with Spanish surnames in City B, median income was $3474. In City A, persons 25 years and older had completed an average (median) of 11.9 years in school. In City B, the average years of schooling was 9.6 years, but for persons with Spanish surnames the median was 5.8 years.

Both cities are business and commercial centers. Both have large military installations supplying jobs for many residents. Neither city is heavily industrial. Both have colleges and universities, and their own symphony orchestras.

The Neighborhoods Where Group Members Lived

Members of some groups lived in neighborhoods well defined by city streets and landmarks. Others were scattered over rather wide areas. In electing to describe their neighborhoods, we have chosen those areas in which most members lived and in which the group's principal gathering points were located. Statistics describing the neighborhoods are for the Census Tracts coinciding most closely with these areas. The more striking discrepancies between the actual residences of members and the tracts are noted below.

In City B, the neighborhoods are described adequately by five adjacent tracts located near the center of the city, but separated from the downtown business center by a freeway and arterial streets. A railroad cut through the district, which was bordered by business establishments. In all of these tracts, the typical dwelling was the single family house, as indicated in Table 9.1. On the average, these houses had four rooms. Tract 41 had a large and modern low-rent housing development in which members of Group B IIIs 2b lived.

As indicated by the fertility rates in Table 9.1, the small homes and apartments were usually crowded with children. A block survey

TABLE 9.1. DESCRIPTIVE STATISTICS ON NEIGHBORHOODS, CITY B, LOW RANK AREAS

	Census Tract Number				
	35 %	34 %	41 %	43 %	60 %
Single family dwellings	86.9	93.7	76.9	79.5	97.9
Fertility[a]	67.1	63.6	90.0	77.9	93.0
Women working	32.5	32.3	35.2	36.5	23.3
Adult laborers	58.2	56.9	56.0	58.5	67.4
Adults completed only 8 or fewer school years	64.4	73.2	76.8	82.6	88.1
Low ethnic status	89.9	91.7	89.1	93.5	93.2
Mexican-born	9.0	15.5	8.8	14.1	8.4
Negro	26.4	12.2	.9	—	—
Lived in same house 5 years or more	62.4	55.9	50.5	51.4	57.0
Median family income	$3,051	$2,851	$2,276	$2,483	$2,725

[a] Ratio between number of children under 5 years and number of women ages 15–44 years.

conducted for this research of every tenth dwelling showed that, on the average, households in Tract 35 had two or three children, while those in Tract 41 had four or five. Our survey of the high-school age population in the city found an average of five children for Spanish-speaking families, compared to an average of two or three for English-speaking families of high school students (Sherif and Sherif, 1960).

In all of these neighborhoods in City B, the majority of employed adults were laborers, about a third of the women held jobs, and the great majority of the adult population had completed eight or fewer years of school. In the block survey and high school survey, we found that approximately 20 percent of the families did not have a father living with the family. Thus, in many cases, working women were supporting the family at rather unskilled, low-paying jobs (C. Sherif, 1961).

Of the tracts in City B, Tract 35 differed from the others in having a somewhat higher average income and about twice as many high school graduates as other neighborhoods. In fact, with respect to years of schooling, the Spanish-speaking population of this neighborhood was well above average for Spanish-speaking residents of the city. This was also the most heterogeneous neighborhood in terms of the ethnic backgrounds of residents, over a quarter being Negro. According to municipal statistics, it had the lowest delinquency rate of the five neighborhoods (about four cases per hundred youngsters from 5 to 20 years), despite the fact that the immediately adjacent tract had the highest rate in the city (about twenty-five per hundred youth). (We have noted Group B IIIm 1b in this area specifically described themselves as "different" from tough neighboring gangs.)

Near each of these neighborhoods, there were parks, playgrounds, or agency centers designed to serve the recreational needs of youth. The groups whose members did not participate in competitive sports were in Tracts 34 and 41, the former having the largest proportion of foreign-born residents. The boys in Tract 43, which had a comparable proportion of Mexican-born, were the ones who asked the observer to help them get team play started, as described in Chapter 1.

In City A, the high rank neighborhood was characterized by attractive and prosperous-looking family houses (see Table 9.2).

TABLE 9.2. DESCRIPTIVE STATISTICS ON NEIGHBORHOODS, CITY A, BY RANK OF AREA

	High (I)	Middle (II)		Low (III)	
		Census Tract Number			
	7	10	24	41	37
	%	%	%	%	%
Single family dwellings	94.6	72.7	63.4	74.6	24.1
Fertility[a]	35.3	31.7	54.8	69.8	59.0
Women working	52.5	46.9	48.6	21.8	42.1
Adult laborers	17.8	23.0	30.0	48.6	48.5
Adults completed only 8 or fewer school years	13.9	22.2	30.8	49.1	63.9
Low ethnic status	2.4	2.1	3.0	3.1	18.5
Lived in same house 5 years or more	44.9	39.9	39.1	44.6	35.5
Median Family Income	$6,446	$5,185	$4,344	$4,480	$2,496

[a] Ratio between number of children under 5 years and number of women ages 15–44 years.

Three members of Group A Is 9a lived outside of this area in an untracted suburb to the north which contains the most elaborate and expensive dwellings in the city area.

Members of Group A IIs 10a lived nearby the high rank area toward the center of the city, most of them in Tract 10, which contained the "uptown" recreation center of a men's civic club where they congregated. Both their neighborhood and that of Group A IIs 11a, some distance south and west of it (Tract 24), are characterized by a transitory population with an average income below the city-wide median (see Table 9.2).

The two low rank areas in City A are not, in terms of the census statistics, as "depressed" as the low rank areas in City B. The group in Tract 41 met at a recreation center in this neighborhood, which is composed predominantly of laboring people with large families living in small houses. Less than a fourth of the adults had graduated from high school. Tract 37 was very near the business district and was the only neighborhood in City A with an ethnically mixed population (18.5 percent of low ethnic status as defined in the census, which is above the city average). None of the neighborhoods in City A housed more than one or two Negroes in 1960.

Social Rank of the Neighborhoods

The method of ranking neighborhoods as low, middle, or high was inspired by the work of Shevky and his co-workers, notably Wendell Bell (Shevky and Williams, 1949; Shevky and Bell, 1955; Bell, 1958). The rationale of rating urban neighborhoods (census tracts) as to socioeconomic-cultural status rests on the general finding that certain demographic measures tend to be intercorrelated. For example, educational level, occupational status, and income in modern cities are associated with certain standards of living. When these are all low, we tend to find poorer nutritional and health conditions, higher infant mortality rates, and so on. Shevky's basic notion was that an area could be characterized meaningfully by adjusted averages of a few measures which would indicate (1) socioeconomic rank, (2) degree of urbanization, and (3) ethnic status of the residents.

This general conception has been supported by Tryon's cluster analysis of census tract data (1955), which showed that at least three factors were necessary to characterize a neighborhood, even though it suggested several revisions of the measures to be used. The Shevky-Bell indexes were also supported by Van Arsdol, Camilleri, and Schmid's factor analysis of census tracts for ten cities (1958), in which they reported that residual correlations after extraction of three factors were small, and that the Shevky-Bell indexes had high generality for these cities. Like the latter authors', our data suggest that the ethnic status of residents is correlated with socioeconomic rank and, inversely, with certain measures of "urbanization," e.g., fertility rates.

Whatever their weaknesses, the Shevky-Bell indexes are empirically based, theoretically meaningful, communicable, and offer definite criteria for ranking neighborhoods (cf. Bell, 1958). In order to assure comparability with findings by other investigators using the Shevky-Bell indexes (e.g., Greer and Orleans, 1962), the computation procedures and conversion factors they have suggested (Shevky and Bell, 1955) were followed.[2]

Briefly, socioeconomic rank is based on proportions of employed workers in a tract who are blue-collar laborers and of adults with eight years or less of schooling. The larger these proportions, the lower the social rank. The urbanization index is composed of three measures: proportion of single family dwellings, proportion of women in the labor force, and the fertility ratio (see Tables 9.1 and 9.2). The lower the proportion of single-family dwellings, the lower the fertility ratio, and the higher the proportion of women working, the higher is the index of urbanization.[3] The third Shevky-Bell index refers to the ethnic status of the population, expressed in terms of the proportion of residents who are nonwhite or members of national groups placed low on the prevailing scale of social distance by native white citizens (cf. Bogardus, 1924, 1947).

Figure 9.1 presents a plot of the standardized indexes for socioeconomic rank (baseline) against the indexes of urbanization for

[2] Since their conversion factors are based on the range of the measures in entirely different cities some years ago, it is obvious that the desirable procedure would be to repeat their original study in the cities of our research. It is just as obvious that this alternative would amount to a major ecological study in its own right. As our research continues, we hope to find available more applicable conversion factors as well as improvements on the measures. By dealing with raw percentages, however, we were able to satisfy ourselves that the composite ranks we have assigned to the neighborhoods in this research were not dependent upon the Shevky-Bell conversion factors.

[3] Bell prefers to take the inverse of this measure, calling it "family status." That is, the more single-family dwellings, the higher the fertility ratio, and the lower the proportion of working women, the higher the family status. However, we find it incongruous to refer to the tracts in City B and to Tract 41 in City A in our research as having high family status, when in fact the families were crowded into small houses and, in City B, almost a quarter lacked a male breadwinner. The concept of "urbanization," which resembles the notion of "acculturation" to an urban way of life, seems more congenial to the facts concerning the Spanish-speaking families in City B and to the working families of rural background in Tract 41 in City A. It is hoped that Bell and other researchers may develop an index better suited to reflect family status.

the five tracts in City A and the five tracts of City B. As already noted, only Tract 37 in City A is above the average in residents of "low ethnic status," while all the tracts of City B are predominantly Spanish-speaking, hence "low" in ethnic status.

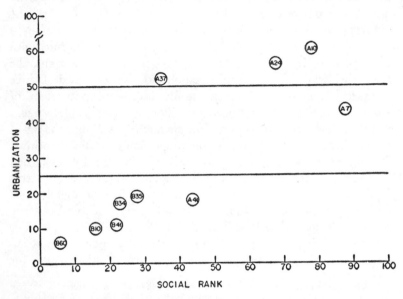

FIGURE 9.1. Study areas in Cities A and B plotted as to socioeconomic rank (horizontal) and urbanization indexes (vertical) according to Shevky and Bell (1955).

In designating the neighborhoods as to composite social rank (low, middle, or high) for purposes of this research, we have also taken into account average income and size of family relative to that income. Since only Tract A 7 had a median family income above the city-wide median, the designation of "high" was reserved for it and other such neighborhoods in future study. Income is an extremely important consideration, especially when the general level of education is as high as it is in City A. For this reason, our cutting point between "middle" and "low" was made at the socioeconomic rank index of 50. Tract A 41 was ranked as "low" because family income was low for the large families in the tract. As Figure 9.1 shows, tracts of "middle" rank are not adequately represented in our research at present. The two middle rank tracts are both highly urbanized compared to the others and their populations transitory. This background is helpful in understanding the fact that the two groups in middle rank areas both contained a good number of school drop-outs. The continuing research program will secure more stable neighborhoods in the middle range.

PREVAILING VALUES OF ADOLESCENTS ASSESSED BY SELF-RADIUS AND GOALS SCHEDULES

How do adolescents living in areas of low, middle, or high rank perceive their neighborhoods and other neighborhoods in the city? Are their models for success and failure uniformly patterned in the images projected in schools and through the omnipresent mass media of communication? Do the alternatives for choice in their settings affect their goals? Do they set their sights at the same levels in various spheres of activity? Do they value and want the same things?

There is a considerable body of research data showing that the goals of adolescents from different socioeconomic backgrounds do differ in various spheres of achievement, for example in occupational and educational spheres (cf. Haller and Butterworth, 1960; Hyman, 1953; Empey, 1956). We have also found that this is the case (C. Sherif, 1961). Does this mean, for example, that lower-class youth reject the idea of "success" after being force-fed with the notion at school and on television? Or does it mean that the self-images of the lower-class and upper-class youth involve entirely different sets of values? Such questions have been raised in current discussions of education, adolescent "culture," and "lower-class subcultures."

In our research, surveys were made of representative samples of high school youth in areas of high, middle, and low social rank in Cities A and B. The surveys were made in high schools serving the neighborhoods where members of the study groups lived. In City

B, the group from the tract with the higher social rank index (Tract B 35 in Figure 9.1) attended a school included in our "middle" high school sample, a student body composed of both Spanish-speaking bilinguals and English-speaking youth. For comparison, we also sampled a "high" rank school attended almost exclusively by English-speaking students in the most prosperous area of the city. Thus, in City B, there were three samples of high school students: 1. High rank—entirely English-speaking; 2. middle rank —separately classified as English-speaking and Spanish-speaking; 3. low rank—entirely Spanish-speaking bilinguals.

The high school samples in City A represent schools serving neighborhoods we have ranked as high, middle, and low with one exception: Two members of the group in a middle rank neighborhood (Tract A 10 in Figure 9.1) had graduated from the high rank high school, one attended it, and the others had dropped out or been expelled. It will be recalled that this tract was ranked as "middle" on the basis of the lower than average income of its residents. Most of the students attending this high rank school came from the north of this tract, and more than 70 percent of them continue their education in college.

Self-Radius and Goals Schedules. Anonymous responses to an "opinion survey for teen-agers" were obtained in required classes and study halls throughout a school day in each school. In this way, the background characteristics of the samples corresponded closely to the population values in school records. The samples were composed of 298 students in City A and 377 students in City B.

In designing the questionnaires, a primary aim was to make the items and the instructions easy to read, so that school achievement would not seriously affect the responses. When the survey was made, the teacher left the room and students were assured that school officials would not see their completed forms. They were not required to sign their names, although information about age, sex, class, etc., was requested. All instructions were read aloud and ample time given to complete the forms.

The items in the schedule varied in form, as indicated in summarizing the findings. In City B, the form included a number of items pertaining to preferences and experiences with Latin American culture. These items were not used in City A, which had very few Spanish-speaking residents, but other questions were added. In both cities, the students were from the upper three classes in high school, and the median age was approximately 16 years in all samples.

Adolescents' Perceptions of Their Own and Other Neighborhoods

When we think of the place where we live, the notion of attitudes defining one's self-radius becomes very concrete. Is this the sort of a house and a neighborhood that is *right* for me? If I could, would I move out of it? If so, where?

The neighborhoods studied in this research did differ in appearance, and many of these differences reflected socioeconomic and cultural differences between the residents. For example, in the least acculturated (and least urbanized) neighborhoods of City B, one frequently saw little houses whose yards had no grass, but had colorful pots of flowers in an "old world" fashion. The high school students recognized this difference in their neighborhoods: Over one-fourth of the low rank sample reported that "most yards in my neighborhoods have flowers, but no grass," as compared with none of the students in the high rank area and only 7 percent of the Spanish-speaking students in the middle rank area ($p. < .001$).

The high school students were asked to fill in the blank in the following statement: "If I had my way, I'd like to live in a neighborhood in the _____ part of the city." Figure 9.2 shows how the youth in City B responded, the baseline giving rank of the area and sociocultural background of the students. The solid line represents the proportion who wanted to stay in the same neighborhood. The high rank sample, which overwhelmingly wanted to stay where they were, lived on the north side of the city. The long dashed line shows the proportion in other schools wanting to move to the north side, and the short dashed line those who wanted to move in another direction. In the low rank area, over 65 percent wanted to move, and most of these to the beautiful north side. In short, there is an inverse

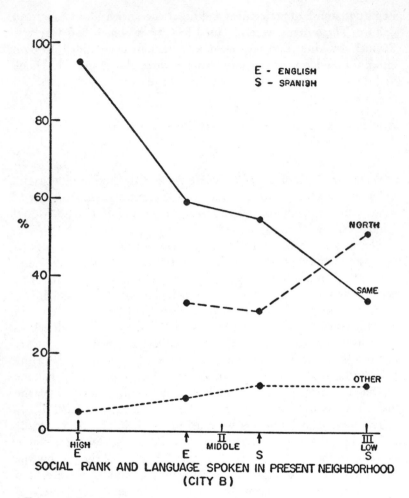

FIGURE 9.2. Contentment and discontent with own neighborhood in areas of different social rank. Proportions of high school youth desiring to move to another neighborhood (*north* or *other*) and to remain in the *same* neighborhood.

relationship between rank of neighborhood and desire to move, and between rank of neighborhood and desire to move north.[4]

A similar relationship was found in City A, except that the preferred directions of the two thirds who wanted to move from the low rank area were equally divided between different sections of town. This split reflects the fact that City A has attractive residential sections on two sides of the city.

A glib interpretation of the finding that so many in low rank areas would like to live in the most attractive part of the city might overlook the fact that it was the living arrangements that were desired, not necessarily other features of the way of life. One member of a group in a low rank area (B IIIs 3b) had in fact moved to a much nicer part of the city with his family, but kept returning to meet with his old pals. He said he could not have fun in his new neighborhood. Even in City A, where the low rank neighborhood was mixed ethnically and lacked the cultural unity of low rank neighborhoods in City B, members of a group which lost a game to boys from a more prosperous area spoke of "us" and "them"—"what *we* couldn't do if we had *their* equipment."

In City B, youth in low rank neighborhoods felt a distance from those "rich Anglos." Over 60 percent of the high school youth in this area preferred Mexican food over any other, and friends who could "speak both Spanish and English." Observers in these neighborhoods frequently referred to the strong feeling for one's neighborhood, in keeping with earlier findings that attachment to neighborhood tends to remain stronger in lower rank youth from childhood through adolescence (Bernard, 1939). On the other hand, we have no evidence of implacable resentment toward high rank, English-speaking youth on the part of the bilingual students. When given the opportunity to state the kinds of people they preferred as friends (using ethnic labels or not, as they chose), almost as many chose "Anglos" or English-speaking friends as "Latins." (C. Sherif, 1961). (Sixteen percent specifically wrote that group membership had

---

[4] In summarizing these data, we speak of a "relationship" or a "significant" difference when its reliability is indicated by an appropriate statistical test (alpha = .05). Frequency data were evaluated through the chi-square test, medians, and means, with reference to their confidence limits.

nothing to do with their choice of friends, a larger percentage than for other groups, although not significantly so.)

Among the informal groups of Spanish-speaking boys observed in City B, there were differences in self-identification. These differences closely parallel the relative acculturation of the residents of their neighborhoods, the most intensely "Latin" self-references occurring in neighborhoods with more homogeneously Spanish-speaking populations and larger proportions of Mexican-born persons. By comparing the boys' evaluations of "Latins" and "Anglos" in the different groups, we found that the language used in group activities reflected the degree of their identification as "different" from Anglos.

Groups in the least acculturated neighborhoods (see Table 9.1) regularly spoke Spanish or, more properly, a patois called "Tex-Mex" heavily loaded with "Pachuco" slang (which seems to have developed among adolescents near the Mexican border). In these areas, the boys made a *point* of putting needed English terms into a Spanish form. For example, he squealed became *se esquila;* airplane was *aeropla;* a phonograph record was *rola,* from the English word roll. Anyone who could speak Spanish but used an English term was *fofaro* (sissy) and was admonished accordingly. Although policemen were customarily called *perro* (dog) by all the Spanish-speaking boys, these groups regarded Latin policemen as tougher than Anglos. English was spoken only to a non-Spanish speaker.

More English was spoken in groups living in more acculturated and heterogeneous neighborhoods. Particularly in Tract B 35 (Table 9.1), where only about 60 percent of the residents had Spanish surnames, the boys mixed English words freely in their spoken Spanish. For example, their sports terms were not translated or adapted into Spanish. They were in frequent contact with non-Spanish speakers (especially Negro boys) even during their own activities. Correspondingly, behavioral manifestations of *intense* identification as "Latins" were lacking.

And what of the youth in the high rank area? Did they recognize the superiority of their situation, as they had of their dwellings? In both Cities A and B, preferences for "white, native-born" friends were more pronounced in high than in low rank areas. In other words, the heterogeneity of ethnic background in low rank areas was *one* source of condescension by high rank students. In City B, with its bicultural population, we asked students to list any people with whom they might not want to make friends. The most frequent response in the high rank school was "Latins," that is, Spanish-speaking persons such as the students attending school in the low rank areas.

Students in City A were asked to name the "worst" high school in their city. There were about a dozen schools to choose from. Yet 53 percent of the high rank sample chose the school attended by our low rank sample, another 28 percent selecting the middle rank school. The high rank school was not mentioned as "worst" by any students in the low rank sample, indicating that the feeling of superiority in the high rank area was not just one side of a reciprocated rivalry in school athletics.

In brief, adolescents living in neighborhoods of differing social rank indicate awareness of that rank and the status accorded the ethnic background of its residents. Those in crowded, shabby areas desire to live in more attractive surroundings. But, as we shall see more clearly, their conceptions of a way of life are not the same as those of adolescents actually living in the "best" parts of town.

Common Values and Variations in Self-Radius

There is one clear and striking generalization about the high school youth which holds in all areas and despite their differing backgrounds: Their values and goals earmark them all as youth exposed to the American ideology of success and wanting the tangible symbols of that success. There were no differences between the youth in different areas with respect to desires for material goods. In addition to comfortable housing, the symbols of success for these adolescents included a car in every garage, a telephone, television set, transistor radios, fashionable clothing, time to enjoy them, and money to provide them. It is obvious, however, that the present accessibility of these items differed enormously for youth in the different areas.

The universal importance of a high standard of material life was reflected in the wishes and ambitions expressed by group members.

Questioning the members of Group A IIIs 12a about their ambitions after he had gained rapport with them, the observer found that only two had clear occupational goals, but all members readily expressed their desires for cars, new clothing and nice houses. Even the boys living in the poorest neighborhoods of City B joined the chorus of praise for the things that American boys come to feel are a birthright, whether they have them or not. The observer of Group B IIIs 6b asked several boys for "three wishes." Here are representative replies: "To be very rich, to have lots of new clothing. . . . I don't know of anything else." "Have a million dollars, a brand new Cadillac, and lots of girls." "To have money, own a large chain store, and travel a lot in my car." "Have a lot of money, to be a famous singer, and plenty of beautiful women."

As statements of goals, these represent common values of the American boys studied. Stated by boys whose families were poor, who had no occupational or educational plans, they acquire a fantasy character. Yet the nature of these goals has something to do with the fact that these boys, who had so little in the way of possessions, had no qualms about stealing from those who had some.

As valued activities, apart from conceptions of achievements in them, high school youth in different settings showed their awareness of the value of education, and occupational choice, and the necessity of work to secure a good life. There were, for example, no significant differences in the proportion of youngsters in different areas who were completely unable to state an occupational preference in response to even one of three items. (The proportions were fairly high, ranging from 20 to 25 percent.) When asked how long a person had to work to earn enough to get along and how much work was the maximum needed to earn a living, youth in all areas set the minimum around eight hours and the maximum between nine and ten hours.

Among the high school students, no one regarded schooling as unnecessary or desired none at all, even though signs of dropping out of school increased strikingly from high to low rank areas, as we shall see. In rating a list of forty-five actions in terms of how socially acceptable or objectionable they were (on linear rating scales), students in all areas showed their knowledge of "right" from "wrong" as defined by the law and in the school. In other words, high school students in different neighborhoods did not differ markedly in *knowledge* of the limits of acceptable behavior and the points at which deviation is subject to sanctions by adult authorities. Nor did the members of groups observed in this research reveal ignorance of societal definitions of serious deviations. Whatever boys in low rank neighborhoods lacked in academic skills and social etiquette, they were keenly aware of the definitions and sanctions for deviant behavior.

If adult norms prevailing in the neighborhoods had diverged, the evaluations of youth from those neighborhoods should have reflected the fact, at least in greater variability of response if not in modal evaluations of some or all of the items concerning what is "right" and "wrong." In fact, the only differences between areas on these ratings was that youth in high rank areas tended to rate statements on deception of adults (e.g., "Lying to parents about why you get in late"; "Skipping a test because you don't have time to prepare") as *less* objectionable than the students in low rank areas.

On the whole, we found that these young people filling out forms in their schools were reluctant to respond in ways that would reflect negatively on their parents. Only about 10 percent indicated, for example, that their parents did not understand them in response to direct questions. With the idea that adult-youth "distance" would be revealed in a topic of frequent discussion, we asked the students what time they wanted to be home at night on school nights and week-ends, then what time their parents wanted them to be home. As Figure 9.3 indicates, there was indeed a discrepancy between adult and youth opinions, averaging around twenty minutes to half an hour. The trend for the discrepancy between youth's desires and parents' curfews to be greater in lower rank areas than in the high rank area is significant. Parents in all areas were, on the average, setting their week-day and week-end limits about two hours apart. These discrepancies can be taken as one index of adult-youth conflict—in an area of considerable importance both to adolescents and their parents. They reflect the intense desires manifested in various ways by youth in all areas to make "our own decisions"—to be "independent."

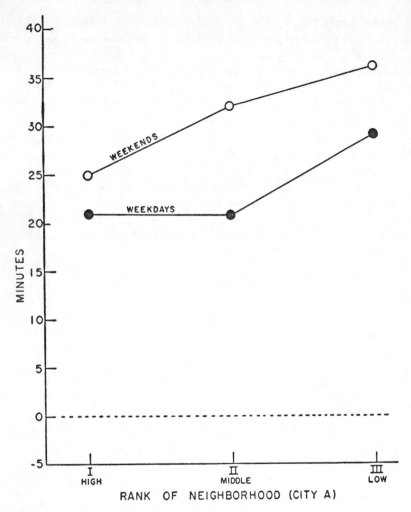

FIGURE 9.3. Discrepancies between youths' decisions on time to come home at night and parental curfews. Average difference between times high school students in different areas want to come home at night and the times their parents want them home.

In addition to desiring material symbols of success, youth in middle and low rank areas revealed the success idea in other ways. There were marked discrepancies between the educational, occupational, and financial levels of parents and the goals of these high school students. Many were setting their goals well above the achievements of their parents in these respects.

In terms of absolute level, youth in low rank areas set their sights lower than those in middle rank areas, with the goals of youth in high rank areas being highest. But differences in the level of goals were not the whole story. The latitudes of acceptable achievement defining the minimum of "what is necessary for me" and a maximum of "what is most desirable" also differed. Hence the paradox that youth in low rank neighborhoods set goals well below those of youth in high rank areas, but see themselves as aiming for "success."

In the sections that follow, other comparative findings on the self-radius and goals of adolescents are summarized, starting with an exemplar of the universally desired high living standard—the automobile—and proceeding to spheres of achievement that are necessary means for gaining that standard legitimately—education, an occupation, and an income.

The Car "Culture"

The extent to which youth in all areas regarded the material benefits of contemporary American society as *necessities* and desired them can be illustrated through our findings about automobiles in City A, where we inquired into the topic extensively. Here the students were asked whether or not they drove a car, and if so, to whom it belonged, its year and model. Then they wrote the year and model of the car they would like to have at present and in the future. Only one girl in the entire sample wrote that she did not want a car. (Girls' and boys' responses were tabulated separately, but they differed only with respect to car *ownership*.)

Approximately one third in the high and middle rank areas did not drive a car, as compared with 71 percent in the low rank area. A fourth of the students in middle and high rank areas had cars of their own (mostly boys), but only 2 percent in low rank areas. The cars driven by youth in high rank areas were newer and more expensive. Over 60 percent in the high rank area drove cars less than six years old, while only about 30 percent in the middle rank area had such recent models.

In order to scale the responses on the kind of cars desired now and later, we classified each car by year and by prestige of the make and model. The latter scale was based on the "blue book" used to determine sale and trade-in values for purposes of obtaining a loan.

Figures 9.4 and 9.5 show the proportion of high school students in the high and low rank areas who wanted cars of five different prestige levels at present (solid line) and in the future (dashed line).

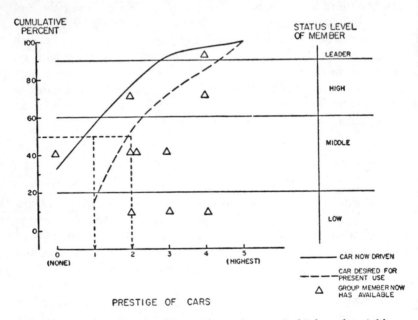

FIGURE 9.4. Attainment by members of group in high rank neighborhood relative to prestige scale for cars prevailing among their schoolmates. Horizontal axis: Prestige of cars from 0 (none) to 5 (highest) by objective criteria. Left vertical axis: Cumulative percent of high school sample having and desiring cars of given prestige. Right vertical axis: Status level of group member (triangle).

The percentages are cumulative from the low to the highest prestige level.

Using an additional scale on the right of each figure, which enumerates four status categories (leader, high, middle, low), we have also located the prestige of cars driven by members of groups who

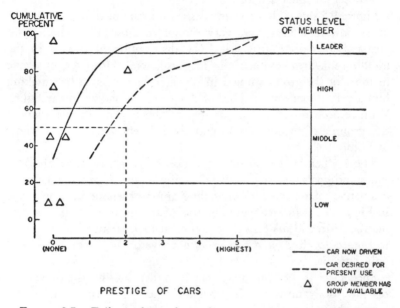

FIGURE 9.5.   Failure of members of group in low rank neighborhood in terms of prestige scale for cars prevailing among their schoolmates. Horizontal axis: Prestige of cars from 0 (none) to 5 (highest) by objective criteria. Left vertical axis: Cumulative percent of high school sample having and desiring cars of given prestige. Right vertical axis: Status level of group member (triangle).

attended these schools and who were observed in this research. The car each member now drives can be assessed relative to the desires of his schoolmates and relative to his own standing in his group.

In Figure 9.4, we see that only one member of Group A Is 9a did not have a car, and that others drove cars of higher prestige than cars desired by over half of their classmates. Further, none of their cars was over six years old. Clearly, members of this group are "successful" with respect to the cars they drive, in the eyes of their agemates. The one member who did not have a car was working part-time to get one of the exact make and year as a member of higher status in the group. This group was, in fact, considered in the "smart set" of their school.

Figure 9.5 shows that current desires for cars of differing prestige in the low rank area were very similar to those in the high rank area presented in Figure 9.4. (The distribution of choices in the middle rank area is practically identical, too.) However, only one member of the group studied in this area had a car, a fact making him a very important member of the group, as shown in the figure. With respect to having cars desired by their agemates, members of this group are obviously in an entirely different situation than those in Figure 9.4.

These schemes demonstrate the possibility of assessing the attitudes and goals of individuals belonging to small groups relative to evaluative reference scales prevailing among their peers. The group in Figure 9.4 is in fact representative of the norm (not the average, but the desired ideal) prevalent in their school. Members of the group in Figure 9.5 all *wanted* cars representative of the norm, but in fact only one member approached it.

Such facts as these are pertinent to understanding the prevalence of "joy rides" and car thefts by adolescents (cf. Perlman, 1959). Of course they do not make such actions less illegal or less morally wrong. But they do indicate that such acts occur relative to a clear and salient evaluative scale shared by teen-agers and concerning an object regarded by them as a "necessity of life." In discussing concerns and activities of individuals in their groups, we have repeatedly mentioned the importance of automobiles to these boys. A recent survey of a stratified representative sample of teen-age boys (Survey Research Center, 1955) reported that care and use of cars ranked high in boys' preference for leisure time activity.

In our research, the intense interest in cars is also revealed by the adolescent's ability to specify the make, model, year, and even the color and engine type of the car he desired. Such specificity is impressive, particularly when compared with the general nature of preferences for occuptions. Precision of taste of this kind is comparable to that of the gourmet or wine expert who loves his hobby and spends long hours of study, care, and preparation to develop a highly differentiated set of categories for evaluating specific foods or wines. The findings almost force one to conclude that the automobile is a major cultural goal of American youth.

Table 9.3 gives the cumulative frequencies for prestige of cars desired by youth in low, middle, and high rank areas later in life, when they are adult. Taking 50 percent as the cutting point, it can be seen that youth in high rank areas set their sights higher, on the average, than those in areas of lower social rank.

TABLE 9.3.   PRESTIGE LEVELS OF CARS DESIRED BY ADOLESCENTS WHEN ADULT (CITY A)

| | Rank of Area | | |
	High N = 110	Middle N = 102	Low N = 85
		Cumulative Percentage	
Prestige Level of Car			
A (highest)	100.0	100.0	100.0
B	70.3	90.2	90.6
C	46.8	67.8	74.2
D	41.9	58.9	53.2
E (lowest)	4.5	1.0	1.2

Spending Money and Other Financial Goals

"Spending money" is something whose meaning every adolescent appreciates. In City B, the boys in all the neighborhoods but Tract B 35 (see Figure 9.1) were regularly broke. As mentioned previously, those who worked had low-paying jobs (around $20 a week) and usually were expected to turn this over to their families, who sorely needed it. In many cases, it seemed that working did not give the boys themselves more money to spend. Perhaps this is one reason why members of low rank groups frequently had little desire to find regular jobs. In the groups of these areas, there were a number of members out of school, out of work, and making little effort to find more than a temporary job to pick up a few dollars for some specific purpose (clothing or a social function with the group). Social workers in the low rank neighborhoods testified to the difficulty of getting jobs for these boys. Jobs were not usually available in their neighborhoods, and they encountered obstacles in trying to acquire them outside of the neighborhoods. Unlike youth in high rank areas, their parents were in no position to help them find jobs.

The actualities of the foregoing situation are reflected in the estimates by students who were still in school in City B of the money they could earn if "I went to work right now." There was a reliable difference in the average estimates made by "Latins," on the one hand, and "Anglos," on the other. The "Anglos" estimated about $45 a week, and the Spanish-speaking high school students about $25 a week. *Both of these estimates are below their respective conceptions of the minimum amount "necessary just to live on."*

In terms of spending money needed by "a person my age," the Spanish-speaking youth estimated a significantly lower figure than their English-speaking agemates in middle and high rank areas (between $3 and $4, as compared with $5 to $6, on the average). In City A, teen-agers in all areas said a person their age needed between $5 and $8.50 (these being confidence limits of the means, which were not reliably different).

Despite the consensus on spending money needed, only boys in the middle and high rank areas actually had such sums. Observers repeatedly referred to the planning and efforts of the boys in low rank neighborhoods to accumulate even a small pool of funds to finance attendance to a dance, movie, game, or party. Such efforts included temporary jobs and pooling anything a boy could get his hands on to sell.

Figure 9.6 represents the reference scales prevailing among adolescents in City B for evaluating weekly income. The baseline shows the social rank and cultural affiliation of the area. The ordinate indicates dollar values per week. The locations of the values represent median estimates made in response to the following items:

"If a person earns $_____ a week, he has just barely enough to live on."

"If a person earns *at least* $_____ a week, he is really well off."

"When I am grown up, I want to make at least $_____ a week." The squares represent the location of the minimum necessary, the

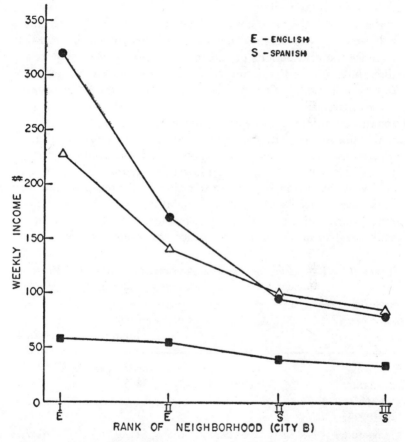

FIGURE 9.6. Reference scales for evaluating income in areas of different social rank. Median estimates in high (I), middle (II), and low (III) rank areas of minimum income for survival (squares), for comfort (circles), and personal goals (triangles). S = bilinguals.

circles show the maximum for comfort, while the triangles show the median goals for oneself.

Confidence limits of the medians in Figure 9.6 indicate that the concepts of a *subsistence* level differ reliably between "Anglo" and "Latin" students, while differences between *goals* (triangles) and concepts of *comfort* (top circle) differ reliably between areas of different rank as well.

Responses to the same items in City A were secured a year and a half later and are, therefore, not strictly comparable to those in City B. Since the distributions of responses in City A were less skewed than those in City B, the means of the estimates were computed, as shown in Table 9.4. The confidence limits of the means indicate reliable differences ($p. < .05$) between the lower and middle rank areas for the minimum needed, between the low and high areas in the maximum for comfort, and between all areas for the personal goals. There were sex differences in responses to these questions, though not reliable, with girls estimating lower figures than boys. The variability of the responses to these questions was greater in the high rank area of City A. This greater variability reflects the fact that the school district of the high rank area includes the transitional middle rank neighborhoods in which one of the groups studied in this

TABLE 9.4. REFERENCE SCALES FOR POVERTY, COMFORT, AND PERSONAL GOALS AMONG ADOLESCENTS IN CITY A

| | | Rank of Area | |
	High	Middle	Low
		Mean Income per Week	
Minimum (Barely enough to live on)	$55.34	$55.27	$45.99
Maximum (Really well off)	$229.96	$152.92	$147.38
Personal Goal ("I want to make")	$188.78	$134.85	$110.24

research lived, in addition to the more luxurious neighborhoods to their north.

For possible comparison with the conceptions and goals of the Spanish-speaking students in City B, data were also obtained at an all-Negro school in City A. Unlike the Spanish-speaking students, however, the Negro youth made estimates differing very little from those of the low rank school in City A, which was an integrated school with only a minority of Negroes and American Indians. The exception was that Negro youth put their own *goals* somewhat higher, on the average, their estimates of the amount needed for *comfort* were lower, and variability was significantly less than for the school in the low rank study area. The high level of personal goals in the all-Negro school was even more striking for education and occupation desired. *In these respects, responses of the Negro youth resembled those of students at the high rank school.* As a result, the discrepancies between their fathers' education or occupations and those desired by youth were much greater than for any other students.

In brief, the picture that emerges is one of differences among youth in different areas in their conceptions of what constitutes a minimum financial standard, what represents "success" for personal income, with associated differences in personal goals. Relative to their own reference scales, youth in every area set their personal goals for success. Those in low rank areas were more ambitious in these *relative* terms than more favored youth. But the level of their goals differs both in terms of socioeconomic and cultural background, as do the amounts of money these young people have to spend at present and the environmental probabilities of their attaining their goals.

Occupational and Educational Reference Scales and Goals

Like their peers in the high school samples, members of the groups studied were, on the whole, *less clear about their occupational preferences and goals than about most other spheres of living.* Almost one fourth of every high school sample was unable to specify any clear occupational goal or expectation.

Members of the group in the high rank neighborhood of City A were all headed for college, like the great majority of their schoolmates, and two of them often talked about their plans to study law and architecture. Members of the group (A IIs 10a), in the transitional middle rank neighborhood which was also included in the same school district, were definitely representative of the minority in the high rank school who aimed only at high school and had no clear occupational preference. The leader of this group had completed high school. His father had gotten him a job paying $1 an hour in a lumberyard. He disliked the work but had no specific alternative of his own. Most of the other boys intended to complete high school, although two were suspended at least for a time.

Most of the boys in the other group located in a middle rank neighborhood in City A had dropped out of school and were required by their parents to work. Two had jobs as deliverymen and another worked as a helper in a restaurant and upholstery shop, pursuits all three heartily disliked. One member bragged that his record length on one job was two weeks. These temporary jobs appeared to bear no relation to what they eventually might do to earn a living after serving their military duty.

Boys in the low rank neighborhood of City A were intending to complete high school, but only two had clear preferences for work— one wanted to be an electrician, the other a cabinet maker. These aspirations are representative of the educational and occupational goals for students in their school, the choice of a blue-collar job being made by almost half of the students and realistically expected ("what I will probably get") by over 50 percent.

In City B, the members of the group in the most heterogeneous neighborhood (Tract B 35) expressed similar goals. As we have noted, this group (B IIIm 1b) was in somewhat better circumstances than others in the low rank neighborhoods of that city. The members went to middle rank schools attended by Anglos, who were in the majority. The boys were so aware of the importance of completing high school that they bragged about how many relatives had done so (very few had), and asked the observer (a college graduate) if he had finished high school.

In part, the difference between attitudes toward school of these boys and the members of the other groups in low rank areas of City B is attributable to family emphasis on the importance of education. In part, their desire to be high school graduates was doubtless affected by the context of the school they attended. As A. B. Wilson (1959) found, the objective socioeconomic status of one's family has a different weight as a condition affecting the goals of adolescents, depending on whether the other students at the school one attends are similar or dissimilar in family status. Thus a lower-class youth attending school in a middle-class neighborhood is more likely to put his sights higher than his counterpart in a school attended largely by other lower-class youth. No doubt even the teachers in the latter schools frequently have different expectations of their charges than those in middle-class areas. Certainly the students foresee less attainment as urgent or necessary for themselves.

However, in accounting for the higher educational aspirations of Group B IIIm 1b, as compared with other low groups in City B, the significance of their own group should not be overlooked. The interactions among these boys were the source of constant support for their aspirations to do as well as possible and to complete high school. As previously mentioned, this group lived in an area near those of the very toughest gangs in the city, and many times expressed their "difference" from the hoods and *pachucos*. *Like the "good boys" in delinquent areas studied by Reckless, Dinitz, and Murray (1956), the self-concepts of these boys were "insulators" against socially undesirable actions.*

It is true that, unlike other groups in low rank neighborhoods, every member of this group was called home by a younger brother at least on one occasion while the observer was with them. The younger members (14–15 years) did not leave the immediate neighborhood without notifying their families (two boys lived with relatives, not parents). However, whatever the role of parents may have been in promoting friendship with "desirable boys" and checking on their activities, it would have been extremely difficult for their sons to maintain their self-concepts had they not found their group of friends a satisfying and supporting locus for their leisure time.

Indeed, the reverse of the coin occurred in Group B IIIs 7b, where the valiant and determined efforts of parents to keep their boys in school were daily diluted by their sons' attachments to friends who had left school and said good riddance to it. These boys, who had been labeled "antisocial" by school authorities, were in fact the most outgoing, active, and loyal members of their group. Their reactions to school reflected very well the conditions productive of boredom and hostility toward school on the part of lower class youth, as characterized by F. Riessman (1962). All of them were bilingual. The observer obtained reading achievement test results on the members in school and the last ones of the members who had quit school. Those who had dropped out had low achievement scores at the time, but so did those still in school, the highest indicating a sixth grade level for a boy who was a first-semester senior in high school. It would be difficult, however, to characterize these boys as "subnormal" in any kind of intelligence other than those skills most directly associated with school achievement and English reading. They were able to plan and carry out complex and coordinated athletic strategies and other skills not involving reading.

Boys in this group who were still in school were constantly kidded about it. As the study progressed, the observer wondered frequently how they managed to stick with the school situation, correctly predicting that one would drop out. A somewhat similar case occurred in City A in the middle rank neighborhood (Group IIs 11a). A boy whose intelligence test scores were above average was actually transferred by his parents to another city where he lived with relatives, in order to keep him away from the other boys, several of whom had been dismissed from school as "behavior problems." He ran away from the relatives to return home to his pals, but his former school in City A refused to readmit him, with his mother's consent.

It is obvious that the findings on educational and occupational goals of high school youth in this research omit those teen-agers who have already dropped out of school, the drop-out rate biasing the high school samples in this way more for lower rank areas than high. Yet, in City B, proneness to leave school was revealed as greater in schools serving low rank areas, even among students still in school. We asked students to indicate whether a "person who wants to quit school because the family needs money" was "like me" or "not like me." (This phrasing was used because it was frequently offered to observers as a reason for having dropped out of school.) "Anglo" students in high and middle rank areas overwhelmingly indicated "not like me," only 8 percent responding affirmatively. The percentage choosing "like me" was double (16 percent) among Spanish-speaking youngsters attending the same middle rank school, but jumped to 23 percent in the low rank school ($p. < .01$).

In City A, the latitudes of acceptance for educational achievement were estimated in each school from the students' responses to three items: "If a person wants to do the things I want to do, he or she needs to complete _____." (This item was followed by twelve alternatives ranging from "seventh grade" to "graduate degree," each of which was translatable into years of schooling.)

"A person is educated if he has finished _____."

"The farthest in school I want to go is _____."

Figure 9.7 represents the median years of school in response to these questions. The median years defining the "educated" person were identical in each case to those defining the "necessary" schooling for someone who "wants to do the things I want to do." The distributions of these responses were not normal. In the high rank school, over 75 percent regarded a college education as both necessary and desirable, even though it will be recalled that financial goals were more variable in this school than others. The distribution of goals in the middle rank school was bimodal, with 44 percent desiring a college education and another 40 percent regarding high school as sufficient. In the school serving the low rank area, there was consensus at the high school level by the majority of students with smaller percentages regarding technical training or college (22 percent) as "necessary," but 41 percent expressing a *desire* for college work.

We have already noted that occupational preferences were more frequently unclear than those in other respects, as revealed in the generality of statements of preferred occupations and the rather high frequency of "no answers." Since the proportions of students

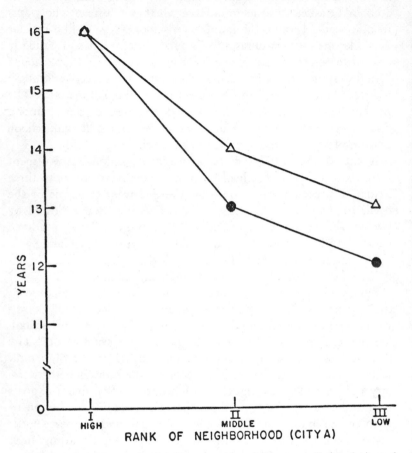

FIGURE 9.7. Years of schooling considered "necessary" (circles) and personally desired (triangles) in areas of different social rank. Median estimates of years in school defining an "educated person" coincide in each case with those considered "necessary."

failing to make an occupational choice did not differ significantly or systematically according to rank of area, the percentages of students aiming at different rungs of the occupational ladder, as ranked by the prestige and income of the occupation, were calculated omitting "no answers." Table 9.5 gives these percentages for City A.

The relationship between distribution of occupational choices and rank of area was even more striking in City B; however, our study

TABLE 9.5. OCCUPATIONAL GOALS OF YOUTH IN DIFFERENT AREAS
OF CITY A

| | Rank of Area | | |
Occupational Rank	High %	Middle %	Low %
1. Highest professional, top managerial	1.2	2.5	3.0
2. Professional, business, technical	26.5	21.3	12.2
3. Semiprofessional, small business	38.6	25.0	24.2
4. Sales and clerical	30.0	23.8	22.7
5. Skilled	1.2	17.5	21.2
6. Semiskilled	2.4	10.0	13.6
7. Unskilled	0	0	3.0

groups in that city were all in low rank areas. In City B, 91.3 percent of the high rank sample who chose an occupation aimed at white collar work higher than category 4 (sales and clerical personnel), as compared to 40 percent of the low rank Latin sample. Furthermore, when asked to state what kind of work they thought they could probably *get*, nearly 20 percent of the low rank sample selecting these more prestigeful occupations shifted to blue-collar occupations (a change which is significant, $p. < .005$). Such downward shift in expectations was not found for the high rank sample in City B. In contrast, a similar proportion of *all* high school samples of City A responded to the item about *probable* occupation by shifting to a lower rank (from 16 to 19 percent change), which again suggests considerable uncertainty about their occupational goals.

In both cities, then, youths' goals for occupation are related to the rank of the area in which they live. Furthermore, as shown in Table 9.6, youth in low and middle rank areas are aspiring to occupations of higher rank than those now pursued by their fathers. In this table, the discrepancies between the proportions aiming at each occupational level and the actual occupational level of their fathers are presented. Over 40 percent of the students in the middle and low rank schools are aiming above their fathers' achievements, while in the high rank school about 8 percent are aiming above and about 13 percent have goals lower than their fathers' achievements. (In an all-Negro school in City A, fully 62 percent aspired to occupations of higher rank than their fathers'.)

TABLE 9.6. DISCREPANCY BETWEEN OWN DESIRED OCCUPATION AND FATHER'S OCCUPATION: CITY A

| | Rank of Area | | |
| | High | Middle | Low |
Occupational Rank	%	%	%
1. Highest professional top managerial	−.8	+2.5	+3.0
2. Professional, business, technical	−12.5	+20.3	+12.1
3. Lower professional, small business	+11.6	+10.6	+17.0
4. Sales and clerical	+10.1	+8.6	+9.7
5. Skilled	−7.6	−25.6	−4.9
6. Semiskilled	−.8	−10.3	−22.6
7. Unskilled	0.0	−6.1	−14.3
Percentage differing from rank of fathers' occupation	21.7	42.0	41.8

In summary, the data do indicate lack of clarity among youth on occupational goals; but both with respect to occupation and education, youth in low and middle rank areas aim above their fathers' accomplishments. It would not seem that lower class youth react *against* the middle-class concept of success. On the contrary, the concept would seem to be more vital in lower than higher strata. What differs seems to be not motivation for, but probability of, success for youth in these differing circumstances, even when the criteria for success are their own goals.

Leisure Time and Agemate Associations

In keeping with the findings of earlier investigators (e.g., Hollingshead, 1949; MacDonald, McGuire, and Havighurst, 1949), the youths in high rank areas typically were more active in both school activities and formally organized extracurricular activities than those in low rank areas. In City A, the students in low rank areas typically spent more time in watching television than those in middle and high rank areas, and they wished that they could spend even more (see Figure 9.8). This is one indication of the simple fact that they had more free time than youth in the high rank school to spend alone or with agemates in unprogrammed activities.

In City B, the students were asked to indicate whether "a person who feels lonely when not hanging around with usual pals" is "like me" or "not like me." The percentages responding "like me" increased from 33.8 percent in the high rank area to 50 percent in the middle rank (English-speaking and bilingual students not differing in this respect), and to 59.7 percent in the low rank area. While the urgency to *be with* other agemates is substantial, it is significantly more general in the middle and low rank areas.

On the basis of observations in different neighborhoods, we find no reason to conclude that youth in high rank areas are actually together less than those in low rank areas. But the former participate with their pals in many formally programmed activities, frequently pursuing their own plans only in preparation for such events or afterward. The groups in middle and low rank areas studied in this research thus far were centered almost entirely upon activities of their own planning. Even when they attended a settlement house or recreation center, it was usually to use the game facilities, to have a place to meet, and to make plans for the day or evening.

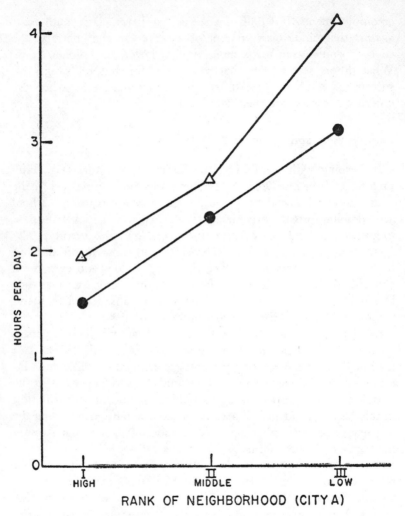

FIGURE 9.8. Television viewing in areas of different social rank as an indicator of unprogrammed free time. Average hours a day spent watching television (circles) and hours desired for television viewing (triangles).

SOME IMPLICATIONS OF THE
FINDINGS ON SELF-RADIUS AND
GOALS IN DIFFERENT AREAS

Neither in schools nor in informal groups of teen-agers—whatever the socioeconomic rank—did we find evidence of youth rejecting the symbols of success as defined in this society: comfortable living arrangements, clothing, cars, appliances, and so on. One might say that American business enterprise and the sponsors of mass communications have been enormously successful in producing a younger generation tuned and aspiring to consumption of their products.

However, youth in areas of low, middle, and high rank did have different scales for evaluating success in a variety of activities essential to acquiring the desired standard of living. Their latitudes of acceptance differed even for the financial achievement necessary to support it. *Relative* to these latitudes of acceptance, and especially relative to their parents' accomplishments, school youth in low rank areas appear as more ambitious than those in high rank areas.

The differences in absolute level of the goals in different activities are significant, but more striking are the differential opportunities available in the different areas for achieving even these goals (cf. Cloward and Ohlin, 1960). In the low rank neighborhoods, the industrious and ambitious adolescent boy who gets a job faces the choice of turning over his paycheck to a family which sorely needs it, or appearing to them and to himself as a selfish, even heartless, son. Even if his parents urge him to forego work until he finishes school, there is no comparison between his experiences at school, where he is often ill-prepared and ill at ease, and his desires to be with his agemates. If some of his pals have dropped out of school, he feels more isolated while following school routine, knowing that they are probably together. Much more than at school, with them he can feel that he counts for something in his own right. This is particularly the case if he belongs to an ethnic group accorded low standing in the social scheme. Those who resolve the dilemma by leaving school usually dislike school actively. But this dislike seems to have much less to do with a "reaction formation" against the *values* presented in school than with the boredom and isolation of the school situation, on the one hand, and the warmth of human contact with fellows like him outside of school, on the other.

Those who leave school—the dropouts—frequently give the excuse that the family needs the money they can earn. This is true. But it is not so easy for them to get jobs, and those they find are low-paying and hard work. To keep at such work without personal benefit of the paycheck is a sacrificial task which only strong dedication to family and great persistence can make rewarding. Until a boy in such circumstances is no longer responsible to his family— through marriage or being drafted—there is little tangible incentive to get a job at long hours and low pay.

In the interim, he gets temporary jobs for small sums of money, spending long hours with pals who provide diversion, recognition, excitement, and a sense of personal worth, all of which boys in more favored areas find more readily both in programmed and informal activities of school and community life. These qualities are valued by individuals in all settings; but boys in favored areas find them in institutional and informal social activities and the instrumentalities afforded by their station in life, notably the automobiles acquired through their own part-time work or through their parents' largesse.

Whatever the restrictions of the self-radius of an adolescent in a low rank area with respect to school and work, he does perceive very accurately the most salient goals of middle-class American life, and he wants them. In terms of sheer frequency of exposure and forcefulness of presentation, the sources of these values are the omnipresent images of "successful" people in the papers, advertisements, the news, the movies, television, and radio, not the schools. The adolescent has learned all about the "good life" in comfortable neighborhoods, complete with fine clothing, cars, appliances, money to spend. It may be that he is told of the positive worth of perseverance, thrift, self-denial, and delayed reward, values which many educators and sociologists identify as traditional "middle-class values." They forget that lower-class youth see their own parents and others in their milieu persevering, postponing rewards, being thrifty and self-sacrificing in contexts and with outcomes almost precluding a positive evaluation of their worth.

Of the youth in low rank areas who remain in school, it may be said that, in view of the level of their goals relative to their own conceptions of achievement, to their parents' actual achievements, and to the environmental probabilities of success, they are more ambitious, more persevering than boys attending schools in higher rank neighborhoods. If there seem to be contradictions in such a conclusion, perhaps they may be resolved by more intensive study of the behaviors of youth who are taken as representative of American "middle-class values" because they happen to have been born into favored circumstances, and behaviors of youth who were not. Such study of social values should not be detached from the actualities of behavior in the interaction processes and concrete settings in which it occurs.

10 *Self-radius of adolescents and attachments to their groups: with emphasis on the impact of other groups*

In Chapter 7, the behavior of adolescents was approached through intensive study of the patterning of their interactions. In Chapter 8, the self-regulation of behavior and immediate pressures from other members toward conformity were reviewed with reference to the norms arising during group interaction. The last chapter focused on attitudes and goals prevailing in urban areas of low, middle, and high rank and on the features of the neighborhoods related to them.

Whether approaching social behavior through study of immediate interaction situations, through study of prevailing reference scales for evaluation, or through the ecological and sociocultural characteristics of its setting, we have found it impossible to deal with one without the others. In this chapter, we will pull together findings and implications from all of these in discussing the impact of relationships between groups on behavior and on group properties, in noting the traditional features of the groups, and in singling out motivational bases for individual attachment to a group. The harmonious or conflicting nature of relationships between groups in a setting, the first topic of this chapter, represents a particularly clear field for appreciating the convergence of ecological, sociocultural, group, and individual factors in shaping the behavior of group members.

RELATIONSHIPS AMONG GROUPS
AND WITH AUTHORITIES

As we saw in Chapter 7, the attachments among individual members of a group are patterned with respect to effective initiative or control, mutual liking, and particular functions in activities of motivational appeal to the members. From their very beginnings, these patterns develop within a particular setting where other adolescents, young adults, families, social agencies, schools, churches, and legal authorities are going about their business, too. The harmonious or conflicting relationships between the major activities and goals of an informal group and other social units are an important determinant of the criteria for achieving status within the group, of the degree of solidarity among its members, and of the degree of individual commitment to group lines of action.

As several studies of high-school youth have shown (e.g., Hollingshead, 1949; Gordon, 1957; Coleman, 1961; Remmers and Rosler, 1957), adolescents in middle and high rank neighborhoods compete for recognition and prestige chiefly in terms of socioeconomic and cultural values widely prevalent in the larger setting. The fact that the primary of these values pertain to material symbols and social skills of an affluent stratum of society, that athletic ability for boys and beauty for girls are surer roads to distinction than intellectual achievements, should not be surprising. High status members in the groups observed in this research in neighborhoods of middle and high social rank tended to be among the affluent in their groups; they were skilled and sophisticated in interactions with adults and other youth; they were able in athletics.

The groups in middle and high rank neighborhoods were very mobile, a condition which frequently made observation difficult, and produced the impression of a fluid, unstable association during early stages of observation. It is noteworthy, therefore, that the greatest solidarity and coordination of performance among members of these groups were found when they were competing as a group with other agemates—in sport, for distinction—or were engaged in activities whose discovery by parents or other authorities would have led to sanctions.

For example, the group in the high rank neighborhood appeared as a highly coordinated, closely knit unit when campaigning for a member's election to school office, when joining their leader to protest unwarranted liberties taken by a nonmember with the leader's girl, in planning and covering up the aftermath of a secret party at a luxury motel. The evidence for this can be stated in terms of the indicators of solidarity stated in our hypotheses (p. 92). Their plans were kept *secret;* who was to be involved and who was not to be included was discussed and agreed upon ("exclusiveness"); individually and in sub-units, the members pursued different tasks without direct leader supervision; and these tasks were well-coordinated. The party, for example, was so secret that the observer found out about it only because members approached him (as a harmless adult) to sign the motel register. (He did not assume responsibility for their actions.) The girls were notified at the last minute to bring swimsuits so that they would have little opportunity to let the plans slip to their parents. Each member contributed to party refreshments and expenses. Afterward, funds were collected to cover the damage done in the motel.

Whether competition and conflicting goals occurred between small groups or involved adult authority, their general effects in every group observed were to increase solidarity within the group, provided only that the opposition did not succeed in physically separating the members. Defeat by a rival group in athletics or physical encounters sometimes led to criticism and recriminations among members for a time, but more usually to assigning blame to persons or circumstances beyond group control (e.g., the referee, the police) and to strategy sessions to improve group coordination in the future (cf. Sherif and Sherif, 1953; Sherif *et al.,* 1961; Blake and Mouton, 1961).

For three of the groups studied, police and agency officials succeeded in isolating members physically, with differing outcomes: In one group, arrest of the leader eventually led to disintegration of the group as a unit (see p. 150). Another group, which was being closely watched by police, voluntarily associated in public in small numbers, two or three at a time, in order to appear to have dissolved without actually doing so. This difficult feat was accompanied by their continuing regrets that they could not, for the time, all get together at once. The third group, in a low rank neighborhood of City A (Tract A 37), had been warned by police not to associate. Then about half of the membership was barred from the settlement house where they usually met. These boys transferred to another social agency nearby. The two sub-units maintained a regular liaison through the only boy who was allowed in both of the centers. The bifurcation was a thorn in their sides, and they spoke often of recruiting new members to fill in the gaps so that two larger cooperating groups would result.

For groups in low rank areas, whether they frequently engaged in illegal activities or not, relationships with other adolescent groups and with police were highly significant aspects of the environment. These groups were much less mobile than those in high rank areas. Leaving the area involved not only considerable physical effort or planning to get a ride, but subjected the boys to suspicious eyes of the police in other areas and occasionally to questioning about their presence.

Given these circumstances, the ecology of the immediate neighborhood becomes a much weightier matter. Competition for facilities and interference from others are eliminated only by the group defining a territory which belongs to them and which they are known to defend. These are the conditions basic to the alliances and conflicts between groups based on neighborhood boundaries.

Thus, groups in low rank areas were aware of other neighborhoods and their boundary streets where they could not go without danger of incident or even violence. They were also aware of friendly groups who could be counted upon to leave them alone, provided they did not interfere with their activities, try to crash their parties, or compete for girls.

The alignments and hostilities between the groups did not strictly follow racial or ethnic lines. Thus the Varga Cats had friendly relations with Negro boys in their neighborhood and avoided other Latin groups outside it. Los Apaches kept a distance from Negro groups, but did not fight with them. They counted on support from the Negro boys in possible clashes with "Anglos," but not with other "Latin" groups. The source of their difficulties and the butt of organized aggression was the Lakeside gang, which occupied an adjacent territory.

On the other hand, Los Apaches had friendly relationships with another large and well-known group called the Spooks. In discussing how they would be able to enjoy the annual city fiesta without interference from the Lakesiders, they confidently predicted that together with the Spooks, they could keep the situation under control.

In view of the rather frequent encounters between Los Apaches and Lakeside, some of them accompanied by violence and knifings, it would be easy to attribute these aggressions by "violent gangs" to the disturbed personalities of members or to their inability to maintain social relationships. The empirical fallacy is that members maintained very close and warm relationships with each other, as evidenced in observations over a period of months. The logical fallacy is that these same individuals maintained friendly relations with the Spooks and with Los Colonias (so-called because they lived in a housing project). The Spooks and Los Colonias were, in turn, just as violent rivals with each other. During observations of Los Colonias, a boy in the neighborhood was jumped by some Spooks, who mistakenly identified him as one of Los Colonias. In retribution for such an act in their neighborhood, four members of Los Colonias found and knifed a Spook.

It is true that such incidents were recalled with excitement by members and with pride in their bravery. But to assess this love of violence and bravado psychologically, it is essential to bear in mind that it was not directed at fellow group members or to members of friendly groups, but to groups seen by the boys as "enemies." Whether by nations, racial groups, ethnic groups, or informal groups, the label of *enemy* justifies to members the use of violence as a means to defeat it (cf. Sherif, 1962).

Explanation of violence in terms of the labeling of the butt of the violence as *enemy* is no explanation at all, unless the dynamics of the labeling and its consequences are understood. It is decidedly relevant, therefore, to summarize briefly what is known about the essentials of these dynamics, which the interested reader may find readily available in other sources (e.g., Sherif and Sherif, 1953, 1956;

Sherif *et al.,* 1961; Sherif, 1962; Faris, 1962; Blake and Mouton, 1961, 1962).

On the basis of extensive surveys of empirical studies of small informal groups, "racial" groups, ethnic groups, national groups, groups with diverging interests (e.g., labor-management groups), several generalizations were warranted: Whenever the goals, interests, and activities of one group imply the defeat of those of another group, the relations between these groups in so many specific situations will be characterized by conflict. This is the necessary condition for the rise of hostilities between groups. Over a period of time, the hostile relationship becomes formulated by the parties involved, in laudatory terms justifying their own groups, on the one hand, and derogatory terms for the other group, on the other. These formulations are expressed by the participants in terms of descriptions of their own group and of the opposing group. The designation of *enemy* is a capsule formula for all of these stereotyped (commonly shared) descriptions which epitomize the justification of one's own group in conflict with another.

The validity of the foregoing sequence of conditions and outcomes has been tested in experiments with pre-adolescent boys and with adults in industrial settings. In the former experiments (Sherif and Sherif, 1953; Sherif, White, and Harvey, 1954; Sherif *et al.,* 1961), great care was taken that the individuals participating in the experiments be closely similar as to background, intelligence, physical appearance, culture, and as free of any neurotic tendencies as possible. Still, the outcome of conflicting goals between groups composed of such like individuals was conflict, the rise of justifying stereotyped characterizations of the out-group, and its eventual designation as an "enemy."

The single individual who comes to perceive *everyone* else as an enemy is labeled as a deviant, psychotic case (paranoid). However, there is a profound difference between the individual case and the case of shared definitions of "enemies." The profound difference is the basis of the classification of others as enemies.

In the strictly individual case, the basis of classification is the experiences of a single individual which are, to a large extent, unique to him, whatever the importance of social relationships in producing them. In the case of shared classifications of others as enemies, the basis is being a member of a group which has conflicting goals and interests with another group. Acceptance of the group's definition and description of the enemy is an integral part of being a group member. This membership basis of group hostility is easily seen in the cases of those who actually leave the group. They are welcomed by authorities or by the opposing social unit, as the case may be, as "defectors" for whom there is hope. They are classified by their own group as "traitors," "squealers," "stoolies"—whichever terms is appropriate. The important point is that by virtue of leaving their own group, their hostility toward the out-group is changed. While leaving one's own group for another is often an exceedingly difficult process, there can surely be no comparison between this difficulty and the tortuous process necessary to change a psychotic individual.

The assessment of the realistic elements in classifying others as enemies cannot proceed solely from the premises of the participants at the moment, but must include criteria based on historical, empirical, and ethical data. In the case of small groups of adolescents who engage in violence, our findings indicate that there are some realistic elements, and that these must be included in any analysis of the behavior or effective remedial measures. There may be cases in which the realistic basis for conflict is so overgeneralized by members as to justify aggression on anyone who is not a group member, a state of affairs which has not been found in this research, but has been reported by others (e.g., Yablonsky, 1962). Still, realistic factors and the group basis of violence and aggressions should be considered in formulating proposals of what to do to prevent their occurrence. It is possible that those who have investigated adolescent violence have focused too exclusively on the violent acts and the reported experiences of participants. This is only part of the picture. An analogy might be exclusive focus upon race riots and the reported feelings of those who participate, without corresponding emphasis on the institutions of racial discrimination and the particular nuclei fomenting violence.

Popular and sociological literature is full of accounts of gang fights and "rumbles," such as those alluded to above. However, in assessing the violence between rival groups, we must counterpose another significant finding: *A major concern of every group studied which engaged in violence against other groups and their members was avoidance of conflict.* This concern was frequently discussed and translated into appropriate precautions just as observable as behaviors of planning an attack, and easier to observe than actual violence. It is surprising, therefore, that the phenomenon is not prominently emphasized in sociological literature on gangs. A recent exception (Yablonsky, 1962) takes a rather cynical view of such concerns, possibly because his fascinating report of "peace negotiations" between hostile groups contains numerous examples of the dynamics of intergroup hostility which haunt parties despite peaceful intent. The incipient renewal of conflict, even as agreement was reached, seems to reinforce Yablonsky's belief that violence is a prime value for the participants and the efforts to avoid it more superficial.

We are impressed with the frequency and intensity of concerns and efforts to avoid conflict in the observers' reports.

Before Los Apaches went into a public place, they sent someone in to be sure no Lakesiders were there. Another group (7b) always chose seats at a ball game as far as possible from any members of a rival group who might be present. These boys were taken by the observer to a drive-in movie, a real treat for them which was almost ruined when they spotted members of a hostile group between them and the washroom. For the entire intermission, they stayed in the car discussing strategies of how to use washroom facilities without making contact with the other group. Though this incident had its humorous aspects, we cannot forget that a basic need was postponed to avoid conflict. There were numerous other examples of active efforts to avoid friction with another group.

Living in a restricted environment where danger is a frequent threat, it is small wonder that masculine toughness—being able to "take care of yourself"—is highly prized and one of the major criteria for standing with one's fellows. To appear unaggressive and mild means not only to be looked down upon, but to confine one's activities to the restricted areas where one is "safe." Living up to such toughness is, in turn, conducive to increasing the probability of further violence with "enemies" who are, in many cases, "traditional." It also increases the probabilities of difficulties with adult authorities.

In many cases, dislike and defiance of adult authorities, especially the police, were also traditional in the small groups of adolescents. Observations of the groups in different neighborhoods reveal many instances of group activities pursued in defiance of adult authority, as though "getting away" with something forbidden by adults was itself a positive value, which brought satisfaction to the participants and recognition for the most skillful members. Actions intended to irritate and heckle adult personnel of recreation centers, for example, were almost a sport for members of some groups, the highest prestige coming from successfully annoying the adult without getting kicked out of the center. (The leader of one group in a middle rank neighborhood in City A confided to the observer that they hoped to annoy one official sufficiently that he would leave or be removed. This boy was skillful, even charming in his contacts with adults, hence was seldom blamed for the activities.)

A more general and sharp cleavage from adult authorities, especially the police, was found in low rank neighborhoods. One observer in City B was a policeman, whose duties never took him into the neighborhood where he observed. He successfully concealed this fact from the group until after his observations were completed. Some time later, they saw him in a downtown area in his uniform. Afterward, he returned to their neighborhood to see what their reactions were. Although these boys had never done anything more "delinquent" than smoke cigarettes smuggled from the grocery store owned by the father of one of the members, they told him that they never would have let him into their affairs if they had known his occupation. As they talked, two boys occupied themselves by drawing derogatory pictures of a policeman on the sidewalk with a piece of chalk. Others questioned him about his occupation, saying that since he was a policeman they were glad that they liked him anyway. This psychological distance from and antagonism toward police was greatly intensified in groups which frequently engaged in forbidden activities or in which "toughness" was a virtue.

The methods of observation in this research (Chapter 6) were developed to avoid, as much as possible, the differential in behaviors of adolescents when dealing with adult authority, on the one hand, and when interacting by themselves, on the other. The reactions to adult authorities observed in the groups amply justify the precautions taken to prevent the boys from seeing the observer as a person with authority over them. Furthermore, they suggest reasons for the difficulties and duplicities frequently encountered by action programs which send social workers, police, or teachers into the field to penetrate adolescent groups and change them.

Traditional Codes in Groups and Between Social Units

In this research, tradition is examined in two ways: through reconstructing the "natural history" of the groups, and through study of the slightly older generation of young adults who were former members of the groups. Natural histories were reconstructed from interviews with parents, social workers, teachers, police, and group members themselves after observations were completed.

For the most part, the natural histories reveal the groups as phenomena of the adolescent period, in the sense that the present members began to associate *as a group* from the age of 12 years or older. In many cases, individuals had played or attended school together even earlier, but had not come together in the particular combination of the present group. The exception, Group B IIIm 1b, was the development of a play group among boys living within a two- or three-block area. Members of other groups were much more mobile than these boys, and their homes were further apart.

In the low rank neighborhoods, the history of several of the groups as recognized and identifiable units in the neighborhood extended back long before the present individuals became members, as long as twelve years prior to observations (that is, when current members were of preschool age). At the time of observation, Group B IIIs 2b (Los Colonias) was associated, on the one hand, with a younger group of boys (who were viewed as something of a bother), and an older group of young adults, many of whom were married but associated in leisure activities. The customs and traditional intergroup rivals of this and similar groups were in large part inherited from the just previous generations of group members as the boys became old enough to be accepted by them.

However, the process of transmitting a tradition does not occur in such groups by adopting an intact group of younger boys into an adolescent group. Instead, one or two at a time, younger boys are recognized as being "grownup" enough to be a help rather than a bother in group activities. They in turn have something to say about others who are accepted. This winnowing process probably accounts for the fact that membership of the adolescent groups is not usually identical with former membership in neighborhood play groups. Attendance at junior and senior high schools serving a wider area than elementary schools is probably another factor.

Having an older brother in an adolescent group may help in gaining admission. Beyond the early adolescent ages, however, kinship and age are less important determinants of standing in the group. In a number of the tightly knit groups, younger brothers sometimes had higher status and more influence in the group than their brothers two or three years older. On the other hand, there were at least two groups in which a still older brother, no longer belonging to the group, had become renowned for prowess in group activities and for "toughness" within their groups and neighborhoods. In these two groups, the mantle of their reputations had fallen to younger brothers, who did their best to live up both to them and to the present memberships' expectations of them as leaders. Both of these boys had other brothers who were less exemplary of the reputation and belonged to the group as members of lower standing. One of these brothers was younger than the exemplar, and one was older. Thus, the matter of embodying a tradition seems to be importantly determined by individual differences in skill, physique, and commitment to the group.

From the point of view of continuity of a group and the models for behavior cherished by members, the just older generation of one group is currently being investigated intensively. The emphasis in this aspect of study is upon actual interactions between former members still in the neighborhoods and the present membership. An interesting contradiction has already been observed in the expressed attitudes of the young adults who were members before marrying and settling down. On the one hand, they regard their own former group as superior, more effective, and tougher than the present generation. On the other hand, they report that they are dropping any active support of the current members, such as giving them rides in their cars, because they are too rowdy. One man said that the last time he gave the *palomilla* (the gang—literally, "little pigeons") a ride, one of their rivals almost ruined his car. Some former members of this group have been in and out of jail for property and drug violations. Those being studied are young adults who have settled down in the neighborhood, most of whom have jobs.

The tacit admission of contacts between the adolescents and the just older generation of young adults is well worth further study. Even in high rank areas, contacts with older college students were highly influential on the boys' behavior. Both methodologically and practically, the extent and nature of continuity in succeeding generations and specific interactions among them become highly significant topics of study.

In other studies in this same region of the country (Dean, 1952; Rahm and Weber, 1958), the existence of more or less continuing traditions of group units, their codes, and their friendly or hostile relations with other groups has been reported. The exact mechanisms by which this continuity is achieved remain a rich field for exploration. It is entirely possible that by understanding the process of influence of the slightly older generation upon adolescents, we may discover the most effective source for changing prevailing norms and other traditions.

IMPORTANCE OF THE GROUPS
TO THEIR MEMBERS

The hypotheses of this research program concerning solidarity of the groups, degree of consensus on norms, their binding nature for individual members, and personal efforts exerted by members to participate in group activities hinge upon the concept of varying importance of the group (Chapter 5). The concept refers to the motivational base for individual association and continuing interaction with other members.

In earlier chapters, we saw that the adolescent period in modern Western societies typically produces prolonged conflicts between urges to be a full-fledged adult with all rights and privileges of adulthood, including the satisfaction of sexual desires, and the contradictions of being partly child and partly adult in terms of responsibility and privilege granted. These conflicts and contradictions form a base of common motives conducive to interaction among individual adolescents. Facing these conflicts, adolescents turn toward one another for the satisfactions and security of standing denied them in the socially institutionalized scheme of things (see Chapter 3).

Through the concept of relative importance of their groups, the gamut of social influences which form the context of individual behavior is joined to the inner influences which prompt the individual adolescent to seek his fellows in pursuing particular goals (cf. Chapters 3, 7, 8, 9). The motives conducive to interaction among individuals and the goals they seek to attain are inevitably affected and deflected by the range of alternatives in the setting. The process of becoming and being a group member generates new aspirations and concerns with oneself as an individual. In general, the behavior of an individual at a given point in time is a function of the pattern of influences from the external physical and social environment he faces and of those from within himself—from the person he is at the time. Together, this patterning of influences external to the individual at a given time and within him constitute the *frame of reference* for analysis of his behavior (cf. Sherif and Sherif, 1953, 1956).

Importance of the Groups in Different Neighborhoods

Although the data presently available are insufficient to permit detailed comparisons *between* neighborhoods, they do reveal differences in the kind and intensity of specific conditions conducive to adolescents' attachment to their groups in neighborhoods of high, middle, and low rank. Furthermore, one important generalization can be made safely at this point in the research: Conditions conducive to strong attachment to one's group are *not* confined to neighborhoods of any one social rank—for example, to low rank neighborhoods.

As noted in the previous sections, the group studied in a high rank area assumed all of the characteristics of a highly solidary unit strongly supported by its individual members when it engaged in activities most relevant to the motives of members to be together, namely, activities directed toward attaining distinction among their peers and carrying out plans independent of adult supervision or censorship. Even a member who did not approve of drinking helped out in their secret drinking party, playing an important part in keeping the affair secret by getting other members home safely.

In terms of the efforts of particular individuals within a group, the dedication of some boys in middle and high rank areas to proving themselves and attaining prestige with peers through working to buy a socially desirable car represents as much personal effort as one could find in any setting. Cases of adolescent groups becoming so important in middle- and upper-class areas as to override the individual's attachment to parents, school, church, and other groups are frequent enough in this research and in the daily papers to warrant the following generalization: Relative importance of an adolescent group to its members is not solely a function of socioeconomic and cultural rank of the neighborhood.

The notion that adolescent groups in low rank neighborhoods serve an entirely different function for individual members than those in middle and high rank areas is probably a product of widespread practical concern and study of adolescent groups in low rank areas, at the expense of studying similar formations in higher strata of society. The structure and functions of adolescent groups in respectable and affluent social strata are glossed over, partly because they are less visible to the naked eye. In terms of what one sees and reads about them, such groups do not seem to present practical social problems calling for immediate remedial or preventive measures, as do some groups in low rank areas of large cities. This may be due to the fact that, in terms of sheer number, upper-class youth are a minority of the youth population. For various reasons related to the resources of their parents, their actions do not usually get counted in social statistics. For these reasons, the usual adult reaction to youthful misbehavior of groups in "favored" areas is one of surprise.

Although the specific conditions conducive to their formation and the specific motives of members certainly do vary in neighborhoods of different rank, the nature of the group formations and the intensity of attachments of individual members do not differentiate them in any way calling for entirely different explanations for behavior. To call groups in low rank areas "gangs" and those in higher rank areas by nicer names does not change the finding that they are all *groups,* with distinctive properties as social units. These properties have unmistakable consequences for individual members, whether group activities are directed toward socially desirable activities, toward sexual satisfactions, experimentation with forbidden drinks and drugs, social distinction, stealing, or establishing a "territory."

The measures stated in the hypotheses for "importance of the group" are longevity and regularity of association, and the variety of activities engaged in by the group. In these objective terms, the groups studied in low rank neighborhoods were, in general, more important for members than those in other areas. It seems reasonable to suspect that our criteria for selection of a group for study, namely, frequency of interaction, tended to make for the selection of groups of considerable importance to members in these areas, those associating more regularly in many activities being more visible. On the other hand, groups more visible in middle and upper rank areas are likely to be those socially more prominent and with less to hide. The resources of youngsters in more favored neighborhoods really make it much simpler to interact regularly in private and to keep forbidden activities secret.

Given these limiting conditions, it was nevertheless obvious that groups in middle and high rank neighborhoods typically associate in a variety of adult programmed activities at school, church, and community groups which cut across their informal associations and reduce the time available to associate informally. Even a group in a middle rank area whose members were cut off from school activity by virtue of dropping out, who did not have church or other community-based affiliations, were forced by their parents to get jobs—

on pain of losing parental support. In terms of sheer time available, youth in low rank areas had more time to be together.

In the low rank neighborhoods, there were fewer formally pro-grammed alternatives to association with other adolescents. Those who were in school—the students who filled in the Self-Radius and Goals Schedule—took part in school activities. But, as observed time and time again in the groups studied, the boys were reluctant to partic-ipate in school and community activities programmed by and for persons of higher social rank than themselves. Even in the all-Latin high school of City B, there were differentials in socioeconomic rank, such that some Spanish-speaking boys saw themselves as "looked down upon." Thus, though skilled in athletics, a boy held back from the effort to "make the school team" when he could be playing in his neighborhood with fellows who accepted him as an equal.

To the extent that the boys perceived a social differential between themselves and others more favored, they were reluctant to partic-ipate in adult-sponsored activities in school and community groups. Even social agencies designed by church or community organiza-tions to help them were ordinarily used as a place to be with other adolescents, as a meeting place, as perhaps the only available spot to get together when one had no money and was watched suspi-ciously by police if he hung around a street corner.

Within the more modest scope of the self-radius and goals typical of his neighborhood, the boy in the low rank area does desire the standard of living represented as the "good way of life." Like any human being of any age beyond infancy, he wants to *belong* some-where and to *count* as a person with *someone*. Even if his family ties are affectionate and strong, as was the case with many boys studied in groups of low rank neighborhoods, his home is small, overcrowded, and burdened with problems of sheer necessities of living.

Failures of parents and the family have frequently been given exclusive blame for youths' fierce attachments to their fellows. It is true that those adolescents who faced extremely unpleasant home situations were eager to get out of them whether the unpleasantness stemmed from conflict between parents or from the crowded quarters. But this condition was not an isolated element in the most secretive, exclusive, well-coordinated (in short, solidary) groups studied in low rank neighborhoods. In these groups, the striking fact was the convergence of conditions at home, at school, and in the neighborhood which presented the adolescent with a picture of himself as someone thwarted, unwanted, looked down upon.

In short, the highest solidarity was found in groups where conditions were most conducive to the members' finding their only locus of pleasurable activity, their only source of personal recognition, their only web of stable relationships, and their only clear personal identity in a group of their peers. For example, members of Group B IIIs 2b had withdrawn or been expelled from school by ages 14–16 for "antisocial" behavior and classroom failure. To them, school had been an unpleasant situation, not an avenue to achievement or a place to be comfortably engaged in extracurricular pursuits. Less than a third of the boys had fathers supporting the family. The mothers of these boys worked hard at poorly paid jobs to support younger children. Life in their crowded homes was far from regular. In most cases, the father had left the constantly growing family after failing to support it. A social worker in the neighborhood tried to help some of these boys find work when they left school. He concluded that their complaints of not being able to find work were entirely realistic. His efforts with business acquaintances succeeded no better than theirs. As a result, the only possible source of money for these boys was stealing, which they did. Some of them even tried to sell the observer a stolen tire, which he declined. The boys spent most of their waking hours together; most of their activities were in company with some members of the group. Their chief source of personal satisfaction was accomplishment in these activities and its recognition by members.

When the observer of this group arranged an athletic competition with another group, so that independent ratings of the status structure could be made, their high degree of coordination was shown under challenging circumstances. These boys did not engage regularly in sports. Adult observers present agreed before the game that, as individual players, they were simply no match for those in the opposing group. Yet, by sheer superiority in coordinated group action, transferred to this game situation, they defeated their opponents, who were better players.

The groups in low rank areas which had the briefest histories and met for briefer periods than others both specialized in athletic games. These groups, one in City B and one in City A, were located in neighborhoods with somewhat higher socioeconomic levels than other low rank areas in their cities (Figure 9.1). Members were attending school, lived for the most part in more stable and comfortable homes, and several members had part-time jobs permitting the accumulation of small sums of money, which they could save because the family needs were not as immediately pressing as in somewhat less favored neighborhoods. Observers of these two groups established rapport with the boys rather easily. They were less secretive about their activities; they talked and played more frequently with nonmembers. In general, these were more loosely knit groups.

Group Solidarity, Spread of Members' Dwellings, and Personal Sacrifice

Whatever the motives bringing adolescent boys together and making membership important to them initially, the actual interactions of members from day to day in their environment produce conditions affecting the importance of the group to individual members. As noted earlier in this chapter, one of these conditions is the relationships with other social units. Competition or threat from other groups and adult authorities particularly draws individuals closer together and generates heightened significance of the group to them. In adolescent groups, threat or opposition from the outside is immediate whenever their activities are socially defined as deviant and are subject to sanctions.

The foregoing dynamics of group functioning make *relative secrecy* of an adolescent group a good indicator of its solidarity. Secrecy can be assessed in terms of the willingness of group members to talk with outsiders (e.g., the observer) about other members and their important activities. It can be assessed through observed "distance" maintained by group members from nonmembers. If great solidarity is productive of strong attachment to the group by individual members, individuals belonging to more secret groups should exhibit greater personal efforts to associate with the group (see Hypothesis A3, Chapter 5).

For groups of boys who must meet by walking on foot, the distances between their homes and their gathering places indicate the personal effort they are willing to make to be together. By first classifying groups simply as "highly secretive" and "less secretive," the spread of dwellings for members of four secret and four less secret groups living in low rank areas and not having automobiles was compared in terms of the areas of the polygons described by their place of residence. Although the number of groups is insufficient for statistical comparison at this date, the findings so far suggest unmistakably that boys in more solidary groups do make great personal sacrifices to get together. The spread of dwellings of the more secretive groups is consistently larger, with no overlap between the sizes of areas for less and more secret groups. An earlier check of the hypothesis using distance between members' homes and their meeting places (Sherif and Sherif, 1960) also supports this finding.

That is, the greater the solidarity of a group, as indicated by its secrecy, the greater are the personal efforts members are willing to make to associate. This implies that the more solidary groups of adolescents are not based primarily on proximity of the individual members, but that, over a period of time, a winnowing process has occurred from which a closely knit and trusted membership emerges. For example, the members of one group converged on foot in an area covering over one hundred city blocks (19 blocks long and 9 blocks wide), despite the fact that one member said that he had quit school because it was too far away to walk.

The strong motivational attachment to a tightly knit group of individual members was also revealed in their behavior when group activities conflicted with obligations to their families, school, church, or even their girls. The departure of one group for an athletic contest scheduled at the last minute was delayed fully ten minutes while the members sought to persuade one of their high status fellows to come with them, even though he had a date with his girl for the same hour. The members were in no position to threaten him, for he was one of their best players, whose defection would have had to be discounted. Nevertheless, their persuasion was effective. He simply did not turn up to see the girl. Many observations indicate the high probability that the group will be chosen over claims from other groups and institutions.

Individuals finding a sense of personal identity and recognition almost exclusively within the bounds of a tightly knit group of peers are less responsive to the rewards, enticements, and threats from outside the group, whether these come from parents, other grown-ups, or are the more distant possibilities of future achievement through neglecting the group and concentrating on school and work. From the point of view of adult society, the behavioral effects of strong attachment to his group of the adolescent may be socially undesirable. This state of affairs does not follow from the sheer fact of attachment, which may encourage individual members to pursue socially desirable goals (for example, to graduate from high school or college), as well as socially undesirable ones. Attachments to some groups in a social scheme are a part of psychological development in any society.

But the criteria for status and other norms of his group have a great deal to do with whether the individual's behavior is socially desirable or undesirable. The goals for achievement that are really effective in regulating his behavior are heavily determined by the interpersonal expectations among those who participate in activities together through their own choosing. The fact that an adolescent group may weigh more heavily than ties with family, school, and community should come as no surprise in the light of the following generalizations from the findings reported in this book and by other investigators:

1. Individuals do not form groups of their own choosing just to be, mechanically, one of a set, or because of any inherent tendency to conformity, or because they want to regulate their behavior in this or that direction. They come together and interact with strongly felt urges and with desires experienced as their own, whether these be desires to be accepted as a person in one's own right, desires to gain social distinction, sexual urges, wishes for desirable objects and instrumentalities, desires for exciting leisure-time activities, searches for recognition, or desires to prove themselves apart from adult

supervision. No matter what the specific content of their goals, no matter whether the aims are socially desirable or not, individuals come together in informal association and stay together because they experience *some* strong motivational basis which is not effectively fulfilled by themselves, individually, or through other existing social channels.

2. No matter what the initial bases of coming together, the interaction among individuals over a period of time becomes the source of satisfactions and frustrations for the individual members, experienced in highly personal terms. The process of interacting with others and developing mutual expectations for behavior is not a coldly intellectual affair, but has direct bearing on the most intimate personal conceptions of oneself. Through the patterned and reciprocal expectations for himself and for others, the individual looks to fellow members for acceptance and recognition in some capacity. The verdicts of others are not just one among a number of alternative evaluations. They are evaluations which *count* for him. It is through the dynamics of patterned interaction with others that he comes to regulate his behavior voluntarily in line with their expectations of him and with other norms shared by all members.

These generalizations point to a serious methodological defect in current literature on the criteria that individuals use in gauging their achievements or failure in various activities. The defect consists of dealing with the individual's concerns over acceptance and rejection, prestige, success or failure in the abstract—as though these were attributes of his personality which could be studied in isolation. On the contrary, these concerns are all relative to some source. For the adolescent those groups of peers with whom he chooses to interact are, for the time, highly significant sources, ranking in importance with the most powerful and attractive adult institutions.

PART IV

Summary
and implications

11 *The individual in his group in the setting: summary*

In this book, our problem has been the study of the individual's behavior as it unfolds within his groups in the context of his immediate neighborhood and the larger setting. This chapter summarizes the problem and approach, then the findings in the research thus far. In the last section of the chapter, the analysis is linked to problems of evaluating conforming and deviating behavior, for good or evil.

PROBLEM AND APPROACH

The groups in question are the doings of the individual members themselves, and their like. Individuals belong to and participate in these informal groups through their own voluntary choice. They are not creations, through blueprint or design, of some external authority, as is the case with many formalized organizations. Being created in the course of interpersonal give-and-take among like souls in a similar predicament, these groups serve as social anchors in the lives of members who actually lack or perceive a lack of social ties desirable to them.

Psychologically, the groups are reference groups for their members. The extent to which such an informal formation becomes the center of the universe for an individual member is proportional to the degree of the disruption of other ties (with family, school, and other social establishments), and proportional to the degree that the group and its activities serve as vehicles for joint action towards the fulfillment of goals he feels denied otherwise (social, financial, sexual, and so on). To this extent, the individual's concerns over social acceptance or rejection, his concern to prove himself as a person who counts, his very conception of the kind of person he is, revolve in no small part around *being somebody* in this group of his own choosing.

The members of the groups in question, both leaders and the rank-and-file, are adolescent boys. We deliberately chose to study this age level and voluntary group formations therein because they dramatize the binding effect of being a member in regulating one's self-conception and behavior. Adolescent group formations are *usually* of relatively short duration, on the order of a few years. From the viewpoint of our problem, we could just as well have chosen voluntary group formations during a more mature age level which are more lasting. For the problem concerns the directive role of groups in defining the individual's self-identity and regulating the behavior of individual members.

Whatever the age level, whenever a number of individuals lack desirable social ties, or strive to establish what appear to them as *more* desirable social ties, they do form groups in which to move and have their being. Whenever individuals share the same predicament (such as deprivation of necessities or lack of what they see as the good things of life which they urgently feel they should have), and when they cannot or dare not do something about the predicament individually, they do open themselves to each other. In the course of this give-and-take, under the promptings of motivational urges they share, they move towards taking things into their own hands in concert with others in the same boat.

The result is formation of groups which become, in time, a major support of their efforts toward attainment of their individually felt goals. The support that individual members derive from their voluntary associations in groups has sometimes been overlooked. In no small part, this oversight has been responsible for the position that the individual and his groups are invariably and eternally opposing entities.

The adolescent is no exception to the general process of group formation. On the contrary, the biological spurt of the period and concern over the transition to the social role of adult in various respects conspire to make the adolescent highly prone to form his own groups with others like himself. Given the promptings owing to disrupted or conflicting social ties, given the promptings owing to deprivations and frustrations he suffers with others like himself, his own group becomes the device for taking things into his own hands.

As a rule, the group formations which adolescents create through their own voluntary interactions are not self-perpetuating, as are similar formations in industries and other institutions. Nevertheless, adolescent groups do possess the essential properties of groups in any sphere of life—properties documented in studies tracing the development of informal groups in religious, industrial, and political fields. In this connection, it suffices to remember the initially informal beginnings, in the recent or distant past, of many social clubs, religious sects, political organizations, and fraternal organizations that flourish today as formal groups or institutions.

Earmarks of a Group and Behavior of Individual Members

The two essential earmarks of adolescent groups, like any other groups, are:

1. Structure or organization of interaction among members, defining the statuses and roles of members in various respects, and thereby defining the proper attitudes of the members toward each other and toward members of other groups.

2. A set of values or group norms shared by group members, over and above the sectors of values they have in common with others in their setting and the society of which they are a part.

The interpersonal expectancies of members and their behaviors within the in-group, and attitude toward and treatment of outsiders, take on a predictable pattern to the extent that the organization of reciprocal positions and roles of members in specific respects is stabilized over a period of time. This property of a group is, therefore, decidedly relevant for behavior of individuals composing it.

Corresponding to the degree of stabilization of the patterns of inter-action, the individual becomes personally concerned with remaining a part of it, maintaining an unquestioned place in good standing in the group, in proving himself in various respects, in showing that he is not a back number in undertakings (which may be good or bad by outside standards), commensurate with the status and role he has achieved. In fact, the individual's concerns over acceptance or rejection, his experiences of personal achievement or failure, that is, the directive components of his warmly experienced ego, in no small part consist of stuff of this sort.

Individual members in reference groups of this sort have had a hand in shaping the organizational and normative properties of the group. Their own personal attitudes and behaviors, in turn, become more and more shaped by them. This shaping of individual attitude and behavior is proportional to the extent that shared ways emerge and become stabilized for conducting activities toward goals that initially served as common bonds conducive to the members' inter-action.

As something they themselves had a hand in shaping, these shared ways of doing things and these rules for conduct are theirs, to be observed without external authority or coercion, even to be cherished. They serve as effective vehicles of solidarity and social control in the group. To the extent that norms of the group's own doing are shared and stabilized, the individual member does *not* experience them as external intrusions demanding arbitrary and functionless conformity. These, their own norms, serve as codified justifications and standards for attitudes and behaviors directed toward more effective handling of problems and plans in pursuit of their common goals—whether for good or evil by other standards.

The group norms that are most binding and most consequential in the members' scheme of concerns are the ones that regulate matters of solidarity among members and that set standards of conduct in the very spheres of motivational promptings that brought them together. These norms define the bounds of what is acceptable and desirable, and the bounds of what is objectionable for personal viewpoint and behavior in matters of consequence to them.

Since members in good standing do share and cherish their own norms, the application of appropriate *sanctions* to behavior that falls outside of their latitude of acceptance in a related sphere is not the sole prerogative of the leader(s) alone. Nor are those of high standing in the group immune from sanctions from others. Correctives become the duly felt business of all group members in varying degree.

To the extent that the individual derives a sense of belongingness and a sense of being somebody to be counted through his membership in the group, the group increasingly becomes the source of his personal security and the context for gauging his personal feelings of success and failure in relevant spheres of activity. Hence, the binding loyalties of the individual, when he has to make a choice, are to his reference group(s). The binding rules, values, or standards for his conduct are those of his reference group(s).

It follows that mere knowledge of rules and standards of society at large and its various agencies does not sensitize the individual, no matter how frequently repeated. When he feels that he does not belong, that he is not wanted, and that his interests are not included in the larger scheme of things, his personal sensitivity is aroused in a context of those who *do* belong to him, who *do* want him, and who *do* take account of his interests. Some of the obvious implications for effective practice will be spelled out in the next chapter.

Motivational Promptings and the Social Setting

Through assessment of influences conducive to the dissolution of ties with adolescent groups, one can point at the motivational promptings that underlie their formation. As reported by a number of investigators with first-hand familiarity with such groups, when members begin to establish themselves in steady jobs, when they marry to establish themselves in ongoing family lives, when they begin to engage in other undertakings that are challenging to them, they are weaned from their adolescent group ties. The adolescent group loses its magic even in the lives of the loyal group members.

When we look at closer range at influences underlying both the formation, functioning, and dissolution of adolescent groups, we start discerning an unmistakable pattern of motivational promptings common both to groups that engage primarily in socially acceptable activities and those that engage in socially objectionable ones. If this be the case, we shall have to cease viewing adolescent groups that engage in socially objectionable activities as the doings of a small number of psychopathic individuals.

The price paid when we view socially objectionable outcomes of group activities as the doings of psychopathic characters is losing sight of the enormity of the problem in its true proportions. In practice, the price paid is resort to measures, such as individual therapy and counseling, which may be appropriate and practical in a relatively small number of cases among the millions who participate in the formation and functioning of groups. There are motivational promptings common to the individuals under the circumstances of their immediate and the larger social setting.

The motivational promptings stem both from biological development of the adolescents and from their setting, but in highly interrelated fashion. Influences stemming from the impulses and urges of a maturing individual and from his setting form a pattern—acting and reacting on one another. Explanations of behavior (whether it is for good or evil) that put the sole weight on the individual's impulses and their vicissitudes, or on the setting alone, have not fared well in either theory or practice.

The gamut of influences shaping behavior composes a system whose parts affect one another (Chapters 3–4). With a changing body reverberating with a dramatic onslaught of the glandular system and its products, the maturing adolescent is throbbing with impulses and desires hard to contain, including sexual urges continually sensitizing the individual for consummation. But even these sexual urges are not one-way affairs. Here too the social setting comes in to define, with sanctions, what he can do and what he cannot do, with all the attendant consequences on the individual (cf. Ford and Beach, 1951).

The same is true of impulses concerned with food to eat, apparel to wear, a dwelling to live in. There are prescriptions, and deprivations as well, the latter owing to constricted family finances, one's station in life relative to others, including the location of the dwelling on this or the other side of the tracks.

It is well known, of course, that the social setting does set limits or bounds within which biological impulses can be carried out, heaping sanctions on the individual who transgresses these bounds. But less seldom is the positive aspect emphasized, using here the term "positive" in a directional sense without judging the efficacy of particular outcomes. The setting provides the adolescent with a framework for a self-picture of the full-fledged male or female in many different and specific respects. This self-picture depicts the characteristics of the approved and the desirable male or female in body proportions, in work and play, as husband or wife, with all the desirable attributes that go with each of these. The setting offers, then, a framework defining the possessions to be attained, the preferable locations in which to live and to aspire to, the particular places and outfits where the individual seeks acceptance as a member in good standing (Chapters 9–10).

In short, for good or bad, the setting depicts affiliations, possessions, social attainments, including *personal* characteristics, that are put at a premium and on a pedestal. These are presented and reinforced through the personal examples of successful men, through books found in drugstores and railways stations, through radio, movies, and television. And, to top it all, one is stimulated by models to get these things *now*—and fast.

But to only a favored few are the instrumentalities for achieving the desired self-picture readily available, and even these are constrained by the very definition of the adolescent period to wait and postpone. It is not a context conducive to a stable identity. Another disruptive influence is an accelerated rate of social change with no recognized alterations in the official prescriptions for the transition. As a consequence, there are varying degrees of cleavage between adult outlook, values, and practices and those seen as necessary, even essential, by the adolescent generation. As noted by various writers, the result is adult-youth conflict. Under the present circumstances, adult-youth conflict in some degree seems to cut across areas of low, middle, and high social rank. The distance between generations is reflected in the not infrequent shift of reference group ties from parents and family to agemates, at least for a period, during the present adolescent generation.

Thus the setting plays its part in bringing adolescents together. All of these motivational promptings impel them toward one another—the deprivations and frustrations of the kinds mentioned above, the self-image to be fulfilled quickly, the state of being caught betwixt and between in a changing world. The informal groups that arise from their interactions are experienced by the individual members as sources of mutual support, vehicles for ventures they would not dare engage in alone, and as secure ground for proving themselves in their strivings to fulfill an identity in the respects depicted by their setting.

To be sure, there are deprivations and frustrations underlying deeds engaged in by individuals in these groups. To be sure, some of these deeds are objectionable. But on the whole, objectionable deeds do not follow directly as a simple consequence of deprivation or frustration. They follow some sort of justification of the deeds provided by the mutual encouragement of other individuals in the same boat, as pointed out by a leading psychiatrist some years ago (Healy and Bronner, 1936, e.g., pp. 7, 63 ff.).

Study Design and Procedures Required by the Gamut of Influences

The gamut of influences summarized above requires a program of research to relate influences stemming from the individual, from his reference groups, and from the setting. Accordingly, the research design reported in this book includes the following facets (Chapters 4–5):

1. Study of the characteristics of the setting. This is the sociological aspect of the program. It amounts to specification of stimulus situations in which interaction among individuals takes place.

2. Study of the self-radius and goals prevailing among adolescents in the areas of study. This aspect provides a bridge between the general characteristics of the setting and behavioral indicators of members of groups selected for intensive study. Attitudes and behavior of group members can be evaluated relative to empirical data on the prevailing self-pictures of adolescents in specific respects.

3. Study of informally organized groups in specified settings over

a period of time. This is the focal aspect of study and includes assessment of the organization and values or norms of the group, its natural history, and case histories of individual members.

Groups, as we have emphasized, are formed to do something about common deprivations, frustrations, and goals of individual members. They are formed to provide individual members with mutual support, a feeling of personal worth, a stable ground for self-identity, intimate social ties conducive to confidence among members chosen to be the "ins." Therefore, even groups which do not, as a rule, engage in socially objectionable activities have their own air of intimacy, their own secrets. In the interactions, there are content and episodes which the members feel should remain within the domain of their intimacy and which are not enacted for the convenience of an investigator with a recorder at scheduled times. In short, groups are not formed for the benefit or convenience of the researcher.

Therefore, we had to use or develop methods and procedures that would not clutter or interrupt the flow of interaction among group members. They are reported in Chapters 5–7. The attempt to adapt methods and techniques of measurement to the flow of interaction, rather than the other way around, requires much more effort and patience than laboratory research. But it offers hope of validity. Through the use of a combination of techniques, some adapted from the laboratory, more precise and reliable measurement also comes into the grasp of field research.

When small groups and their members are studied relative to the settings, and the settings relative to the groups, the dichotomy between "small group" and "large group" is bound to disappear, in time, into thin air. And the "psychological" and "sociological" approaches to social behavior supplement one another, instead of being monopolistic prerogatives of the respective disciplines.

This approach accommodates study of the contributions of individual members to any desired degree of elaboration, from the point of view of unique personal characteristics, idiosyncracies, and skills. Interactions of individuals prompted by common motives which can be satisfied through concerted actions invariably result in formation of a group organization with its set of norms. This phenomenon is the invariant product under such circumstances. But *which* member

will occupy *what* position in the organization, and with what overtones of personal feeling each will respond to the norms, are also
determined by the personal skills and idiosyncracies that individual
members bring to the group. The contribution of these personal
skills and qualities is not in the abstract, however. It is made relative to the activities and situations which are important to the
individuals in their concerted undertakings, as well as any shared
evaluations of socially desirable qualities they bring to the interaction situation. In essence, this was Gibb's conclusion in his defini-
tive survey of studies on leadership (1954). It is equally applicable
to any other members of a group.

SUMMARY OF FINDINGS

Sociocultural Setting, Self-Radius and Goals of Its Youth

Our larger setting is American society—still rather sharply graded
with respect to material and social opportunities for different strata
of the population; economically a system of private enterprise becoming more and more urban and industrial; increasingly homogeneous in ideas and goals as the mass media of communication and the
public schools grow larger and more uniform in content. The 1960
Census reflects these characteristics. A recent analysis by a government statistician for *The New York Times* (Miller, 1962) reveals
the income differentials. The Census Tract Statistics reflect the
extent to which different neighborhoods in the cities are beneficiaries
or victims of the trends.

Within this society, our research focused on large cities located
in the Southwest and down into neighborhoods of low, middle, and
high social rank. The rank of a neighborhood was determined by
communicable and reproducible indicators (Chapter 9). The neighborhoods differed in the comforts and facilities afforded, the economic and educational levels of residents, and their cultural backgrounds.

Does growing up in such different neighborhoods result in differences in youths' conceptions of themselves, in their values, in goals for the future? Or are the self-radius and goals of American youth fundamentally similar despite their varied experiences?

We conceived of the individual's self-picture in terms of related attitudes defining the bounds of acceptability for him, with minimum and maximum limits relative to which he sets his own goals for achievement. Our findings from representative samples of high school students in low, middle, and high rank areas show that youth in these areas have *common* values, traceable to membership in the larger society, as well as *variations* in self-radius and goals related to characteristic differences in their neighborhoods. The striking finding was what the commonalities and differences concerned.

The values and ambitions common to youth in all areas spell the image of *individual success* in American life as purveyed by the magic world of TV, movies, papers, magazines, and popular books. The ingredients of the image are comfortable living, cars, attractive clothing, money to spend, leisure, and entertainment. Regardless of present conditions, most youth are more discriminating and more precise in specifying down to the last detail the kinds of automobiles they want now and in the future than they are about their choice of a life's work. The uniformity and urgency of desires for the good *things* of life are mute testimony to the enormous success of large-scale salesmanship.

To have the sweet smell of success as an adult, all the teen-age students know that some effort is required. But what of the achievements in those areas of life so essential in this country for attaining the desired standard of living by legitimate means—education, an occupation, adequate income to support it? In these respects, the youth in different neighborhoods differed in several ways.

In summarizing the variations, it should be stressed that the differences were relative, not absolute or categorical. Even taking into account the school dropouts in different areas, it cannot be said that there is among any large segment of youth a total devaluation of education. Debunking the values accruing from schooling does become a norm in certain small groups in both lower and middle rank areas. This does not give it the status of a *cultural* norm prevailing among youth in an entire stratum of society or among those with a particular cultural background. In fact, it was not shared by many of their parents who had only two or three years of schooling themselves. Similarly, it cannot be concluded that youth of different sociocultural and economic backgrounds differ as to *knowledge* of right and wrong, as defined by legal, school, and parental authorities.

However, with respect to the amount of education, income, and occupational prestige that the adolescent sees as a minimum for himself, on the one hand, and the level he labels "success," on the other, the self-radius of youth in the different neighborhoods does vary significantly and systematically. The latitudes of acceptance in low rank areas in these respects simply do not extend as high up the ladder of achievement as those in high rank areas, and they start at lower levels.

The variations of self-radius from less to more favored settings have to be appreciated to assess the considerable differences in personal goals typical of the different areas. As earlier investigators have also reported, youth in high rank areas set their goals higher than those in low rank areas. However, relative to their own conceptions of success, youth in low rank areas set their goals at high levels. Youth in high rank areas frequently allow a comfortable margin between their own goals and the level of achievement that they view as really successful.

With reference to the achievements of their parents, with reference to opportunities clearly available in their settings, and with reference to their own conceptions of success, we found that youth in low rank areas are, on the whole, more ambitious, more "achievement-oriented," than those in high rank areas. This state of affairs is a paradox only if one insists on treating the individual's motivations and his goals as though they were simply functions of *him* as an organism—apart from his prior learning experiences, his view of his own environment, and his daily interactions with agemates and adults in it.

The discrepancies between what youth have in the way of success symbols and what they desire are decidedly least in the high rank neighborhoods, despite the higher level of their goals. Furthermore, in the schools serving areas high in social rank, the conceptions and goals of the students were more uniformly at the same level. Of course, this fact could cause considerable discomfort and feelings of deprivation to the minority of students coming from more moderate circumstances in the same school district. But in the middle and low rank areas, there were splits, even cleavages, among the youth as to their attitudes and goals—or more properly, bimodalities in their distributions within an area. These heterogeneities within areas reflect the movement of population in the middle rank areas and the tides of acculturative processes in low rank areas with bicultural populations.

For example, the distributions of preferences for automobiles were very similar from neighborhood to neighborhood. But goals for education were overwhelmingly for a college degree in high rank areas, while youth in other areas varied considerably. In middle and low rank areas, the proportion aiming for college became smaller; conversely, there were larger proportions in school indicating proneness to drop out before completing high school and, in fact, increasing rates of actual drop-outs from high to low rank areas. In the schools serving primarily low rank areas, it is the student aiming for the university who is not in the majority.

The survey of prevailing values and goals for oneself gives a static picture. But it provides a framework within which the discrepancies between overwhelmingly desired success symbols and the actualities faced by the adolescent can be gauged (see Chapter 9). It also shows the ranges of socially supported choice available for youth in different settings, thus enabling us to locate an individual's course of action relative to evaluations of others in his setting.

The prevailing values do not mechanically determine the choice processes of individuals when there are alternatives; nor do individuals make decisions in quiet solitude through sheerly intellectual deliberation. An individual perceives the value alternatives in his setting through the web of interaction with other individuals, the filtering process acquiring its highest value among individuals who face common problems and interact with the desire to do something about them.

Conforming Behavior in Adolescent Reference Groups

The recurrent findings so far may be summarized with reference to the major hypotheses in Chapter 5. For this purpose, we need not attempt at present to evaluate those predictions which require study of a larger number of representative groups and neighborhoods or those predicated on experimentation. These are tasks of the continuing research program.

As predicted in our first set of hunches (labeled A, pp. 90–91), adolescents who interact together frequently and regularly reveal in their behaviors and joint actions a motivational basis for their association. Cutting across all groups studied thus far was the boys' overwhelming desire to do things adults do, *on their own,* without programming or intervention by the older generation. The "things" they wanted to do pertained, for the most part, to goals which we found valued by youth in all areas—to cars, clothing, entertainment, sexual relationships and social contact with girls, companionship with those of like mind, and, except in the least acculturated neighborhoods, sports.

Owing to the differential facilities and the boys' resources in the neighborhoods, however, these focuses of desire led to different forms of activity. For example, in a high rank neighborhood, the boys we studied had cars—an enormous advantage in pursuing any of the above goals, especially seeing girls. On the other hand, having a car meant spending a great deal of time in caring for it, thinking and talking about the *next* model, and giving friends a ride. Not having a car, as was the case for most of the boys in less favored neighborhoods, did not decrease one's desire, particularly since one encountered great difficulties in being alone with a girl without one. If one could get a job and his parents were not in dire need, he could save for a car. Otherwise, a lot of effort went into arranging to get a ride, to borrow, or, if necessary, take one.

Frequently, this doing things adults do involved activities not deemed proper for the adolescent age level, or immoral and illegal by parents and other authorities (e.g., sexual activities, smoking, drinking, drug usage, racing automobiles, unsupervised parties, theft, and more serious violations). Such acts were reported by members of groups in every neighborhood. To the extent that such activities were frequent, the greater was the wall of secrecy shielding members from adults in particular and outsiders in general (cf. Hypothesis D3, Chapter 5).

In assessing other specific kinds of motivations bringing boys together, we relied on objective evidence from activities characteristically engaged in and from individual life history material. However, the inferences about motivations were made relative to the physical and social character of their settings, including the reference scales and goals prevailing in them and the facilities available for reaching these goals. In these terms, it is significant that activities violating the limits of acceptance for adults occupied only a fraction of the time members spent together, even in groups officially labeled "delinquent" in their localities.

In making the above generalization, we ignore the lack of etiquette, good table manners, and politeness, and the rowdiness of behavior, typical in some groups. They are grounds for sanctions only from an adult brought up in a more refined atmosphere. Of course, such behaviors may become cause for intense concern and anxiety to adults trying to their jobs (for example, teach) in the same way they would with youth in neighborhoods where politeness to adults and good table manners are deeply ingrained from childhood. There certainly is more rough behavior in some neighborhoods than others; but we are speaking here of serious violations of parental or legal norms, not variations in etiquette. (One of our observers actually got an older used car to protect his recent model from the ravages of his group when he took them places. The boys were most appreciative of the rides and were not deliberately harming his car. The actions of concern to him were the scuffling of boys in a neighborhood where boys were expected to scuffle some, and where parents had no shiny new cars which they taught their children to protect.)

The greater absolute frequency in some groups of actions subject to sanctions by adults, if discovered, was proportional to the greater regularity and duration of their interactions. It is decidedly relevant, therefore, to look into how often and how long boys in different neighborhoods congregated informally.

In a favored neighborhood, the adolescent boys were involved in a much more varied and time-consuming schedule of adult-sponsored activities at home, in school, church, and clubs. They associated in these activities as well as informally—a primary gratification for the individual member being his identification with this "smart set" among his schoolmates. However, they did not have the time available to get together informally that boys in less favored neighborhoods had. We have no evidence that their informal reference group was unimportant to the individuals, for on numerous occasions they revealed in many ways that it was very important to them. Yet the members were all related in varied and overlapping ways to other small groups and institutions, besides their families, all of which made some demands for time and loyalty.

In the low rank neighborhoods, activities of adolescent boys are frequently blamed on lack of supervision by their families, broken homes, and lack of parental love for children. The correlations between broken homes and commitment in institutions, however, do not prepare one to find, as we did, that many of the boys in less favored neighborhoods had affection and loyalty to their families—even when only one parent was present—and that some participated in socially undesirable activities with their fellows, even though their families were stable and their parents would have disapproved.

In the low rank neighborhoods we studied, the homes were small and crowded, offering few facilities for entertainment. As many studies have shown, participation in programmed activities at school, church, and community was less. Frequently, boys felt that they were out of place, looked upon with disapproval in school and community affairs. Not taking part in them meant long hours to be together, which, in any event, was more pleasant.

These observations are relevant to our hypotheses about the importance of a group to its individual members (Hypotheses A4, B1). The most tightly knit, solidary groups were found in neighborhoods where the boys had a great deal of time on their hands. In particular, the most solidary groups were those in which the backgrounds of their individual members contained not just one but a *set* of unfavorable environmental conditions conducive to thwarting and deprivation (e.g., inadequate and overcrowded housing, instability in the family, inadequate clothing, lack of money, failure at school, poor job opportunities, etc.). Such conditions are decidedly pertinent to understanding the *susceptibility* of an individual to commit himself to others in a similar plight who do accept him, even if they engage in activities that he knows, intellectually, are punishable.

To understand more fully the individual's commitment to his informal reference group, his conformity to its norms or to the norms of other reference groups that may conflict with them (family, church, school, etc.), we have to examine the properties of the groups and the consequences of being a member. Many boys undergoing similar deprivations and thwartings do not thus commit themselves, either because parental rules prevent it, because they do not gain acceptance, or because, in some way, they see and hold close other alternatives. This has been a puzzle for students of adolescent psychology and juvenile gangs. To begin to unravel it, we have to look not only at individuals but at the properties of groups which do become the center of things for their members.

Patterns of Conformity in Groups. Being a part of regular and recurrent interactions among contemporaries who congregate of their own choice means, for the individual, regulation of his behavior relative to others (Chapter 7). We found that interaction among adolescents was patterned in a variety of ways (i.e., in various dimensions), notably with respect to the relative effectiveness of initiative attempted by individual members, the degree of control over what happened in the group, and the regard of others for them in these respects (Hypotheses B, B2).

The patterning of interaction in informal groups in terms of *power* was measured in terms of effective initiative, including the ability to invoke sanctions (e.g., punishment). In these terms, each group had a leader—that is, an individual with undisputed top standing at the time—even though members often said in response to a direct question, "We don't have a leader. We're all equal here." The patterns of power were measured reliably over periods of time through a combination of independent techniques. They were validly measured in the sense that objective measures "from outside" the group were highly correlated with measures secured from the members themselves (sociometric choices in this dimension).

However, the existence of a power structure does not mean that regulation of behavior was achieved in such structures solely, or even chiefly, by punishment or its threat. On the contrary, the great bulk of patterned behavior and conformity to group norms occurred without sanctions or threat of sanctions in these groups.

From outside, adults often wonder why youth "submit" to group norms, especially when they know resulting actions are punishable. They wonder why they do not have a "healthy conscience" or "strong superego" without analyzing in functional terms what these words imply. What the adults mean is, "Why don't they stick by the moral values which parents, school, church, and government promulgate, rather than the trends of activity in smaller circles? Why don't they feel guilty or sorry when they betray values which we know are worth upholding?" Phrased in this fashion, we would explore the question not only in terms of the individual adolescent, but in terms of the efforts made by adults to promote these values, what they mean to the adolescent, and the actualities he faces—including the actualities of these smaller circles of agemates.

One reason why this issue does constitute a puzzle is that many adults fail to grasp the reasons for which individuals participate in groups of their own choosing and the fact that, in so doing, their self or ego is involved—including their "conscience," for good or evil. If we think of group structure only in terms of brute force, on the one hand, and submission, on the other, the puzzle is real. But this is not typical of informal reference groups. For one thing, the hierarchical ordering in terms of power, or effective initiative in controlling group interaction and sanctions, is not the only dimension of group organization. Mutual liking also forms a pattern, so that individuals are patterned in terms of popularity.

In addition, as our findings show, the group is patterned to give wide play to individual differences in ability to contribute, personal characteristics, and skills in various activities, *within* the power structure and norms of the group.

If we take all relevant dimensions into account for a composite view of group structure, we can conceive of the individual's *role* in the group as a nexus of all the relevant dimensions. Thus conceived, the individual's role provides a constellation of linkages with others in the group. It is forged in interaction with others, both through their treatments and reactions to him and through his own behavior, idiosyncracies, and contributions—or lack of them. No wonder, then, that in the course of frequent give-and-take in his group, he may come to think of himself in terms of this nexus and to regulate his own behavior quite willingly in its terms. Individuals do, voluntarily and even unwittingly, regulate their behavior in line with their face-to-face reference groups.

Individuals are sometimes dissatisfied with their standings and roles in their groups. A number of instances of active efforts to change one's standing or other features of his role were observed. Some were successful. Such efforts take considerable personal skill and patience. By far the most propitious circumstances for the attempt were those coinciding with changed circumstances—an altered emphasis in the group's activities, or a change in relationships with outsiders (other groups of agemates or adult authority), as suggested by Hypotheses D and D4, Chapter 5.

Collective bestowing of praise for upholding group norms was more common than negative sanctions for deviation beyond the latitude of acceptance. Both were important events, but the latter were crises, in some degree, for the individual members receiving them. In this research, it was found that the latitude of acceptance was narrowest, deviation most promptly and unanimously reacted against with sanctions (e.g., general cold-shouldering, exclusions, physical punishments) for matters concerning the maintenance of a group and its perpetuation as a unit (Hypothesis C3). This was particularly apparent in relations with other groups and adult authority, where the latitude of acceptance was narrowest of all.

Within the range of acceptable behavior, the leader and high status members had the narrowest latitude of all, inasmuch as their actions might imperil other individuals as members. In less consequential issues, the leader frequently was permitted greater leeway, even for actions clearly violating norms which other members were expected to follow.

Achievement of high status in these groups did not rest solely on ascriptions from outside the group, which could either help or hinder the individual, depending upon the situation. It was associated with strong personal commitment to the group, skills and personal qualities highly valued by members, but also acumen, ability to plan beyond momentary interaction situations, and to coordinate the actions of others. In short, achieving status was accomplished by those more able, in some respects highly valued by other members, by individuals exceptionally aware, responsible, and loyal. These characteristics, it should be noted, are not descriptive of neurotic or psychopathic personalities.

On the other hand, the uncertainties associated with marginal or fringe membership and with expulsion from a group produced behaviors at times markedly erratic and "irresponsible." One boy who had been high in status, but who ran in a moment of danger, thereby deserting other members, was depressed, even despondent. As we have noted throughout the book, the boys most loyal and responsible within their group were, in a number of cases, characterized as "asocial" by adult authorities in school and recreation centers. Some notation on the direction of "socialty" and ability seems to be needed.

The content of group norms does vary from neighborhood to neighborhood and within neighborhoods (cf. Hypotheses C1 and C2). Each group had certain catchwords and customs distinctive to the membership. And, to an important extent, traditions, fads, and fashions distinctive to neighborhoods of a given social rank *become* norms for particular groups within them. There is a kind of filtering process, whenever a given neighborhood presents alternatives. We do not mean to suggest that this is a simple event, or that it always results in either socially desirable or undesirable outcomes. For example, members of one group observed were set upon not being hoodlums and upon graduating from high school. They lived in a low rank neighborhood within a three-by-four block area. It would be easy to attribute these aims to their families, who certainly played a part. Yet it is also true that these boys went to a school attended mostly by students of middle socioeconomic status where the dropout rate was not so high. It is also true that they derived great pleasure from athletic sports and conversation together, and assiduously avoided association with tough gangs.

On the other hand, a tradition of toughness and defiance of adult authority also reflects a filtering process, whereby individuals selectively turn toward these alternatives in their collective interactions and, in turn, are chosen by others as fit company, or ignored, or rejected, as the case may be. So does a tradition of social distinction and "smartness." Such norms are transmitted especially from a just older generation when the younger generations face similar motivational and practical problems. The process of transmission in terms of direct contacts between just succeeding generations remains one of the fascinating problems of continuing research. Our present generalizations are drawn from natural histories of the groups and individuals currently members.

Taking up the mantle of a tradition does not seem to be a process of simple imprinting from an older generation. Instead, traditions are transmitted successfully when individuals facing similar motivational problems and similar obstacles or opportunities for dealing with them do interact in sufficiently patterned relationships to translate common values into actions.

Whether the tradition is socially acceptable or objectionable to outsiders, the particular individuals most successful in the process of selecting a tradition and translating it into action are those capable of monitoring their actions closely in terms of others in their set and in terms of the goals of the joint activity. The importance of out-of-the-ordinary personal skills in translating tradition into contemporary action is one reason why age and kinship are not the most significant determinants of status in successive generations of youth in a neighborhood. The younger brother of a fraternity president does not automatically get into the club, especially if his brother has graduated. Even if he does, his standing is not inherited from his brother. Similarly, the younger brother in a low rank neighborhood does not automatically follow his brother's footsteps (which may lead to either socially desirable or undesirable paths). Aside from the problem of being accepted by a group, which is not always easy when the group is tightly knit, achievement of status requires continuing contributions in the group's terms. Thus, we found coming and going of members in the informal groups we studied, especially at the low levels of status, and in more tightly knit groups the members frequently resided over widely scattered parts of a neighborhood, even when they had to walk to get together.

In other words, this selective process means that proximity alone is not the crucial factor in group formation and transmission of norms, if distances permit association at all. On the contrary, we have suggestive evidence that the more solidary a group, the more secretive its activities, the more effort members are willing to put forth to associate, as measured by the spread of the dwellings of members who must congregate on foot (Hypothesis A3).

Intergroup Relations in Neighborhoods

Several of our hypotheses concerned group solidarity (Chapter 5). The most tightly knit groups observed were those whose members had fewest stable ties with other groups and institutions, hence whose belonging was highly important to them (Hypothesis B1). High solidarity was also associated, as noted earlier, with prolonged and regular interaction in a variety of activities. However, these same groups were also those most in opposition to adult authority and most frequently plagued with problems with other groups of agemates.

At this stage, therefore, we are in no position to make strong generalizations about group solidarity or cohesiveness in terms of member relationships solely *within* the groups, such as extent of mutual liking, or steepness of the hierarchy. Even the less cohesive groups became more cohesive when their activities, or circumstances, brought them into conflict with outsiders (Hypothesis D2). The expulsion of such a group from a recreation center and warnings by the police not to associate eliminated the immediate "trouble" from the vicinity. It did not result in dissolution of the group, but strengthened the internal ties among members. The one clear case of disintegration of a group following authoritative sanctions involved the leader's activities outside of the group circle—in another town, in fact—which members regarded as unnecessary, foolhardy, even betrayal, since they were not involved.

In Chapter 10, we discussed some of the ecological and organizational circumstances conducive to conflicting relationships among groups and with adult authorities in a setting. As noted, every individual involved contributes his bit to the over-all picture characterizing a particular neighborhood in this respect. Yet, on the basis of experimental evidence on intergroup conflict, as well as surveys of the literature and the findings in this research, we are forced to conclude that intergroup relations emerge as a set of conditions which continuously affect group properties and member behavior (Hypotheses D1–D4).

The actions of particular groups certainly affect the continuing character of intergroup relations. But primary praise or blame for the character of member attitudes toward out-groups cannot be assigned to strictly individual characteristics of the members, or even to the characteristics of the structure of a single group (Hypothesis C5). On the contrary, some groups and their members maintained friendly relationships with certain groups and hostile relationships with still others. Furthermore, of two groups with friendly relations, one was often friendly with a third, while the other regarded the third as an "enemy."

Thus, our most striking finding is that interpersonal relationships within these informal groups are not insulated from relationships with other groups and adult institutions, or from the character of the setting. Conclusions about them can make sense only when behaviors in give-and-take within a group are considered relative to other groups in the neighborhood, both agemate and adult, including the images fostered so effectively in the larger setting.

EVALUATION OF CONFORMITY
AND DEVIATION IN GROUPS

In this research, we have explored conformity in adolescent groups which was socially acceptable from the adult point of view, and socially objectionable from the adult point of view. In doing so, our aim has been to analyze and understand, not to justify.

Now, certain conclusions will be drawn which have far-reaching implications for theory and action programs. They are based on our data concerning behaviors in spontaneously organized groups, on our experiments on group formation and intergroup relations, and on similar findings in the literature.

One of the strongest promptings of human beings is to establish stable, secure social ties with others, for the following reasons:

1. To have a dependable anchor for a consistent and patterned self-picture, which is essential for personal consistency in experience and behavior, and particularly for a day-to-day continuity of the person's self-identity. Some stability of social ties is a prerequisite condition for the individual to experience himself as the "same person" from day to day, with his characteristic attributes and moorings. There is very considerable evidence that lacking such ties, the individual has great difficulty in establishing a clear self-identity, and that, once developed, the absence of such ties promotes experiences of estrangement and uncertainty, accompanied by erratic and inconsistent behaviors.

2. To provide the individual effective support and vehicles for carrying out the business of living, which requires a shelter and yet a better shelter to live in, food and preferred foods to eat, clothing and better garments to wear, a sex partner and the desirable sex partner, and so on.

The social ties that provide these things for the individual are, as a rule, linked with his membership in groups—in a family, club, church, work group, school group, clique, and so on. These groups are not entities apart from individual members. Lacking individual members, they are consigned, at best, to pages of history books. In view of the still prevailing position that the group and the individuals are entities apart—even dichotomies—it should be reaffirmed that groups exist and continue to exist because of the membership of individuals and because of their active participation in them. In fact, if individuals' existing groups are not functioning as effective vehicles for the business of living and for attaining strongly desired goals, if the groups cease to serve as dependable anchors to center the experience of consistency and continuity as an individual, then individuals do form new groups more effective and more functional in these respects.

On the other hand, to the extent that existing or newly formed groups are stabilized with their organizational systems and norms set, to that extent do individual members experience their place in the scheme of things, their mutual expectancies in interpersonal relations (with regard to the "ins" and "outs") in terms of the prevailing patterns. To that extent, the binding rules for the individuals which they observe with inner conviction are the rules of their groups. The values they uphold and cherish as theirs are the values of the group—thus minimizing the need for punitive sanctions by other members.

Thus, it can and does happen that individuals comply or conform in attitude and behavior to the organizational and normative system of their groups out of requirements of an inner voice (conscience), sense of loyalty, sense of responsibility, even sense of decency relative to follow members. Stepping out of the bounds of propriety defined by his group, thus out of his own role expectancies and self-picture, arouses one's *shame* or *guilt* feelings, and calls for appropriate sanctions from fellow group members. After all, fellow members are important persons in the individual's scheme of things, proportional to the importance of the group in providing support for his personal identity and as an instrumentality for fulfillment of his needs.

These conclusions should not be taken as an apology, justification, or approval of socially objectionable and harmful deeds committed as a function of membership in any group. They are based on study of the outlook and behaviors in actual groups. Realistic analysis of conforming and deviating behavior in groups must look for the standards to which individuals *are* conforming. The weight of the role system and norm set of reference groups in shaping the outlook and behavior of individual members is something one finds. It does not follow, in the least, that the role system, the norms, or the attendant conformity in behavior are something to be glorified and justified.

The role system that enables an individual to contribute his bit to the perpetuation of group formations engaging in antisocial activities, and that provides mutual support for members in these activities, should, as a rule, not exist. Likewise, norms in any group that serve as justifications for personal injury, harm, personal or sexual exploitation, with attendant attitude that "the hostile world owes me these things," should not exist and should be eliminated.

This is one thing. But it is another thing to ignore groups as such, to pretend that only "other people" belong to groups. It is another thing to minimize the importance of groups in shaping behavior, as though groups and individuals were distinct entities and behavior was determined only from within the individual. It is another thing to ignore the decisive weight of the norms of groups in shaping the individual's attitudes which become directive attributes of his self-system. It is as though an individual conscience could form in a vacuum, independent of social ties.

Conformity and deviation refer to behavior relative to some standard—no matter what the contemporary connotations of these terms in current literature. It is perfectly feasible to evalute conforming or deviating behavior in terms of standards of the larger social scene or human well-being. But it is also essential to know what a particular behavior is conforming *to* or deviating *from*. It does not wipe out groups that are antisocial in terms of more encompassing human values to damn groups *as such* or to minimize their influence. Groups are facts of human existence. There are groups which engage in socially laudable and socially obnoxious activities. There will be groups, created by individuals, long after theories and studies that ignore or caricature their properties are in the graveyard of many other artifacts of human history.

Human individuals do live in groups; they form new groups when old groups cease to serve as anchors for their personal experiences, when they become obstacles rather than instrumentalities for pursuing the essentials of living. When a member of a group, an individual does observe the rules as guides of attitude and behavior, including the individual who is the bohemian, the anarchist spurning any government, and including the great majority called "delinquent."

If antisocial groups are to be dealt with effectively, if social norms conducive to debasing, ignobling, and servile conformities are to be dealt with, the first step is to cease condemning groups or conformities *as such,* to stop pretending group organization and their norms are illusory. The basis of human morality is observance of a set of rules or norms—exemplified in such laudable short-cuts as "Thou shalt not kill," "Thou shalt not steal," "Do unto others as you would have others do unto you."

Social isolation, particularly of rejection in a desired setting, is unbearable for the human individual as a permanent state. The state of normlessness is, for the human individual, a state of personal conflict or loss of personal identity. Why, then, denounce groups as such, or norms as such, or conformity as such? Instead, our efforts should be directed toward evaluating particular groups and particular norms in terms of the state of interdependence of human beings in given societies and in terms of enduring, lasting human values in contemporary settings—where what one does relative to others is no longer his own business. What one group does has come to be the business of all groups.

The huge task this implies also entails realistic assessment of the motivational promptings coming from the individual under the particular circumstances and influences impinging on him from his immediate and larger settings. If his group and its values are socially objectionable, it does not profit the knowledge of human action or practical ends to consider him apart from them. Nor are the problems solved simply by isolating him from his objectionable ties if these provide the moorings of his existence. The task is not as simple as erasing his observances and conformities. It is the task of providing group moorings with socially desirable values and goals as integral parts of these moorings. Only in this way can he develop a new sense of self-identity, for observance of values that are not in conflict with the human sense of challenge, that are not in conflict with the enduring and lasting values of his larger setting and other groups in a shrinking world.

12 Implications for a grim picture

The concern of this concluding chapter is the implications of the foregoing analysis of research findings on the shaping of socially acceptable and objectionable behaviors. Throughout, the analysis has stressed the importance of studying both acceptable and unacceptable behaviors in order to understand either. In the present context, the implications of the analysis are relative to behaviors that contribute to a grim picture in the lives of adolescents and that have aroused growing concern among parents, teachers, youth workers, and government officials.

Doubtless there is a tendency for every adult generation to see the youth of its time as going to the dogs. Without implying that things were better in the good old days, we will, nevertheless, look at the proportions of socially objectionable deeds that came to official attention in recent years. The picture is grim, because it is part of what has been called an "affluent society," offering more, not fewer, opportunities to youth.

Next, measures which have been proposed to ameliorate or prevent the problems associated with youthful misdeeds and criminal acts are reviewed briefly. Finally the implications of research are stated for programs aiming at effective preventive measures for coping with problems of juvenile delinquency.

A GRIM PICTURE

The adolescent period in this country is regarded as the time of preparation for adult responsibilities, including completion of at least the minimum schooling needed in a modern technological society— a high school diploma being the standard. A high school education is available in public schools to all but a diminishing minority of youngsters, yet some forty percent of the children in the fifth grade fail to graduate from high school (Lichter, Rapier, Seibert, and Sklansky, 1962, p. 2). It is easy enough to dismiss this proportion which fails to meet the minimum goal as "dullards." Yet studies of school dropouts invariably show that more than half have succeeded in evidencing at least average ability, and some are superior, even by tests which tend to favor children of literate middle-class parents who can provide considerable background for their children's educational ventures (cf. F. Riessman, 1962).

Add to this disheartening statistic the fact that in 1960, the number of delinquency cases *officially* handled by courts in the country increased for the twelfth straight year (Children's Bureau, U.S. Department of Health, Education and Welfare, 1961). Figure 12.1 presents this picture in terms of number of cases by thousands yearly, which can be compared with the lower curve showing the population between 10 and 17 years of age during the same period. As this figure shows, out of approximately 25 million youngsters from 10 to 17 years old, over 800,000 were *court* cases during 1960. Over half a million were brought to court for reasons other than traffic violations (all of which are not included in these statistics). It is also clear that the rate of court cases has increased at a faster rate than the number of youngsters of these ages.

Whether or not one is concerned about year-to-year increases or decreases, it is a fact, as H. D. McKay stressed (1959), that a sizeable proportion of youth is involved. Court cases are only a fraction of police contacts and arrests. Probably as many as three fourths of the latter are handled by police without courts, by various social welfare agencies, and by parents (Perlman, 1959).

After examining the statistics, we agree with the considered judg-

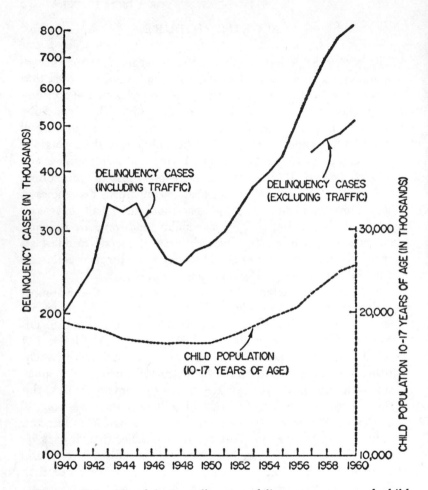

FIGURE 12.1. Trend in juvenile court delinquency cases and child population 10–17 years of age, 1940–1960 (semi-logarithmic scale). From *Juvenile Court Statistics,* 1960. Washington, D.C., U.S. Department of Health, Education, and Welfare, Social Security Administration, Children's Bureau Statistical Series, No. 65, 1961.

ment of I. R. Perlman (1959) that the rising curve depicted in Figure 12.1 could hardly be accounted for by more children, by better
reporting, or better law enforcement, though any one of these may
be very important in a particular locality. It could be argued that
police are more prone to arrest and prosecution is more likely than
in former years. It is equally likely that police are less prone to do
so, living as they do in a society with numerous agencies established
to help youth in trouble.

In fact, really long-term data on arrests and court cases in Buffalo,
Cleveland, and Philadelphia suggest that, half a century ago, many
of the cases of arrest of youth would now be regarded the province
of local relief, welfare, or school officials (Monahan, 1961; Juvenile
Court of Cuyahoga County, 1954; Buffalo Youth Board, 1960). In
truth, the definitions of "delinquency" have changed, and we now
have specialists to handle many cases that crowded the courts in
former years.

Perhaps the most remarkable fact about the climb in official delinquency rates is that they occur not during a depression or war, not
even in the immediate post-war period, but *after* the greatest dislo-
cations attributable to the war have been adjusted. They occur at a
time when writers discuss the problems of an "affluent" society. A
similar rise is currently reported in countries which were more
directly affected by the war and its aftermath—Norway, France, the
United Kingdom (Gibben, 1961, p. 22). Of the western European
countries, Denmark alone reports no change in the rate of juvenile
crime.

The phenomenon of youthful misbehavior has often been associated with rapid social change. We have noted the importance of
this factor in discussing adult-youth conflict. Yet it is noteworthy in
this connection that a sharp increase in juvenile delinquency at present is not characteristic of certain countries, such as Yugoslavia,
Israel, and Poland, "undergoing the most rapid social reconstruction
or development, although there are local situations which in other
countries would be readily accepted as reasons for an increase"
(Gibben, 1961, p. 23). It is necessary, therefore, to pose the question
of what kind of social change is correlated with increasing youth
problems.

Many writers have stressed the difficulties in interpreting official statistics, particularly in making comparisons between communities. However, in a period of prosperity, in a period when opportunities for education and occupational training are on the whole greater, in a period when hundreds of agencies are working for the welfare of youth, youthful misbehavior and school drop-outs are properly labeled by government and community leaders as a major social problem. In fact, the official statistics are only part of the grim picture.

At best, as Perlman observed (1959), the statistics are that portion of an iceberg above the waterline. By examining the composition of the exposed iceberg, we may learn something about who is involved. Even from our own research, we know that many punishable acts go undetected. Is there any resemblance between the boys observed in our research who engaged in socially objectionable activities, for the most part undetected, and the individuals on official records?

Who is Involved?   On the official records, boys outnumber girls five to one. The most frequent charge, by far, is some form of stealing property. Of the court cases of individuals between the ages of 10 through 17 years, only a fraction (between one fourth and one third by various estimates) reappear in court more than once. The most probable age to be caught is between 14 and 16 years. And the great majority of boys, particularly in cases of theft and violence, committed the deed in the company of others.

In summarizing the analyses of court statistics by Shaw and McKay and the Gluecks, Barron (1960) indicates that between 70 and 90 percent of adolescent crimes occur with companions, the percentage for cases of theft being nearly 90 percent. These, be it noted, are estimates based on what official records show. Among the boys in this research, there were several cases who appeared on court records as "loners" but who were actually accompanied by fellow members at the time. Being caught, they loyally refrained from naming the others. Conversely, those who had been caught and told on their companions were considered objects of disdain by their fellows.

The group-related character of much juvenile delinquency is not distinctive to contemporary American society. It is also characteristic in most western European countries (United Nations, 1955, p. 178). In a broad perspective, this fact shows the inadequacy of attributing juvenile misbehavior to "bad company." Granted that there may be occasional innocents incidentally involved and tragically caught by circumstances. But in such overwhelming figures, who is to decide which ones are the "bad company"?

Despite the popularity of referring to delinquents, especially those who engage in acts of violence, as "psychoneurotic," "psychopathic," or, more recently, "sociopathic" cases, there is no convincing evidence that such designation is warranted. The prevailing expert opinion is that individuals who warrant the label of "pathological" are decidedly a minority in contributing to the statistics (U.S. Senate, Subcommittee to Investigate Juvenile Delinquency, March 9–10, 1961, p. 1590). Indeed, pathology is suspected in cases of violent acts, especially murder, toward friends and family members.

But it is considered much less probable in violent acts toward members of other groups and by bystanders (U.S. Senate, Subcommittee to Investigate Juvenile Delinquency, April 18, 1961, p. 13). Coupled with the fact that homicide accounts for considerably less than one per cent of juvenile court cases (Perlman, 1959), this would seem to make individual pathology a rather minor aspect of the problem.

In fact, as evidence in this book shows, the importance of group formations in socially undesirable behaviors by youth almost precludes great importance to individual pathology as a causative factor. Being a responsible, reliable member of a group, who can be counted upon by others even in secret and dangerous activities, is simply not possible for any period of time if one is severely disturbed emotionally, subject to acute anxieties, depression, persecution, or other such symptoms. If one persistently fails to follow what his fellows feel is "right" and does what they denounce as "wrong," his presence will not be tolerated by other members. Yet, to adult outsiders, the boy who does follow actions of the group which are socially objectionable, and subsequently justifies his actions, is frequently labeled a "psychopath" because of it. In fact, one could say with considerable truth that the label "psychopath" and its variants are frequently used in cases of lack of guilt for violating social norms, owing to the individual's dedication to other norms.

In recent years, numerous social agencies have intensified work with adolescent gangs. There is a tendency to look upon them as unique to certain situations and neighborhoods, to regard them as categorically different from "cliques," friendship circles, and other designations for informal groups, and to label them as pathological formations. Yet, as we have seen in this research, adolescent groups do exist in all kinds of neighborhoods, and are directly involved in the great majority of official cases of misbehavior. We would suspect that the latter is true in more favored neighborhoods even to a greater extent than in underprivileged ones. The occasional newspaper accounts of "middle-class delinquency" involving theft, vandalism, sexual orgies, drug usage, almost invariably involve groups of youngsters.

Whether more or less than in previous years—and most studies indicate more—there are cases of juvenile delinquency among more "favored" or "middle-class" families (Wattenberg and Balistrieri, 1950, 1952; Wattenberg, 1948; Thrasher, 1944). There is a reluctance to admit that such neighborhoods have "gangs," and a reluctance to admit that the "gangs" of poorer neighborhoods have any similarity to the groups in theirs.

In line with our own experiences in this research, the U.S. Senate Subcommittee to Investigate Juvenile Delinquency (April 18, 1960) reported after visiting twenty-six cities that there was "based on our investigations, discussions, and contacts made with gangs, gang workers, police on the beat, teachers, and citizens, a wide discrepancy between their off-the-record statements and the official reporting regarding the existence of gangs, their antisocial behaviors, and the degree of problem they created" (p. 12). The Subcommittee attributes the discrepancy to "the attitude that the mere existence of any gang or gang problems constituted a failure in the responsibility of those agencies so that the type of reports made by these agencies were less than complete."

In the middle-class neighborhood, admission of the existence of cliques—not to speak of "gangs"—seems similarly to challenge the school, church, and family. We do not suggest that the label alone will change anything about the picture. We do suggest that the group-related character of much juvenile misconduct and crime needs to be recognized, and special categories for groups in different neighborhoods be dropped. This would at least permit analysis in functional terms of the sets of influences involved in various cases. Groups are, after all, a fact of human existence. Recognition of this fact would make it easier to get candid reports from those best situated to know what the groups in their locality are doing.

Before turning to measures which have been proposed to prevent youthful misconduct, a few more facts about those who are brought to the courts' attention may help define the problem. It is sometimes thought that the crowded neighborhoods of large cities are the only seats of juvenile misdeeds. In fact, two fifths of the court cases are contributed by suburban, small-town, and rural areas, the noncity courts having the largest rate of increase in recent years (Perlman, 1959; U.S. Senate Subcommittee to Investigate Juvenile Delinquency, 1960).

The problem is by no means exclusively a big-city problem, nor exclusively a problem of the poorer classes, although both—having more numerous populations and less recourse to private solutions—do contribute more to the official court statistics. Nor is the problem just one of particular ethnic or racial groups, although the rates for many of the less favored are often higher. As McKay (1959) pointed out, the ethnic communities once considererd trouble spots in Chicago were the Irish and Germans. If a city has a sizeable population in poor and crowded neighborhoods composed of an ethnic minority, the probability of a high delinquency rate for that minority is greater.

MEASURES PROPOSED TO
PREVENT YOUTHFUL MISBEHAVIOR

What steps have been taken or proposed with the aim of making the adolescent period one of preparation for a socially fruitful future, rather than a period of marking time or pushing toward the real and imagined privileges of adulthood in socially objectionable ways?

What is being done is well-intentioned, of course. There is quite general agreement that in the process many important and essential services are being performed by the agencies, schools, and other institutions involved. There is also general agreement that no single measure being taken, nor all together, are adequate for meeting the problem (cf. Perlman, 1959; U.S. Senate, Subcommittee on Juvenile Delinquency, April 18, 1961; United Nations, 1955, pp. 179–180).

In commenting on various measures in this section, we shall restrict ourselves to primarily preventive efforts, rather than corrective institutions. Despite the fact that repeated violators, who are usually the ones to be institutionalized, constitute a great problem, they are not the largest problem either numerically, or theoretically, or practically. Really effective institutionalization is in no small measure dependent on conditions outside the institution which can perpetuate and enhance its positive effects.

Our comments on the measures concern their probable effectiveness in dealing with the gamut of influences which bring youngsters together into informal reference groups and which affect their goals and self-pictures as they interact with one another. From this point of view, it is fairly clear why casework with individuals can have limited success as a preventive or ameliorative measure. Individual casework was the earliest and is still the most prevalent form of remedial work, and constitutes a necessary service in many contexts. However, no matter how deeply it probes the troubled mind of the individual adolescent, no matter how warm the relationship established with social worker, counselor, or psychotherapist, casework concentrates on the individual's feelings, skills, interpretations of his problems. Important as these are, reinterpretations of individual experience and changes of attitude cannot solve the adolescent's dilemma with agemates and adult institutions, because it cannot *reach* them.

Even family casework is limited in touching the reference group more weighty in the scheme of things for the youth who belongs to an adolescent group. The disappointing outcome of the most ambitious research program utilizing individual-social worker contacts— the Cambridge-Somerville project (Joan and W. McCord, 1959)— was to be expected in terms of this analysis. Polsky's research (1962) in a "therapeutic community" designed for correction of delinquents is illuminating in this regard. In a nutshell, he shows how the individual psychotherapy and counseling sessions remained for the boys *insulated* experiences, those which really *counted* for them being their day-to-day interactions with one another in their living quarters, school, and work.

Even assuming unqualified success in a portion of the cases, it is not realistic to suppose that individual casework and therapy can make a dent on a problem of this magnitude. Considering only *court* cases—that is, youth already in trouble—adequate casework would require about forty thousand trained professionals spending all of their time on the estimated number of youth to appear in court in 1965, which is expected to top one million. Each professional would have to handle from twenty-five to thirty cases at a time. Additional personnel would be needed for preventive efforts.

Recreation programs are another widely used medium for delinquency prevention. Such programs have an important community function quite apart from any possible role in preventing undesirable behavior. Their effectiveness in the latter respect is limited by several features (cf. Novick, 1960). For one thing, organized recreational activities represent only part of the interests of any youth group, particularly after the earliest adolescent years. Frequently, as others have also reported, we found that recreation buildings and equipment were *used* by groups—as meeting places, as instruments for pleasant activities—then left behind when the members wanted to do something they regarded as important. In some instances, the "more important" activities involved breaking laws.

Social agencies, such as settlement houses and youth centers sponsored by the community, have a definite function in providing artistic, educational, social and athletic facilities to supplement those offered by schools, especially during the vacation periods. It is obvious that the staff of a recreation or welfare center must maintain some order and protect the rights of others using the center, as well as its property. The usual practice, by and large, is to expel individuals, and groups as a whole, to get rid of discipline problems on the premises and to maintain the good name of the agency. At times this is a temporary discipline measure designed to promote better behavior. At others, it is clearly used to protect the agency. For example, in a neighborhood studied in this research, one such agency expelled a troublesome group, though by no means a delinquent one, with the threat that they would be arrested by the police if they set foot in the agency again.

The result is that such centers are more effective in serving younger children and those older youth less likely to get into trouble. This does not mean that all the youth who do not cause discipline problems while on the premises are lily-white. For many of them, the facilities provided by the agency correspond only to limited spheres of activity and concern. They behave within the bounds of the rules while in the agency in order to use its facilities. But they also engage in activities more interesting to them in other hangouts.

A related measure is the youth recreation center staffed and run by teen-agers with adult sponsorship and with activities of their own choosing. Thrasher (1942–44) describes a prosperous, middle-class suburb (Manhasset, Long Island), in which problems of vandalism, drinking, and other offenses were reduced when a youth recreation center was instituted with the rules made by the teen-agers themselves. Such endeavors seem to be most successful in communities having a fairly homogeneous population. Youth see those who participate in making the rules and running the center as like themselves. When there are wide differences in background in a community, however, such a youth center can easily become the scene of a power struggle between rival groups of youth, or one segment of the community may use it while others stay away or are kept away by their parents.

Occupying the days of youth in school and recreation centers with educational, cultural, athletic, artistic activities is, of course, desirable, and the facilities for doing so should be expanded for all. But if such programs do not engage or create motivational promptings *high* in the scheme of success and fulfillment of the youngsters themselves, a relatively short period on their own may be sufficient to upset the long hours spent in socially acceptable programmed activities. Let us make the point concrete with an illustration.

In the mid-1950s, student fraternities were banned by the administration of a high school attended by youngsters from middle- and upper-class neighborhoods—one of the best schools in a city of about 300,000 people at that time. This measure was taken both to insure participation in school functions and to deal with discipline problems that were bad for the school's good name. The student clubs did not actually disband. They disappeared, but went underground. One of them had their get-togethers on some occasions in a vacant house about ten miles away from the city, owned by an elderly lady.

On the night in question, the boys had their supply of drinks and went to this house. In their give-and-take while drinking beer, in their claims and counterclaims, one thing led to another, as the participants of such parties well know. The tangible result was that during the evening these youngsters engaged in vandalism of the house on the order of three to four thousand dollars, as reported by the local papers. These kids, who entered the house, destroyed windows, walls, even pushed out a pillar supporting the porch (a display of strength?), came from middle- or upper-class families. They were not failures at school. Several were on a school team. They did not come from a social stratum that is supposed to be maladaptive in economic matters, destructive, adventurous, revengeful of middle-class values, as depicted in some currently fashionable theories of delinquent values as "reaction formation." Fortunately for the owner and for the boys, their parents were in a position to take care of the damage, with the happy result that these youngsters did not get into court statistics on which some theorizing about juvenile delinquency is based.

There are other handicaps in "building-centered" programs alone (school buildings included). Among them is the psychological distance between adults and youth in general and, in particular, between "respectability" in the person of a recreation worker, social worker, or teacher and youth who see their kind as "lower" down the social ladder. In combination, this and other handicaps led to the concept of the "hard-to-reach" youth, who are generally untouched by organized recreation or by youth clubs, such as the Boy Scouts, Boys' Clubs, etc.

These "hard-to-reach" youth are often responsible for some of the thefts, acts of vandalism, and violence which surprise the community and police. Of course, the police should increase its vigilance to stop the occurrence of such youthful offenses and violations. But perhaps too much responsibility is sometimes laid upon law enforcement agencies. You cannot put a policeman to watch over every fifth or even every tenth youngster among the 25 million in this age bracket. Even when the police pinpoint actual or potential offenders, they cannot always be responsible for their actions. Groups whose members know they have been pinpointed, as we found, quickly adopt the policy of lying low or dispersing for the time being, until the police relax their close watch and turn to other duties.

Necessary as law enforcement is, the influences that shape behavior, for good or evil, are not primarily a job for the police. The influences are more widely rooted than the sanctioning power endowed in the police. By the time behavior develops to the point that police action is required, most of the drama in attitude and behavior has already taken its course. The recent trend of having the police be friendly towards possible violators is one of a thousand or so steps in the right direction. As we have seen in this research, attitude toward the police in some neighborhoods verges on enmity, hardly a praiseworthy attitude for adolescents, and not conducive to detection by police either. But the value of friendly policemen and police-sponsored activities to get acquainted with "hard-to-reach" youth should not be overrated.

Such efforts were praised in an editorial in the *El Paso Times,* in a city contributing probably a little over its share to the grim picture, owing to a number of circumstances, and occasionally declaring a curfew as a drastic measure to keep potential offenders off the streets and away from meeting places at night. The editorial wrote: "Another point to be considered is that the police, by trying to make friends with those youngsters, may succeed in cracking the wall of secrecy which usually surrounds activities of the gangs" (*El Paso Times,* 1959, p. 6–A). The fact that there has been no appreciable change in juvenile offenses in that city reflects the futility of putting too much reliance on the law enforcement officer's efforts to be friendly.

Inspired, perhaps by the success of sociologists and anthropologists in studying small groups or gangs through participant observation, a number of agencies "extended" their work from their buildings and institutional settings through the so-called "detached worker." The detached worker or extension worker is detached spatially and in method from the agency setting, but in purpose he is not detached—he is an "extension" of the agency's purposes. Detached workers have been used in New York City and other large cities. As a result of difficulties in arousing continuing local interest and in finding local adult leaders, the Boys' Club has embarked on a project utilizing the technique, the power of which lies in the simple human fact that adolescents are drawn to human beings who approach them without condescension or threat, and with interest, even if they are adult.

From the point of view of fact-finding, the "detached worker" method has been useful in confirming the existence of adolescent cliques or groups, in making contact with their members, in learning about their values (e.g., Crawford, Malamud, and Dumpson, 1950). Those with the purpose of rechanneling the group activities toward constructive ends have probably realized their aims only partially. Some workers have reported decreases in group "warfare," greater interests in sports, less preoccupation with "adventure" for its own sake, and so on. But none to our knowledge has claimed "reform" or throughgoing changes in the values of the group.

Detached worker programs have the decided advantage of dealing with social units which are psychologically meaningful for the adolescent. By their nature, they presume that it is possible to change small group activities, and hopefully the goals of members, without substantially changing the pattern of influences impinging on the group, or the motivations which bring the boys together. This assumption probably is responsible for disappointment in many cases.

By virtue of the skills and persistence required, the detached-worker program cannot grow large. The Children's Bureau (cf. Novick, 1960) reports, in fact, that fewer candidates are turning to this type of social work. Certain unforeseen difficulties have also developed. For one thing, in some neighborhoods, having a worker attached to one group results in its being attacked by groups which do not, thus increasing conflict between informal groups in the neighborhood (e.g., Miller, 1959). Apparently, as Miller suggested, having an adult worker signifies that the group is really a "tough" one, therefore a challenge to defeat.

In observing the operation of detached workers in New York City, Yablonsky (1962) reports other difficulties: Without considerable training and practice (and we may add, some valid criteria), a detached worker is liable to "inaccurately diagnose group structure" and to fail to distinguish between the core members and the fringe or hangers-on. Even a trained observer can easily be misled without a clear notion of group properties. For example, the above author bases much of his account of the "sociopathic" leader of a "violent gang" of adolescents on the behavior of a 26-year-old man, despite the fact that the account of relationships with adolescents seems to show that the man is a go-between or fringe member of adult criminal organizations. He is certainly not an adolescent nor a member of the adolescent group.

Yablonsky also concludes that there is a danger that a detached worker may become a "social director" for a group—opening community facilities for its use—without modifying its "behavior patterns." He may tacitly furnish justification for the group's antisocial activities. This conclusion also seems to have a basis in fact, since almost any human adult who focuses his attention on one group in a neighborhood fraught with traditional rivalries between informal groups will be highly prone to see the situation in terms of their plight alone.

However, our purpose is not to support or dispute the above conclusions, but to inquire why such things might happen as a result of the detached-worker approach. Briefly, aside from the worker's training, the reasons must involve limitations of the method. The worker's task presumes that it is possible to lead group activities into socially desirable channels without altering the common problems that brought the boys together or the concrete circumstances in which they operate. Under some conditions, in some neighborhoods, this may be possible.

One of the groups studied in this research (see Chapter 1) became highly preoccupied with competitive athletics, even though they had not come together for that purpose and even though their environment had changed only by the presence of an adult who could help them with athletic tactics and get games for them. But, as the observer noted, despite their antisocial activities, they were already interested and skilled in sports. A traumatic incident in the neighborhood, the words of an interested social worker on the value of sports for growing boys, and the terrific prestige of sports on the national scene had all had their impact on the boys' interests.

The preoccupation with sports and concentration on efforts to win did result in a change of leadership from a free-wheeling tough guy to the most effective sports captain. As a result, the entire group did cooperate to keep things on a keel that would enable them to continue to play and compete, even making positive efforts to raise the threshhold of the erstwhile leader's aggressive tendencies (efforts which, as we have noted, were not resented by the former leader, who was just as anxious to have the best team as the next fellow). The fact remains that competitive sports were only a part of the activity of this group. The rest still involved the pool hall, the taverns, and a good many "antisocial" actions, even though the observer protested them in his presence.

The observer in our research was not a detached worker making active efforts to change the group, but on the contrary was warned that this was not his function. Nevertheless, the findings on this group are instructive. The concern of the parents over a tragedy in the just preceding generation of adolescents, their heed to the words of a social worker about sports, the urging of the just older youth who had stayed out of jail—all of these suggest the power of relatively untapped resources in poor, even crime-ridden, neighborhoods.

Conversely, the resistance of parents and young adults, as well as adolescents themselves, has been given as a cause of some of the failures of well-intentioned efforts. In its initial stages, the Quincy, Illinois, project (Bowman, 1959) attempted several measures which it later abandoned. Placement of youth in more favorable foster homes encountered, naturally enough, resistance from natural parents and a paucity of foster parents. Aggressive casework with youth and their families proved not only time-consuming, but found support among only a few parents of the youth involved. At a higher level of community organization, no agency could be found willing to take on special recreational programs, and parents in nice neighborhoods objected when it appeared likely that their children would be exposed to "objectionable" youth. The project turned to the schools, where interest was found. Brown and Dodson (1959) attributed certain failures to make Boys' Clubs a part of some neighborhoods, in contrast to their own success, to a lack of "community-oriented social forces" present in those neighborhoods.

Such untapped community resources were the keystone in the conception of the Chicago Area Project, begun in 1934 under the inspired leadership of Clifford Shaw (Shaw, 1944; McKay, 1959; Kobrin, 1959). In its general outlines, Shaw's conception was that youth are responsive to their reference groups ("primary groups"), more than to "outside" agencies coming into their neighborhoods to "help" them, and that the greatest assets a community had in improving the chances of their youth were the "talents, energies, and other human resources of the people themselves."

By the "people themselves," Shaw meant the residents of the neighborhood, including parents, tavern keepers, storekeepers, young adults who had been delinquent in their time, even racketeers and former prisoners who could be interested in any way in improving the lot of their youth and induced to do something about it—if such people were part of the neighborhood in question. Since he meant it, Shaw was criticized at times by welfare agencies and businessmen who saw their task as reaching *down* to *uplift* youth, without muddying their coats through contact with the very persons most influential for the youth in question. Shaw, in turn, saw the latter as "psychologically unsound because it places residents of the community in an inferior position and implies serious reservations with regard to their capacities and their interest in their own welfare" (1944, p. 2).

Shaw himself saw the project as a real-life experiment designed not only to prevent the spiralling of members of adolescent gangs into adulthood as criminals, but to see what could be done on a community level, discovering, thereby, more about the roots of socially desirable and undesirable behavior. Over the years the procedures used in the project have been adapted to the different kinds of neighborhoods in which it has been involved. Although all have been "poor" neighborhoods, they have differed with respect to the existing forms and stability of the local power structures (Kobrin, 1959, p. 25).

In general, the basic approach has been to arouse local residents to the need of some efforts for youth, encouraging them to organize their own committees with the project as an aid, to collect funds, and to do something appropriate about their local problems. A tangible index of the project's success in arousing residents of some of the poorest neighborhoods in Chicago is, for example, the fund of over $21,000 collected in the year 1943 by residents of six of the poor areas. In these six areas, the adults set up twenty-two centers serving 7500 children, sent over 1500 children to camp, worked intensively with nearly 600 juvenile and adult offenders. The limited number of project personnel could not possibly have handled such numbers. At every step, young adults and parents (including previous offenders) helped and worked with them, feeling that the outcome depended on them, as it did.

Whatever its limitations, this conception of Shaw's points to one practical requirement merely to get enough older youth and adults to work with adolescents on constructive projects. A recent survey by the U.S. Children's Bureau (Novick, 1960) found "that the majority of preventive projects are small, most having professional staff of no more than ten people" and that "few children and youths are reached by them" (p. 9). Even aside from this psychological soundness of Shaw's approach within the scope of the immediate setting, the hard facts of life force the conclusion that his is the only feasible approach to get enough people involved in youths' future to make the efforts count on a community level.

With similar aims, the Youth for Service program in San Francisco has reported considerable success for volunteer work projects for youth with community participation and support for tools, space, equipment, and adult helpers (U.S. Senate, Subcommittee to Investigate Juvenile Delinquency, 1959, pp. 1123–1134). Founded in 1957, the project reports completion of a hundred work projects involving three hundred teen-agers in poor neighborhoods of San Francisco. Interestingly enough, one of the first projects involved work on cars

—a project which initially attracted many boys, because, as one boy participating reported: "I feel that in a boy's life from 16 to 18 or 19, a car is inevitable in their mind. So, if they are going to have cars, and they are not going to die out, they might as well have some place to work on them" (*ibid.*).

From the approach and findings of the present research, we can detect a hint of some inevitable limitations on area projects as presently in operation. On a local level, they can reach only the local aspects of the gamut of influences shaping behavior and are relatively powerless to touch larger social conditions affecting the goals and success pictures of the boys and their life chances to fulfill them. As we have seen, the goals and success pictures of youth in different areas are influenced by larger institutions, including the mass media of communication.

They do, for example, all want cars—*now,* as soon as possible. But it is unrealistic to expect that area projects could set about getting a car for every boy who does not have one, nor is this necessarily a desirable goal. It seems more likely that effort at this local level could transform other goals more easily—for example, the desire to shine in fighting to the wish to excel in a work project that benefits oneself and his community—than those of the success symbol so persuasively presented in mass communications.

To every public outcry about the kinds of success images, the violence and sexual emphasis in the mass communications, conscientious citizens decry a trend toward censorship; and purveyors of the communications challenge anyone to prove a connection between the content of their communication and the behavior of individuals. Yet, as the Conference on Impact of Motion Pictures and Television on Youth reported to a U.S. Senate committee (Subcommittee to Investigate Juvenile Delinquency, 1961, pp. 1574–1577): *"The amount of time and number of television programs involving crime, horror, violence is conspicuous"* (p. 1575). As examples of familiar, frequently repeated images, they give:

"The weak, comic, or brutal father and his representatives, the stupid, ineffectual, callous police. . . .

"The well-meaning but ineffective or naive mother. . . .

"The teen-ager devoted only to pleasure-seeking and depicted largely as a noncontributing, if not actually dangerous, member of society. . . .

"The criminal who has prospered for many years before his downfall in the last three minutes of the program."

They conclude in a vein which any psychologist of any persuasion could support, that it is the "acccumulated effects of such programs over long periods of time" whose consequences are to be feared. The committee did not refer to advertisements, which absorb some of the best talents in the country, which picture successful people with "zing" who are "going places."

Area projects, such as those inspired by Clifford Shaw's work, foresaw human resources, even in the most poverty-ridden neighborhood, as their greatest asset. This conception is one of the oldest and most honored conceptions in this country. Perhaps what is needed is a "project" among the sponsors, agencies and performing personnel of the mass communications to arouse their dedicated interest in youth's future—to entertain, inform, and instruct in ways conducive to more constructive self-images.

Meanwhile, several of the major cities in the country have instituted coordination of community services, an aim devoutly to be desired. Still larger efforts, labeled with such laudable titles as "Mobilization for Youth," seek not only the coordination of existing agencies, but the training of personnel, special task forces, improvements and changes in school programs, special study programs. The White House has lent its prestige to the notion of a Peace Corps for the home front.

Certainly efforts to improve public education, to involve youth in creative work projects and healthy activities, to find constructive work for youth, jobs preparing them for the future, to utilize agency resources effectively, are to be lauded. Despite the sums being appropriated in some large cities (e.g., over $12.5 million in New York City), nationwide the great bulk of public expenditures for youth are in the fields of usual services of public education, recreation, police detection, court processing, and correction. Certainly, more funds and more efforts are called for. But, regardless of money and effort from individuals, what measure of success can be expected and what are the conditions for such success?

POINTERS FOR POLICY AND
ACTION

Research findings are valid to the extent that they have bearing on the actualities of related events and enable us to make predictions to control these events in the service of bettering human life. In the present context, then, the urgently required contribution from research on adolescents is effective lines of action toward curtailing the grim picture of the frequency and rising trend of violations and offenses that are socially harmful, and harmful to the violators themselves.

As we have seen, the grim rate of violations committed by youth, in rural areas as well as in cities, is increasing in spite of all the efforts of police and courts. It is rising despite the increase in settlement houses staffed by trained social workers, despite the increased availability of counseling services and thriving psychiatric and clinical activity. The violators, in the long run, are the greatest victims of the trend, which occurs at a time when appropriations for recreation facilities, for reinstating school dropouts, for "talent conservation," have been increased or newly created.

Pointers and implications for action are derived from the present research findings with reference to the grim picture and the measures being taken to change it. These findings are in line with those of many other researches as well, as reported in our various surveys of the literature (e.g., Sherif and Cantril, 1947, Chapters 8–10; Sherif and Sherif, 1953, Chapters 7–8; Sherif, 1963). In fact, our research program was formulated after surveying the available research findings.

There is no claim that our research or any other can point to something altogether new under the sun. Nor are the implications presented as a cure-all to replace measures currently being used, some of which were discussed in the last section. However, the findings do have something to say for establishing pertinent criteria with which the soundness of policy and action projects can be evaluated, independently of the claims of various projects competing to gain an edge over others. They do suggest the necessary conditions in which measures for prevention may be more effective.

The leads derived from the data are, in fact, implicit in the design of the research, which studied socially acceptable and socially objectionable behaviors in terms of intersecting sets of influences which contribute to shaping them: 1. Person-to-person relations in groups of the members' own choosing, studied within the context of 2. prevailing conditions and values from the immediate neighborhood and 3. values and success images of the larger societal setting.

Thus, if the implications have a distinctive character, it is that they emerge not merely from individual data and case histories alone; not from study of small groups alone; not from ecological and sociocultural data alone. They emerge from all of these, and they pertain chiefly to the interrelationships among them. The findings permit us to locate the domain of influences a particular measure is likely to affect, thus providing a criterion for assessing the effectiveness of the measure in question. The over-all implication is, as we shall see, the necessity of rounded and coordinated programs with measures capable of affecting each set in the gamut of influences.

Objectives for Policy and Action.   The many-faceted nature of the shaping of adolescent behavior—for good or evil—implies formulation of definite aims for policy and action. One reason that the causation of delinquency is inadequately understood and that so many research and action projects are disappointing is that the objective is negatively defined: "To prevent delinquency."

Clearly the objective must be a positive one: for youngsters to internalize, to make their own, and to create values and goals that are acceptable, that are laudable, from the point of view of enduring human developments and their own potentialities. The aim is, or should be, for youngsters to dedicate themselves toward work targets, vocational and professional goals, constructive activities, whose attainment will enrich themselves and human society.

This objective implies, in the long run, building of a self-image in which success is gauged in terms of its harmful or laudable effects on others and on oneself as a person, not of getting there as fast as one can, not of acquiring symbols of success no matter what the means.

Thus in evaluating particular policy steps and action programs, the yardstick should be their contribution to this end: namely, the end of youth personally involved in enduring human values and positively building a personal self-picture dedicated to challenging tasks and life goals that are not at odds, in every step, with the interests, claims, possessions, and lives of others.

Just as our findings suggest the inadequacy of policy aimed at "prevention," rather than at encouragement of positive directions for all youth, whether delinquent or not, so they clearly show that it is almost foolhardy to evaluate the effectiveness of a "delinquency project" merely in terms of the decrease in violations in a given area within a short period of time. For one thing, decrease in violations may be merely due to the fact that the youngsters are in the lime-light.

A Digest of Indications. For the convenience of the reader, the major research findings were presented in summary in the last chapter. Here, to sum up, are conclusions with which effective policy and action must deal.

The behavior of adolescents that counts, like that of adults, is not ordinarily impulsively dictated by the ups and downs of appetites or even lasting deprivations and frustrations. It *is* motivated and goal-directed. But this goal-directedness is regulated, even in the case of sexual urges, by standards, rules, or norms that the individual is committed to, that he upholds and cherishes.

Those who violate the norms of the mainstream of society are deviates in an ethical and legal sense. But, psychologically, they are no exception to the general rule. Psychologically, they are not necessarily nonconformists and deviates in all cases. Psychologically, the great bulk of such violators, including anarchists, most delinquents, and many criminals, are acting in conformity with the rules of the game standardized in their own give-and-take, or in groups of their own choosing. These rules they consider as their own. They are the binding ones for them.

In fact, to the extent of their conflict with the mainstream of society, they are strict in the observance of their own norms. Mere knowledge of the rules prevailing in the mainstream, even knowledge of the consequences of violation, is not sufficient, for they are not theirs. Consequently, they are to be bypassed or evaded whenever they can manage to do so with impunity. This is not to deny that there are lapses, circumstances, and events in which violations do violate the individual's own rules. But the point is, which rules does the individual feel *guilty* about if he violates them?

The important people to adolescents, the people whose words are really to be heeded and who test one's personal worth, are those in the same predicament or fortune, as the case may be. Being in the same boat, adolescents create their own set, which provides them criteria for adjusting their outlook, and for gauging personal success and failure in various respects. Thus, exhortations by teachers, officials, parents, and other adults may touch them, but not appreciably or in a lasting way.

The clique and gangs, like clubs and professional formations, are formations that serve as devices of mutual support as they search for something to anchor them in a stable way. They are formations that serve as effective devices to attain goals, to fulfill needs that one cannot or dare not fulfill by himself.

Whence are these goals derived? Whence are these needs fomented? Some of them are integral to the adolescent period as the physical growth and transition to adulthood are currently defined in society. But even those most clearly biological urges are regulated, and the regulation goes beyond the bound of the adolescent's small group. Their sources are in the social setting—not only the immediate neighborhood and city, but also in the larger setting, and not to a lesser degree.

Relative to this inner ferment and these goals, the individual is bound to do something about them:

1. When the neighborhood and the larger setting abound and are saturated with examples of fast success;

2. When one feels that he utterly lacks things that others like him have in abundance as he sees them in the neighborhood, at school, in the movies, on TV, on the covers of books in the drugstore;

3. When he is caught in a depriving or frustrating home situation, or has to suffer a life with parents whose world is at variance with his;

4. When he comes to feel that the world owes him a car, nice things to wear, money to spend, girls to entertain;

5. When, to top it all, he feels that he is looked down upon as inferior because of his origin, race, or religion;

6. When he finds that the line of work he is good in brings no recognition or holds no future promise.

These and other predicaments in some combination are inevitably relative to the setting in which he moves.

As he finds out that there are others in the same plight, they gravitate toward one another to pour out their hearts, to find comfort and support in one another's company. The result is a small and closely knit human formation providing stable moorings they lack elsewhere. The ideas, verdicts, and formulae that are crystallized, in time, as guides and justification towards their ends in concerted action may support socially desirable ends or antisocial ones from the larger point of view.

Faced with recruiting and occupying youth with constructive goals, policy and action programs must contend with this picture. Regardless of what is the aim, they must face questions about the place of various activities in the scheme of things for youth. What is the place, the function of the school in the scheme of things of those in school and of the dropouts? What concerns for immediate success, what criteria of success, are so compelling that they cannot be postponed through the long channel of school years? How does the dropout see the avenues that school opens? What if youngsters who are experiencing the same deprivation—real or imagined—decide to take things into their own hands to try for the easy and fast success whose images are projected day in and out through personal example, the magic episodes in magazines, pocket books, TV, and movies? What if a group of agemates in their daily give-and-take stabilize the verdict that a trade, a profession, a school degree are not the effective ways to fulfill themselves, or not worth forgoing what they can have together here and now? What if a bunch of youngsters in a blighted area see the ceilings of attainment drawn for them, see themselves as different from those in public institutions?

The statistics on juvenile violators summarized briefly earlier in this chapter should at least teach us a basic fact for laying down policy and action programs. Only a fraction of the youthful violators operate as lone wolves. This small fraction properly belongs within the domain of clinicians or psychiatrists. Let the clinicians and psychiatrists concentrate and do their effective work with this small fraction of psychopaths who follow neither the rules of society or of circles within it.

As we have found, the line between the "delinquent" group and other adolescent groups becomes very thin when one discovers that in concert they do engage in socially unacceptable activities, whether they are caught or not. The comparative ease with which minor and undetected violations may be followed under exceptional circumstances by a tragedy is reflected in the words of the youthful murderer of an innocent nurse as she returned home after her night duty in Ann Arbor, Michigan, in 1951:

"Normally I wouldn't get into trouble and Max either by ourselves. I suppose his parents think I was a bad influence on him and mine think he was a bad influence on me. And Dave too. But it isn't that. We all got together and something was bound to happen" (Martin, 1953, p. 124).

Whether or not these informal associations fit some scholar's formal definition of a "group," they are, as we have found, patterned organizationally and they do have sets of rules or norms. And they do *count* for the youth involved in them. Such groups are no places for the recluse, the mentally deranged, or the lone wolf. Ironically, one has to have social skills to be accepted at all and to rise up in the eyes of his fellows. He has to say and do appropriate things in various contexts. He has to fulfill the expectations of his fellows to have any self-respect. He has to be resourceful and alert in joint undertakings. Relative to his fellows, he has to be altruistic and even, at times, sacrificial.

It is easy to denounce the individuals in such groups which do violate the human values of society as morbid and pathological. It is easy to blame the groups, as though individuals could, psychologically, be bereft of moorings with others. It is easy to denounce conformity in the abstract, as though conformity were not as essential for moral as for immoral behavior of the kind in question. But it is time to stop and desist from such futile luxuries.

The influences that lead to socially acceptable behaviors and socially objectionable behaviors are not altogether separate, distinct, and different. Thus the aim must be to alter those sets of influences that are inimical to adolescents' developing personal commitments to challenging activities in their groups—whose existence and whose goals are in harmony with the large and enduring values in the society. The particular intersections of influences shaping socially undesirable behavior also take their toll on the human development of youngsters who stay within bounds, or are not detected.

There are some activities, such as sports, that do provide human association, beneficial activity, and are both high in youth's scheme of things and in the mainstream of values in this society. A conversation with a young undergraduate at a fairly large university will illustrate the point in its simplest and concrete form. He was an athletic star on the campus. We were talking with him in a city park where a serious crime had recently been committed by a group of adolescent boys. The young athlete was from the neighborhood and had played in the park as a youngster. Pointing to a bunch of boys who had been expelled from the park recreation center, he said: "Probably I would have been a character like those if it weren't for my strong interest in becoming an athlete to prove myself that way." Later he elaborated. He had had a group of buddies. But he had to keep himself in good shape physically. Therefore, he kept away from wild parties, drug experimentation, drinking, and the like. His athletic accomplishment brought him new friends, recognition, human warmth, and opened paths to higher education. He was greatly encouraged in all this by helpful adults.

This young man, too, had followed a path to success and to recognition. But not all youngsters are lucky enough to have his physique and coordination to start with. Of course, they may have other skills, but who would know or care? The young man was lucky to have the aptitude in an area, like sports, that brings recognition and rewards so quickly that the future looks nearer. How many other such areas are there, except for the prodigy?

SOME CONSIDERATIONS FOR
POLICY AND ACTION PROGRAMS

The function of the researcher is not that of the executive in the policymaking position. But the researcher cannot justify an attitude of aloofness in regard to actualities that touch on his research problems, including action programs. Even on scientific grounds, he has to be concerned with the problem of validity, if the model or generalization he is formulating is to have any bearing on the actualities of events, to be more than empty logical tautologies.

On the other hand, the researcher, especially in human relations, cannot with scientific conscience assume the role of complacently passing down prescriptions. In the human sciences, learning is necessarily a two-way street. He has to follow the actualities of events at their grass roots, as confronted by men of action. The researcher can learn from actualities accessible only to front-line men like the classroom teacher, school counselor, group worker, individual policeman, probation officer. In order to evaluate the fate of predictions made on the basis of his formulations and those of his colleagues, he has to follow actual events closely.

Measures Prompted by Urgency of Problems.   The grim picture of a rising tide of adolescent violations, briefly depicted earlier in this chapter, rightly has created the feeling of urgency to do something about it. As a consequence, various kinds of action programs and activity projects are engaged in dealing with the problem. As we have seen, these include detached workers services, intensive coordination of community services, intensive group work, casework, parent education programs, youth employment programs, and recreation programs (Novick, 1960). In addition, more effective utilization and training of police, probation officers, and juvenile court personnel are proposed.

Special mention should be made of various area projects like those in Boston, San Francisco, and New York. Notably, these include the Chicago Area Project started nearly thirty years ago. It conceived of behavior and misbehavior as shaped by reference group (primary group) ties, and, hence, insisted on the necessity of mobilizing all formal and informal groups, agencies and prestige persons in the area (including ex-delinquents and ex-convicts) toward revitalizing wayward youth along socially acceptable channels. No area project today, no coordinated community services plans, no theory on the shaping of outlook and behavior in small groups and neighborhood can, with integrity, deny the impact of the Chicago Area Project initiated by Clifford Shaw, who devoted a lifetime to ecological and longitudinal research as well as to the action program (Shaw, 1944; Kobrin, 1959; McKay, 1959).

One cannot help finding, in the various measures used in action programs instituted across the land with a feeling of urgency, explicit or implicit assumptions as to 1. the effectiveness of various measures in bringing about changes in attitude and behavior, and 2. the causes of misbehaviors.

It is a waste to resort to a measure because it is customary or readily available if one wants to change attitudes in a lasting way. Such wasted effort will be curtailed through consideration of the research findings on attitude change and resistance to change of attitudes to which a person is committed. These findings indicate that it is not only the content, mode of presentation, or threat of consequences that count. At least of equal importance is the value for the recipients of the source of the advice or exhortation (who said, who wrote, who sponsored it). The context of a person's social ties and his ongoing concerns and activities also need to be considered.

The implications of the findings on attitude change are clear with reference to adolescents' attitudes toward neighborhood agencies, police, probation officers, teachers, and parents who wish to alter youth viewpoints. Their words will not find receptive ears unless there are some ties of trust, unless the content touches the concerns and activities that *count* for the adolescent. This is why adults (law enforcement officials, social welfare agency staffs, parents, and teachers) do need to work toward at least a neutral, and preferably a helpful, image in adolescents' eyes. Otherwise their words may be heard, but not heeded. The content may boomerang.

Assumptions of Causation and Some of Their Consequences. The assumptions made of the causes (etiology) of youthful violations, whether explicit or not, do have decisive consequences for the whole manner with which the problem is approached and handled. Until very recently, the dominant views have been colored with notions of sickness or disease, derived by analogy from medical pathology. The conceptions of causes inevitably affect the *investigation* of causes and the adoption of *measures* to deal with the problem.

Conceptions of youthful misdeeds in terms of disease and pathology have curtailed the search for causes in the multifaceted scope the problem requires. This analogical tradition, coming from nineteenth-century thought, is rapidly being corrected, as reflected by the increasing number of social scientists participating in policy positions and action programs, including the study of human relations in medical schools themselves.

Despite these developments, which broaden the directions in which causes are sought, the analogical mode of thinking is still with us. It still exerts its heavy hand, sometimes with unforeseen consequences. Consider, for example, the individual adolescent offender who has shown a high degree of insight and sense of responsibility in the intricate interpersonal relations within his own group. Consider how he feels when he is treated as a psychopath or sick person. The stereotyped label is accompanied, not infrequently, with vindictive black adjectives. Theoretically it is not appropriate for analyzing the gamut of influences involved in shaping his attitudes and behavior. And from a practical point of view it tends to contribute to intensifying his hostile attitudes.

Or, consider the case of a school dropout who (though apathetic or hostile at school) has exhibited skill and resourcefulness in planning and executing activities in his group, some of them legally punishable undertakings. Put him through an intelligence or academic achievement test, in which success is of little concern to him. On that basis, enter him in a class for those with "low IQ" or for "underachievers." What have we achieved from the point of view of changing his attitude toward school and "conserving" his talents? We have not even assessed adequately what he went through in the test situations, or what constitutes achievement and success for him.

There are certainly cases of offenders whose problems bring them within the proper domain of the psychiatrist and clinician—let there be no implication to the contrary. But in assessing causes of youthful misbehaviors, we should give due weight to what we learn even from the official statistics. As noted earlier, the great majority of misdeeds calling for social or legal sanctions are committed by members of groups, in concert with one another. As sociologists have reported time and again, there are definite patterns of locations and changes in the patterns of such misbehaviors.

In searching for causes, we must be aware of changes in the locations in which misbehaviors occur and their perpetuators dwell. The following extracts are illustrative of the point:

> On August 2, 1960, the Pennsylvania Chiefs of Police Association, meeting in Philadelphia, adopted a strongly worded report on juvenile delinquency which said in part that ". . . the broken home and unemployed and socially handicapped type of youth" can no longer be solely blamed for juvenile crime. National and state police officials report that there are muggings, burglaries, larcenies, and crowd disturbances emanating from the ranks of those who have no reasons for committing these crimes except for so-called thrills.
>
> In Washington a group of boys ranging frrom 14 to 17 from prosperous families were accused of 11 thefts, 4 housebreakings, 2 stolen cars, and 10 outbursts of vandalism. In New Jersey, 17 youths on a "burglary for kicks" spree amassed $10,000 in valuables and sold them for $3,000. Questioned by police, they admitted they had fair allowances. They participated in the burglaries "'because it was thrilling."[1]

Whence these thrills? Why the large proportions of offenses on property and human life committed, not alone, but in concert with others? We suspect that these "thrills" have something to do with the differential effects generated in interaction with fellow group members.

When individual members interact in pursuit of proving themselves to each other, outdoing one another in activities which appear

[1] From U.S. Senate Report of the Committee on the Judiciary, April 18, 1961, pp. 2–3.

to them man-sized and risky, they do get feelings of importance, of being admired by someone who counts, of excitement. When the activities are in conflict with legal and adult values, the ties among members are further tightened, as the findings indicate. The differential effects of membership and absorption in the group snowball to the point that members see themselves as "big shots" out of all proportion.

There were concrete instances of this snowballing of excitement, mutual praise, mutual solidarity, and glorification in the groups studied in our project. Under proper circumstances and with laudable goals, these same differential effects of interaction in a tightly knit group can serve to heighten individuals' efforts in socially ennobling directions. We suspect that a similar analysis can be applied in tracing the beginnings of drug usage (which of course could not acquire such frightening proportions without formal and informal organizational ties making it available), of sexual orgies, and of the self-justification of many school dropouts.

If we are concerned about the validity of our theorizing, we have to go beneath official statistics. Otherwise, we will perpetuate some myths about "delinquent subcultures" that imply that "antisocial" groups with "maliciousness, unaccountable hostility, and negativism" are peculiar to one large class of people. The conclusion of Richard Perlman, Chief of the Juvenile Delinquency Studies Branch, U.S. Children's Bureau, is instructive in this regard: "Not only do such studies show that the number of hidden delinquents is great, but they also reveal that the number of undetected delinquents is large among the middle- and higher-income groups—the groups which appear in strikingly small numbers in official statistics" (Perlman, 1959, p. 7).

On the basis of all the evidence, the enormity of the task of assessing causes of juvenile misdeeds is clear, for the causes are multifaceted. As such they are beyond the ken of any one academic discipline. They stem from the needs of the organism, from the human craving to establish stable moorings when they are impaired or unsatisfactory, from the success pictures the adolescent builds as man or woman through living examples in the neighborhood, in the immediate face-to-face situations of his groups, in the larger setting, and, probably to no lesser degree today, through TV, movies, paper-backs, magazines with ubiquitous content.

Steps Toward a Fresh Approach. For effective policy and action, what is needed is more down-to-earth assessment of the causes of adolescent misbehaviors—which range from those of relatively minor consequence (occasionally skipping school, occasional parties with some drinking involved) all the way to those very serious indeed (vandalism, robbery, rape, and murder). In view of the enormity of the picture, assessment of causes is a whale of a job. In the long run, it will more than pay, by curtailing wasted and disjointed efforts, to tackle this whale of a job. But the feat cannot be accomplished simply by putting together the various theoretical pieces advanced by scholars with commitments to particular theories, nor by adding fragmentary data or experiences of practitioners to this assortment of doctrines. Unless approached and carried on within the frame-work that accommodates the gamut of influences on behavior, the multifaceted parts of the dragon are seen by each from his particular angle, particular position, particular organizational commitments.

A fresh approach is needed to promote the coordinated efforts required. One series of feasible steps is the following:

First, putting away, for the time being, theories and explanations advanced by researcher and practitioner alike. This is only the initial condition for taking a fresh and unbiased look, in order to make the second step fruitful.

Second, examining the available hard statistics on the occurrence of misbehaviors, as to their kind, trends over time, locations, patterns in change of location; also gathering together all available cases of hidden, undetected offenses reported in the scattered research and in the personal experiences of police, social workers, researchers, parents, educators, and so on.

Third, presenting these facts, or a truthful summary of them, to qualified representatives of practitioners of varying persuasions; researchers from relevant academic disciplines; theorists of various persuasions; legislators and policy-makers at community, state, and federal levels; and—not the least important—authors and executives in television and the movies and authors and publishers of comic books, magazines, and paperbacks.

We are convinced that the picture of cold facts and incidents personally experienced by people in direct contact with youth will impress the onlookers and will suggest the following:

1. The *multifaceted* sources of the causes that need closer study.

2. The *interrelated* nature of various aspects of the sources, and the different weight or significance of these in varying combinations —thus putting a question mark on the utility of amassing disjointed technical studies of the "delinquent" and "nondelinquent" with over- or underemphasis of this or that aspect according to preferred theory or organizational commitment.

3. The particular contribution each can make to the concerted effort to gain a rounded picture and to coordinated, effective measures according to his appropriate function.

To be sure, the immediate and readily located instigators of misbehaviors are found in the individual's experienced lure of an empty car on a street, of a girl walking around the corner, of money in a passerby's pocketbook or a cash register; or in the gratification of proving oneself a big shot through subduing fellows in the neighborhood who claim to be big shots, too. To be sure, the mutual encouragement and mutual confidence that trigger misbehaviors are those from trusted buddies with whom a youngster has daily give-and-take, with whom he feels binding ties and a singleness of fate. Nevertheless, we would be cutting the roots from these immediate instigators, so striking to the naked eye, if we do not ask questions:

Why did the youngster come to feel with urgency that he wants a car, *has* to have one, the world owes him one?

Why did he come to feel that if he is to be a man worthy of his salt, he must *prove* himself by having ready cash to entertain a girl or have parties (orgies) with all the trimmings?

Why does he think that securing and using drugs are *feats* to be accomplished?

How did he come to feel that such "accomplishments" are more important proofs of his manhood than success in school subjects, homework, or work in a trade?

To reach the roots of such conceptions, we have to go behind what catches the eye in the immediate situation. As documented in Chapters 9 and 10, and in reports of other research, certain objects and actions are common to the "value systems" of the great majority of adolescents, regardless of their neighborhood. Since we know that this has not always been the case in all places or at all times, these common values must reflect common exposures.

We do know that the adolescent is bombarded day in and day out with quick success stories in the neighborhood and elsewhere, exposed to symbols of success in the outpourings of the mass communications—flashy cars, shapely girls running around with trimly dressed males, he-men who knock their opponents down and beat them up, exciting accounts of the "thrills" of illegal or immoral activity.

In fact, we suspect that the appalling increase in delinquency rates in rural and semirural areas is not a simple reflection of the influence of city on country or of suburbia. We suspect it has something to do with the penetration of mass means of communication—especially television, with its concrete imagery of what is thrilling and successful coming to youth in the intimacy of their very homes.

The facts of juvenile misbehavior may be likened to an iceberg, with its exposed portion the official statistics and its hidden portion the undetected incidents not on the records. But the better analogy may be some extraordinary plant growing partly above and partly below ground with common roots—tangled, spread in many directions—some laid down long before new shoots are sent forth, others extending almost simultaneously with new buds.

The task, then, becomes tracing the roots, their growth, their intertwined patterns, to sketch a rounded picture of causation. The task involves a picture of how a youngster, trying to establish himself as a man worthy of his salt, acquires his notions of attainments urgently to be desired, of what is thrilling and what is not, of how he can fulfill all these—in short, how his self-picture, comprising variegated roles and targets, emerges.

This task implies as complete an account as possible of the influences coming from at least the following sources:

1. The fact of membership in groups created or chosen by adoles-

cents in which desires, secrets, and confidences are freely shared, ways and means of doing something about them discussed, plans and their execution laid down in a mutually binding way.

2. The immediate setting, with its particular brand of opportunities or lack of them, its facilities, its particular brand of heroes and villains, its brands and patterns of formal and informal practices, its particular distribution of white and Negro, gentile and Jew, Anglo and Latin, privileged and underprivileged.

3. Attributes of the length and breadth of the larger scene, of which the areas and their small groups are parts. This larger scene provides common features for the adolescent on the threshold of becoming a full-fledged adult, depicting the essentials of what he has to do and to attain in various roles.

The three sets of influences act and react on one another, falling into patterns. If we become fixated on face-to-face, intimate aspects, or on immediate settings, we get only part of the picture—distorted by our close focus on it. On the other hand, if we fix our sights only on the larger scene, we are bound to telescope some stubborn actualities of the immediate neighborhood and community—for example, the power of face-to-face interaction. Application of principles derived from the whole grand picture will thus be difficult, and the gap between theory and action magnified.

If action starts with efforts to mobilize the residents of an area, securing the participation of formal and informal agencies of influence, including the good will of the youngsters and their local idols, we have a start in the right direction. But neighborhoods are not insulated compartments. The role of adolescents; how they experience deprivation and frustration, and how it is to be met; the ways a youngster can prove himself to be somebody; how spheres and images of achievements and success are built—all these lack decisive ingredients if influences coming from the larger setting are not included in the picture. There are common threads woven in the larger social fabric, as well as different strands in particular locations and areas. Ignoring the common threads and their connections is not conducive to good theory. In practice, it breeds frustration for well-intentioned efforts.

On the other hand, if carried out in their overlapping perspectives, the assessment of the gamut of influences may well provide pointers towards an imaginative and bolder pattern of measures which is preventive in its effects. The search for preventive measures, instead of merely ameliorative ones, is the desired goal for all, but admittedly still presents baffling problems today.

Action and Criteria for Its Adequacy. The efforts required to build the total picture of influences shaping adolescent behavior in socially desirable or undesirable directions are far beyond the capacities of any one area of study, as currently defined by academic disciplines, let alone any one or several research projects. The scope of the efforts is great enough to call for the research skills and experience of all those involved with the destiny of the younger generations: social scientists of varying academic descriptions; psychologists in various problem areas; psychiatrists; statisticians; teachers; social workers; counsellors; occupational advisers; law enforcement personnel.

If their efforts are to count, they must be concerted, not simply large, intensive, or simultaneous. And yardsticks are needed to assess progress. Fitting together their efforts implies assessing each set of influences, as well as its intersections with others—that is, those locations at which change within one set of influences implies change in another. In this way, and probably only in this way, can a rounded and valid picture emerge.

Meanwhile, those who face the problems of adolescent misbehavior urgently need criteria—some yardsticks—for appraising the measures they institute to change the grim picture. We propose as a general standard that the consequences of the measure be assessed relative to which of the three sets of influences it is designed and capable of affecting. Through such a yardstick we can learn more from the results of concrete measures about the relationships of small group, neighborhood, and larger setting, and their crucial interdependencies. We can even learn from the limitations and unanticipated consequences of measures taken. It is to be hoped that such concerted efforts will be forthcoming with widespread support at local, community, state, and national levels. With this hope, we narrow our perspective to the main focus of the data in this research.

Reorienting Behavior of Group Members in Their Settings. Although this research was conceived and is carried on to secure data from three sets of influences on behavior, its focus has been explicitly on small groups and member behavior within them. As social psychologists, our aim has been to keep this focus without losing sight of the continual interplay of influences from group, neighborhood, and larger setting.

At this stage of the game, there is decided relevance for emphasizing the group-related character of many adolescent deeds and misdeeds. On the one hand, we are besieged with literature about the large organization and "organization man," about the trend toward a "mass society." But seldom does this literature emphasize that these trends are also conducive to the rise and proliferation of small informal groups and to absorption of the energies and affections of individuals in such groups. Yet this is precisely the case.

The sense of aloneness and uncertainty that the individual caught in such trends experiences is not unlike that of the adolescent. And like the large organization, like the "mass society," the adolescent world is not composed of unrelated, individual atoms. It is not totally disorganized, despite the chaotic and even violent eruptions which emerge from time to time. It appears to be chaotic because it is patterned to such a large extent informally. We are startled by the misdeeds and occasional violence, and find them without apparent cause because we are not aware of the informal organization. As adults, we are unable to see why youth fall under the sway of mass communication for their tastes, their ideas of excitement and adventure, because we do not see its influence in the web of their daily interactions.

The extent of the blackout in knowledge between the larger social scene and individual behavior is revealed in the incidents quoted on page 12 of the report of the U.S. Senate Subcommittee (April 18, 1961), of a pistol-packing "gang of twenty or more" called "Ramblers," whose existence was altogether unknown to the adults working in the area:

Community organizations at work in the areas where the youth are alleged to have committed the crimes had not heard of the Ramblers before the police roundup and one youth's detailed account, backed up by others in custody, of highly organized holdups, yokings, and purse snatchings.

Playground officials, the Recreation Department's roving leaders, and

Junior Police and Citizens Corps, the LeDroit Park Civic Association, and the Youth Aid Division of the police department had all been unaware even that a group of youths using the name "Ramblers" existed.

So, practically as well as theoretically there are reasons for recognizing the existence and the significance of small informal groups which become, for the members, reference groups defining conformity and deviation for *them*. Their very existence is not unrelated to the social scene in which they occur, but explaining them in terms of the larger setting makes them no less real, present, and immediate for individuals in them.

From a practical point of view, one might think, therefore, that many problems of adolescent misbehavior would be erased simply by breaking up the groups whose norms justify, to members, actions contrary to the well-being of otherrs. The solution is not so simple, if only for the psychological reason that individuals caught without moorings feel that they must have some, and will look for them anew if temporary solutions are dissolved. Furthermore, adolescent groups are not confined to certain neighborhoods where extra policemen are assigned. In our research, socially objectionable activities were found in groups whose neighborhoods are not the kind where one looks for "gangs."

In surveying the literature on juvenile cliques, gangs, crowds, sets, and the like, we have found that most attempts to set up classificatory schemes for adolescent groups not only contain internal contradictions, but do violence to the facts. For example, there are groups in middle-class neighborhoods just as tightly knit as many "gangs," which are supposed to be phenomena of lower-class neighborhoods. Very few adolescent groups, even gangs, seem to have been organized deliberately with the explicit aim of illegal activity; and they usually engage in many other activities besides. The so-called "retreatist" gangs whose members use drugs usually also engage in other illegal activities, and so on. In the interests of *analysis* of the effects of membership and taking *steps* to correct their directions, it may be helpful to deal with all of them as *groups* having, in varying degrees, informal structures with some solidarity and some common norms or values.

In this research, we have seen evidence of the binding nature of individual loyalties to small organizations during the adolescent period, of the terrible importance of activities they undertake in concert, of the patterned character of communication and other interactions within their framework. We have seen the power of groups, for good or evil, in achieving coordination of individual efforts, in generating mutual excitement toward productive and destructive ends. It is something one would rather have working for the common good than against it.

Then is breaking up adolescent groups a generally realistic or effective solution to problems of adolescent misbehavior? We can foresee circumstances in which the drama had been played so far that this is the only feasible climax. But, ordinarily, the process takes drastic measures—physical separation of members. The adult who simply forbids group members to associate is deluding himself, perhaps creating a more cohesive unit, and usually sending its problems elsewhere.

We will also point out that the attempt to "rechannel" activities, or reorient attitudes, must be conceived as a long-term proposition, ordinarily involving much more than the appearance of a sympathetic adult on the scene or programmed activities offered from above. For one thing, such attempts are bound to run up against problems stemming from the interdependence of influences affecting the wants, the attitudes, the targets of individual members. Small groups are not closed and airtight. They are highly permeable to influences from their settings. Even though some members may have obvious talents in some direction, they may not care at all about pursuing them.

Many efforts to "rechannel" group directions have offered athletic sports as the "new direction." Since sports are highly resonant with the value placed on athletics in the society at large, it does have appeal to many, if not all, American boys and girls. But are competitive games all that can be offered on the scale of the school programs, little leagues, city, state, and regional competitions? And, do athletic sports—as *recreation* for all but the highly talented and dedicated few—really encompass a large enough slice of the adolescent's interests to turn him in directions of new attitudes and interests?

Are sports and camps and busy-work really adequate to encompass the concerns of adolescents, excepting those few who are exceptionally talented in them? We think it would be well for those who have to face the difficult problems of reorienting groups of youth which have taken undesirable dirrections to remember that adolescence is, in fact, the prelude to adulthood, and that it is supposed to be a period of preparation for adult responsibilities. If, as adults, we would not abolish the adolescent period as such a transition stage, then we had best reevaluate the opportunities for youth to grow in creative directions—not just opportunities for "delinquent" youth, but for all young people searching for their own places and contributions as adults.

The report of the approach and findings of a research project—which this book is—is not the place for specifics of a blueprint for action policies and measures. However, one thing is certain concerning the relevance of the findings for policy and action, and should be emphasized in conclusion. Whatever the explicit or implicit rationale and established generalizations on which action policy is based, it should be conceived in full realization of an over-all finding that stood out strikingly throughout this research, and is in line with the research literature surveyed.

Any policies or action measures, including professional and technical skills for guidance and training, will be self-defeating if they are conceived with the run-of-the-mill assumptions of the sort: "The scholar knows best"; "the executive knows best"; "the expert knows best"; "enforcement agencies know best"; "teachers know best"; or "parents know best."

The crux of the matter for effective policy and action is not the busy-work *as such,* not the programmed activities *as such,* or even the end products of training to exhibit for public display. The cardinal point is to ensure throughout (whatever the activities) the youth's feeling of having a *function* in their initiation, development, and execution.

What we do not take part in initiating and developing and producing, what we engage in without our own choosing and aspiring, 's not felt as ours. What we do not feel as ours lacks in the experience of inner urgency and in sense of responsibility. The important thing to actualize at the very start is not immediate technical proficiency, but the feeling of participation, the feeling that we have functions in the larger scheme of things, the feeling that we have indispensable roles with others in things that all feel should be done.

Any activity, any program should be in the nature of a challenge to youth, requiring concerted planning and action. Involvement in the planning and execution affords, at the same time, the occasion for the individual to test his acceptance or rejection by others, an occasion for him to prove himself to others, and an occasion personally to excel in the process.

When policy is formulated, action programs outlined, and facilities provided in harmony with this principle, a self-image will emerge in the youth that he feels as his own free creation and, hence, something to be cherished and lived up to in its practical implications. The alternative in which programs are worked out only *by* adults *for* the benefit of youth with the intent of doing something *to* them is bound to share the fate of all such ill-conceived policies.

When we are made to take part in programs which are not of our own free initiation or free choosing, we simply go through the moves. The benefits are only transitory at best. We may drag our feet or evade them when we can with immunity, as has been the case with regimented programs and activities in which the individual himself is not ego-involved as a personally committed and aspiring active participant in concert with others important in his eyes.

References

ATWOOD, B. S., 1933. Social participation and juvenile delinquency. *Indiana Bull. of Character and Correction,* **210**, 208–211.

AUSUBEL, D. P., 1954. *Theory and Problems of Adolescent Development.* New York: Grune & Stratton.

BALES, R. F., 1950. *Interaction Process Analysis: A Method for the Study of Small Groups.* Reading, Mass.: Addison-Wesley.

BARRON, M. L., 1960. *The Juvenile in Delinquent Society.* New York: Knopf.

BASS, B. M., 1960. *Leadership, Psychology and Organizational Behavior.* New York: Harper & Row.

BELL, W., 1958. The utility of the Shevky typology for the design of urban sub-area field studies. *J. soc. Psychol.,* **47**, 71–83.

BERNARD, JESSIE, 1939. The neighborhood behavior of school children in relation to age and socioeconomic status. *Amer. soc. Rev.,* **4**, 652–662.

BERNARD, JESSIE, 1961. Teen-age culture: An overview. *Annals Amer. Acad. pol. and soc. Sci.,* **338**, 1–12.

BLAKE, R. R., AND MOUTON, JANE S., 1961. Competition, communication, and conformity. In I. Berg and B. M. Bass (Eds.), *Conformity and Deviation.* New York: Harper & Row.

BLAKE, R. R., AND MOUTON, JANE S., 1962. The intergroup dynamics of win-lose conflict and problem-solving collaboration in union-management relations. In M. Sherif (Ed.) *Intergroup Relations and Leadership.* New York: Wiley.

BLOS, P., 1941. *The Adolescent Personality. A Study of Individual Behavior.* New York: Appleton-Century-Crofts.

BOGARDUS, E. S., 1924. Measuring social distance. *J. appl. Sociol.,* **9**, 229–308.

BOGARDUS, E. S., 1947. Changes in racial distances. *Internat. J. opin. and attit. Res.,* **1**, 55–62.

BORDUA, D. J., 1961. Delinquent subcultures: Sociological interpretations of gang delinquency. *Annals Amer. Acad. pol. and soc. Sci.,* **338**, 119–136.

BOSSARD, J. H. S., 1948. *The Sociology of Child Development*. New York: Harper & Row.

BOWMAN, P. H., 1959. Effects of a revised school program on potential delinquents. *Annals Amer. Acad. pol. and soc. Sci.*, **322**, 53–62.

BROWN, R., AND DODSON, D., 1959. The effectiveness of a Boys Club program in reducing delinquency. *Annals Amer. Acad. pol. and soc. Sci.*, **322**, 47–52.

BUFFALO YOUTH BOARD, 1960. *Trends in Delinquency and Crime*. New York: Buffalo.

CLOWARD, R. A., AND OHLIN, L. E., 1960. *Delinquency and Opportunity. A Theory of Delinquent Gangs*. New York: The Free Press.

COHEN, A. K., 1955. *Delinquent Boys*. New York: The Free Press.

COLEMAN, J. S., 1961. *The Adolescent Society*. New York: The Free Press.

CRAWFORD, P. L., MALAMUD, D. L., AND DUMPSON, J. R., 1950. *Working with Teenage Gangs*. Welfare Council of New York City.

DASHIELL, J. F., 1930. An experimental analysis of some group effects. *J. soc. Psychol.*, **25**, 190–199.

DASHIELL, J. F., 1935. Experimental studies of the influence of social situations on the behavior of individual human adults. In C. Murchison (Ed.) *Handbook of Social Psychology*. Worcester, Mass.: Clark Univer. Press.

DEAN, DOROTHY, 1952. *Juvenile Delinquency in El Paso, Texas. A Border City Culture*. M.A. thesis, Univer. of Oklahoma.

DE SOTO, C. B., AND BOSLEY, J. J., 1962. The cognitive structure of a social structure. *J. abn. soc. Psychol.*, **64**, 303–307.

DIMMOCK, H. S., 1937. *Rediscovering the Adolescent*. New York: Association Press.

DRESHER, R. H., 1957. Seeds of delinquency. *Personnel Guid. J.*, **35**, 595.

El Paso Times, 1959. Editorial, Sunday, June 7, p. 6–A.

EMPEY, L. T., 1956. Social class and occupational aspiration: A comparison of absolute and relative measurement. *Amer. sociol. Rev.*, **21**, 703–709.

FARIS, R. E. L., 1962. Interaction levels and intergroup relations. In Sherif, M. (Ed.), *Intergroup Relations and Leadership*. New York: Wiley.

FARIS, R. E. L., AND DUNHAM, W., 1939. *Mental Disorders in Urban Areas*. Chicago: Univer. of Chicago Press. Reprinted 1960.

FIREY, W., 1947. *Land Uses in Central Boston*. Cambridge: Harvard Univer. Press.

FORD, C. S., AND BEACH, F. A., 1951. *Patterns of Sexual Behavior*. New York: Harper & Row.

GIBB, C. A., 1954. Leadership. In Lindzey, G. (Ed.) *Handbook of Social Psychology*, Vol. II. Reading, Mass.: Addison-Wesley.

GIBBEN, T. C. N., 1961. *Trends in Juvenile Delinquency*. Geneva, Switzerland: World Health Organization, Public Health Papers, No. 5.

GORDON, W. C., 1957. *The Social System of the High School*. New York: Free Press.

GREER, S., AND ORLEANS, P., 1962. The mass society and the parapolitical structure. *Amer. sociol. Rev.*, **27**, 634–646.

HALLER, A. O., AND BUTTERWORTH, C. E., 1960. Peer influences on levels of occupational and educational aspiration. *Soc. Forces*, **38**, 289–295.

HARE, A. P., 1962. *Handbook of Small Group Research*. New York: Free Press.

HARE, A. P., BORGATTA, E. F., AND BALES, R. F. (Eds.), 1955. *Small Groups: Studies in Social Interaction*. New York: Knopf.

HARTLEY, RUTH E., 1957. Personal characteristics and acceptance of secondary groups as reference groups. *J. indiv. Psychol.*, **13**, 45–55.

HAWLEY, A. H., 1950. *Human Ecology, A Theory of Community Structure*. New York: Ronald.

HEALY, W., AND BRONNER, A. F., 1936. *New Light on Delinquency and Its Treatment*. New Haven: Yale.

HOFSTÄTTER, P. R., 1956. *Gruppendynamik. Kritik der Massenpsychologie*. Hamburg: Rowohlt. Esp. Zur psychologie der versuchsperson, pp. 43–45.

HOLLINGSHEAD, A. B., 1949. *Elmtown's Youth*. New York: Wiley.

HOMANS, G. C., 1950. *The Human Group*. New York: Harcourt, Brace.

HORROCKS, J. E., 1962. *The Psychology of Adolescence. Behavior and Development*, 2nd ed. Boston: Houghton Mifflin.

HYMAN, H. H., 1953. The value systems of different classes. A social-psychological contribution to the analysis of stratification. In R. Bendix and S. M. Lipset (Eds.), *Class, Status, and Power*. New York: Free Press.

JUVENILE COURT OF CUYAHOGA COUNTY, 1954. *The Community Concern about Juvenile Delinquency*. Cleveland, Ohio, Annual Report.

KELLEY, H. H., AND THIBAUT, J. W., 1954. Experimental studies of group problem solving and process. In G. Lindzey (Ed.) *Handbook of Social Psychology*, **2**, 735–785.

KEY, V. O., Jr., 1956. Strategies in research on public affairs. *Items*, **10**, 29–32.

KOBRIN, S., 1959. The Chicago Area Project—A 25-year assessment. *Annals Amer. Acad. pol. and soc. Sci.*, **322**, 19–29.

KUHLEN, R. G., 1962. *The Psychology of Adolescent Development.* New York: Harper & Row.

LICHTER, S. O., RAPIER, ELSIE B., SEIBERT, FRANCES M., AND SKLANSKY, M. A., 1962. *The Drop-Outs.* New York: Free Press.

MACDONALD, M., MCGUIRE, C., AND HAVIGHURST, R. J., 1949. Leisure activities and the socio-economic status of children. *Amer. J. Sociol.,* LIV, 505–519.

MARTIN, J. B., 1953. *Why Did They Kill?* New York: Ballantine.

MAYS, J. B., 1961. Teen-age culture in contemporary Britain and Europe. *Annals Amer. Acad. pol. and soc. Sci.,* **338,** 22–32.

MCCORD, JOAN, AND MCCORD, W., 1959. A follow-up report on the Cambridge-Somerville youth study. *Annals Amer. Acad. pol. and soc. Sci.,* **322,** 89–96.

MCGUIGAN, F. J., 1961. The experimenter—a neglected problem. Paper presented at American Psychological Association, annual meetings, New York (mimeographed).

MCKAY, H. D., 1959. Juvenile delinquency. Testimony before the Subcommittee to Investigate Juvenile Delinquency of the Committee on the Judiciary, U.S. Senate, 86th Congress, First Session, May 28 and 29.

MILLER, F. B., 1954. "Resistentialism" in applied social research. *Human Organization,* **12,** 5–8.

MILLER, H. P., 1962. Is the income gap closed? "No!" *New York Times Magazine,* November 11, 1962, 50–58.

MILLER, W. B., 1958. Lower class culture as a generating milieu of gang delinquency. *J. soc. Issues,* **14,** 5–19.

MILLER, W. B., 1959. Preventive work with street-corner groups: Boston Delinquency Project. *Annals Amer. Acad. pol. and soc. Sci.,* **322,** 97–106.

MILLS, C. W., 1959. *The Sociological Imagination.* New York: Oxford Press.

MONAHAN, T. P., 1961. On the trend in delinquency. *Soc. Forces,* **40,** 158–168.

MORENO, J. L., 1935. *Who Shall Survive?* New York: Beacon House, revised edition, 1953.

MURPHY, G., 1947. *Personality.* New York: Harper & Row.

NOVICK, MARY B., 1960. *Community Programs and Projects for the Prevention of Juvenile Delinquency.* Washington, D.C.: Children's Bureau, Social Security Administration, U.S. Department of Health, Education and Welfare.

ORNE, M., 1959. The demand characteristics of an experimental design and their implications. Paper to symposium "The Problem of Experimenter Bias," American Psychological Association, Annual Meetings, Cincinnati (dittoed).

ORNE, M., 1961. On the social psychology of the psychological experiment: With particular reference to demand characteristics and their implications. Paper presented at American Psychological Association, Annual Meetings, New York (dittoed).

PERLMAN, I. R., 1959. Delinquency prevention: The size of the problem. *Annals Amer. Acad. pol. and soc. Sci.,* **322,** 1–9.

POLLIS, A., AND KOSLIN, B., 1962. On the scientific foundations of marginalism. *Amer. J. Econ. and Sociol.,* **21,** 112–130.

POLSKY, H. W., 1962. *Cottage Six—The Social System of Delinquent Boys in Residential Treatment.* New York: Russell Sage Foundation.

PORTERFIELD, A. L., 1946. *Youth in Trouble.* Fort Worth, Texas: The Leo Potishman Foundation.

PRADO, W. M., 1958. Appraisal of performance as a function of the relative ego-involvement of children and adolescents. Ph.D. thesis, Univer. of Oklahoma.

RAHM, H. J., AND WEBER, J. R., 1958. *Office in the Alley. Report on a Project with Gang Youngsters.* Austin, Texas: The Hogg Foundation for Mental Health.

RECKLESS, W. C., DINITZ, S., AND MURRAY, ELLEN, 1956. Self-concept as an insulator against delinquency. *Amer. sociol. Rev.,* **21,** 744–746.

REDL, F., 1956. In Helen L. Witmer and Ruth Kotinsky (Eds.), *New Perspectives for Research on Juvenile Delinquency.* Washington, D.C.: Government Printing Office, 60–65.

REMMERS, H. H., AND RADLER, D. H., 1957. *The American Teenager.* Indianapolis: Bobbs-Merrill.

RIECKEN, H. W., *et al.,* 1954. Narrowing the gap between field studies and laboratory experiments in social psychology: A statement by the summer seminar. *Soc. Sci. Res. Council Items,* **8,** No. 4, 37–42.

RIECKEN, H. W., AND HOMANS, G. C., 1954. Psychological aspects of social structure. In G. Lindzey (Ed.), *Handbook of Social Psychology,* II, 786–832.

RIESSMAN, F., 1962. *The Culturally Deprived Child.* New York: Harper & Row.

ROSE, A. M., 1954. *Theory and Method in the Social Sciences.* Minneapolis: Univer. of Minnesota Press.

Rosen, B. C., 1955. Conflicting group membership: A study of parent-peer group cross-pressures. *Amer. sociol. Rev.,* **20,** 155–161.

Rosenthal, R., 1961. On the social psychology of the psychological experiment: With particular reference to experimenter bias. Paper to symposium, American Psychological Assoc. Annual Meetings, New York (mimeographed).

Schmid, C. F., 1937. *Social Saga of Two Cities.* Minneapolis: Univer. of Minnesota Press.

Sears, R. R., 1960. The growth of conscience. In I. Iscoe and H. W. Stevenson (Eds.), *Personality Development in Children.* Austin: Univer. of Texas Press.

Seidler, M. B., and Ravitz, M. J., 1955. A Jewish peer group. *Amer. J. Sociol.,* **61,** 11–15.

Shaw, C. R., 1930. *The Jack Roller.* Chicago: Univer. of Chicago Press.

Shaw, C. R., 1931. *History of a Delinquent Career.* Chicago: Univer. of Chicago Press.

Shaw, C. R. (Ed.), 1938. *Brothers in Crime.* Chicago: Univer. of Chicago Press.

Shaw, C. R., 1944. Memorandum submitted to the Board of Directors of the Chicago Area Project, January 10 (mimeographed).

Shaw, C. R., and McKay, H. D., 1942. *Juvenile Delinquency and Urban Areas.* Chicago: Univer. of Chicago Press.

Sherif, Carolyn W., 1961. Self radius and goals of youth in different urban areas. *Southwest. soc. Sci. Quartl.,* December issue.

Sherif, M., 1948. *An Outline of Social Psychology.* New York: Harper & Row.

Sherif, M., 1951. A preliminary experimental study of intergroup relations. In J. H. Rohrer and M. Sherif (Eds.), *Social Psychology at the Crossroads.* New York: Harper & Row.

Sherif, M., 1954. Integrating field work and laboratory in small group research. *Amer. sociol. Rev.,* **19,** 759–771.

Sherif, M., 1959. Operational report to the Hogg Foundation for Mental Health, The University of Texas. Description of research on natural groups (1958–1959). Norman, Oklahoma: Institute of Group Relations (mimeographed).

Sherif, M., 1960. Individual behavior and group processes in differentiated sociocultural settings. Paper to American Sociological Association, New York (mimeographed).

Sherif, M., 1961. Conformity-deviation, norms, and group relations. In

I. Berg and B. M. Bass (Eds.), *Conformity and Deviation*. New York: Harper & Row.

SHERIF, M., 1962. Intergroup relations and leadership: Introduction. In M. Sherif (Ed.), *Intergroup Relations and Leadership*. New York: Wiley.

SHERIF, M., 1962. The self and reference groups: Meeting ground of individual and group approaches. *Annals of N.Y. Acad. Sci.*, **96**, 797–813.

SHERIF, M., 1963. Social psychology: Interdisciplinary problems and trends. In S. Koch (Ed.), *Investigations of Man as Socius: Their Place in Psychology and the Social Sciences*. Vol. 6, *Psychology: A Study of a Science*. New York: McGraw-Hill.

SHERIF, M., AND CANTRIL, H., 1947. *The Psychology of Ego-involvements*. New York: Wiley.

SHERIF, M., HARVEY, O. J., WHITE, B. J., HOOD, W. R., AND SHERIF, CAROLYN W., 1961. *Intergroup Conflict and Cooperation. The Robbers Cave Experiment*. Norman, Oklahoma. Institute of Group Relations. Reedited and expanded version of mimeographed report, 1954.

SHERIF, M., AND HOVLAND, C. I., 1961. *Social Judgment. Assimilation and Contrast Effects in Communication and Attitude Change*. New Haven, Conn.: Yale.

SHERIF, M., AND KOSLIN, B., 1960. "Institutional" *vs.* "behavioral" approaches with special reference to political science. Norman, Oklahoma: Institute of Group Relations (mimeographed).

SHERIF, M., AND SHERIF, CAROLYN W., 1953. *Groups in Harmony and Tension. An Integration of Studies on Intergroup Relations*. New York: Harper & Row.

SHERIF, M., AND SHERIF, CAROLYN W., 1956. *An Outline of Social Psychology,* rev. ed. New York: Harper & Row.

SHERIF, M., AND SHERIF, CAROLYN W., 1960. Self-radius and goals of group members and their age-mates in differentiated sociocultural settings. Norman, Oklahoma: Institute of Group Relations (mimeographed).

SHERIF, M., WHITE, B. J., AND HARVEY, O. J., 1955. Status in experimentally produced groups. *Amer. J. Sociol.*, **60**, 370–379.

SHEVKY, E., AND BELL, W., 1955. *Social Area Analysis*. Stanford: Stanford.

SHEVKY, E., AND WILLIAMS, MARILYN, 1949. *The Social Areas of Los*

Angeles. Analysis and Typology. Berkeley: Univer. of California Press.

STOGDILL, R. M., 1959. *Individual Behavior and Group Achievement. A Theory: The Experimental Evidence*. New York: Oxford.

SURVEY RESEARCH CENTER, 1955. *A Study of Adolescent Boys*. Ann Arbor: Institute of Social Research, Univer. of Michigan.

TALBERT, R. H., 1956. *Cowtown—Metropolis*. Fort Worth: The Leo Potishman Foundation.

THRASHER, F. M., 1927. *The Gang*. Chicago: Univer. of Chicago Press.

THRASHER, F. M., 1944. Prevention of delinquency in an overprivileged neighborhood. *Proceedings of the National Conference of Juvenile Agencies*, XL (April), 96–106.

TRUMAN, D. B., 1955. The impact on political science of the revolution in the behavioral sciences. In *Research Frontiers in Politics and Government*. Washington, D.C.: Brookings Institution.

TRYON, R. C., 1955. *Identification of Social Areas by Cluster Analysis*. Univer. of California Publications in Psychology. Berkeley: Univer. of California Press.

TURK, H., AND TURK, THERESA, 1961. Personal sentiments in a hierarchy. *Soc. Forces,* **40,** 137–140.

UNITED NATIONS, 1955. *La prevention de la delinquence juvenile dans certain pays Européens*. Department of Economic Affairs, U.N. publication, IV, 12.

U.S. CHILDREN'S BUREAU, 1961. *Juvenile Court Statistics—1960*. Washington, D.C.: U.S. Department of Health, Education and Welfare, Social Security Administration.

U.S. SENATE, COMMITTEE ON THE JUDICIARY, 1959. Hearings before the Subcommittee to Investigate Juvenile Delinquency. Part 5, November 9–12, 17, 19–20. Washington, D.C: U.S. Government Printing Office.

U.S. SENATE, COMMITTEE ON THE JUDICIARY, 1961. *Investigation of Juvenile Delinquency in the United States,* Part 9. Role of the Federal Government in Combatting the Juvenile Delinquency Problem. Hearings before the Subcommittee to Investigate Juvenile Delinquency, 87th Congress, First Session, March 9 and 10. Washington, D.C., U.S. Government Printing Office.

U.S. SENATE, COMMITTEE ON THE JUDICIARY, 1961. Report to the Committee by its Subcommittee to Investigate Juvenile Delinquency. 87th Congress, First Session, April 18. Washington, D.C.: U.S. Government Printing Office.

VAN ARSDOL, M. D., JR., CAMILLERI, S. F., AND SCHMID, C. F., 1958. The generality of urban social area indexes. *Amer. sociol. Rev.,* **23,** 277–284.

VOLKMANN, J., 1951. Scales of judgment and their implications for social psychology. In J. H. Rohrer and M. Sherif (Eds.), *Social Psychology at the Crossroads.* New York: Harper & Row.

WATTENBERG, W. W., 1948. Boys who get in trouble. *J. Educat.,* **131,** 117–118.

WATTENBERG, W. W., AND BALISTRIERI, J. J., 1950. Gang membership and juvenile misconduct. *Amer. soc. Rev.,* **15,** 744–752.

WATTENBERG, W. W., AND BALISTRIERI, J. J., 1952. Automobile theft: A "favored group" delinquency. *Amer. J. Sociol.,* LVII, 575–579.

WIENER, N., 1961. *Cybernetics, or Control and Communication in the Animal and the Machine,* 2nd ed. New York: Mass. Institute of Technology Press.

WILSON, A. B., 1959. Residential segregation of social classes and aspirations of high school boys. *Amer. sociol. Rev.,* **24,** 836–845.

YABLONSKY, L., 1962. *The Violent Gang.* New York: Macmillan.

ZACHRY, CAROLINE B., 1940. *Emotion and Conduct in Adolescence.* New York: Appleton-Century-Crofts.

Appendix

Instructions to Observers of Groups

These sets of instructions were developed during four years of research for observers in the intensive study of groups in different sociocultural settings. They incorporate experiences gained in the direction of this aspect of the research. They are included in the book to specify the way the approach presented in Chapters 2–4 and the research design in Chapter 5 are made operational in collecting data on attitudes and behaviors of group members, and to meet the numerous requests from colleagues in research, in community social work, and in training programs on group process for information on this aspect of the research.

Instructions and forms pertaining to assessment of self-radius and goals in the research (Chapters 9–10) are not included in the Appendix. They are available on request.

I
Phase I in Study of Groups

MAIN OBJECTIVE OF PHASE I:

Singling out a group for intensive study through *your own observations* of repeated associations of the same set of boys.

METHOD FOR PHASE I

Observation is the method for gaining information about a group or its members at this stage. The only direct questioning permissible in this phase is of individuals *unrelated* to the site of observation or the boys observed. For example, in becoming acquainted with a neighborhood, it is all right to inquire *in general* terms about where youths spend their leisure hours from some adult in a position to know. However, it is *not* all right to inquire about a particular cluster you may see from the boys themselves or others who know them, *at this stage*. Observation should include special alertness to any information that comes your way without your asking for it directly. You should make a special note when information is volunteered to you, giving the circumstances, persons involved, etc.

PROCEDURAL STEPS

1. Choice of a locale as an *initial* base of operations *in the area selected* for study. The site may be a social agency, a park, soda fountain, or some other "hangout." It is emphasized that this choice is for an *initial* base and that the observer's success in later phases is dependent upon his becoming able to encounter a group in other locations or to accompany them out of the initial base of operations.

2. After becoming sufficiently acquainted with the neighborhood that you know one or several locations where youth associate, observe the interactions among boys *primarily* between the ages of 13–18 years. This does not mean that a group has to be *exclusively* between these ages, since natural associations are not always so strictly age-graded.

2a. To help remember the individuals you see, it may be helpful to assign a tag or nickname that seems to characterize their appearance to you. If any of these individuals reappear, it is easier to note this fact by use of the tag until you learn names.

2b. If you use actual names, specify how you learned them.

3. After observation of various interaction clusters, the aim is to select a group for intensive observation consisting of a "hard core" of at least six or seven members, primarily between the ages of 13–18 years, with additional members and a "fringe" around this hard core.

4. During Phase I, the *sole data* for singling out a group for intensive study will be your own observations from *outside* the group. There are several considerations which this criterion imposes:

4a. At this phase, you are not to approach group members or others who know them with direct questions about them or their activities.

4b. On the other hand, if individuals approach *you,* you should not only respond but carefully record the entire incident. Such incidents should be carried off by the observer as naturally as possible under the circumstances. He is not to *avoid* contacts initiated by the boys.

4c. Even at this early stage, you should be aware that your appearance on the scene may arouse efforts to *place* you and to explain your presence. Therefore, your appearance in the particular locale should be from the very start as natural and self-evident as possible. Any close attention to particular individuals or clusters, following the boys so they can become aware of being followed, or *obviously* listening may be labeled as "suspicious" or "spying." Therefore, *at this phase,* avoid showing obvious interest in the individuals who appear to you as most likely to be selected for study. Until a group has been singled out, as described below, appear to be as interested in others as you are in them. It is not even necessary to be physically close to the group you are most likely to choose at this phase.

4d. In later phases direct questions to group members and others will become appropriate. Later, information from other sources will be used as a reliability check. Questioning friends or associates of group members at this phase will spoil the possibility of the later use of such information.

5. A group will be selected for intensive study through your own observations of *recurrence of interaction* (frequency of association) among its members. It will consist of boys who, during at least four observation periods made within approximately two weeks, interact together consistently. Interacting together includes arriving together, departing together, conversing, playing with one another, taking sides with one another.

5a. Recurrence of interaction need not necessarily mean that *all* of the boys associated with a group are seen together at once. It does mean, however, that clusters occur in a patterned way. For example, one might see A, B, C, and D; then B, D, and E; then A, C, and E; then A, B, D, and F: then B, C, E, and F, etc. The recurrence of a core of common individuals associating in this way can be built up over successive observations.

5b. Of course, in addition to sheer recurrence of interaction, *any* evidence of "sticking together" in an unmistakable way, of mutual secrecy from others, of exclusiveness, of *unsolicited* manifestations of being a part of a group should be *carefully* recorded. These observations should not be in the form of an "impression" on your part, but should include the *specific behavioral incidents which occurred*. These incidents or remarks should be written down in detail and specified as a basis for the conclusion that these individuals may be members of a group, satisfying the criteria of the definition.

5c. In the past, observers have sometimes tended, in this phase, to move around too much in their search for recurrent interactions, especially if the same youngsters failed to show up in the same locality within a few days. While it is important to learn several possible bases of observation in the area, these should be restricted to the given area agreed upon in conference with the principal investigator, provided the locale or agency you choose is actually inhabited by boys of the

13–18 age range. In the long run, it proves to be more effective to keep going back to a few locations every two or three days. In this way, we are taking advantage of probabilities. Of course, once a recurrent pattern of interaction is spotted in one place, it should be followed to other locations and activities.

6. In writing observations, in general and especially in this early stage, always be careful to write down what you *actually* observe. If you have comments, impressions, or evaluations, please write them also, but specify that you are making an inference or a judgment. In other words, clearly label what you saw or heard, on the one hand, and what you think it means or general impressions, on the other hand. The latter can be very useful if they are backed up by specific detail of behavioral incidents, but are difficult to utilize if they are not. In writing your reports, separate your impressions or evaluative remarks from behavioral events by writing them in a separate paragraph, *indented from the margin* of the observations. In reporting incidents or remarks, specify the individuals acting or otherwise involved by name or symbol (abbreviated description or label if you don't know names yet), and *underline* these names or symbols in your reports. This will help you to be aware of the actions of all of the individuals involved, and also helps in later analysis of data.

7. The study will proceed to closer range observation of interaction processes and to more intimate data on members and their relationships *only after this first step of identifying a group* and singling it out for study is completed. Detailed instructions for procedures of observation and writing reports will be given after this phase and explained in detail in conferences, as needed.

8. In the next phase, it will be essential that you establish *rapport* with the group members. However, in this first phase, do not try to speed up establishing rapport in a way that will be considered an undue imposition of yourself on the members of a potential group for intensive study. As elaborated in personal conference with you, one of the main concerns of the project is to study the interaction between group members and relations with non-group members, *without cluttering the flow of interaction* as they would carry it on among themselves (at least, cluttering it as little as possible). Your role is *not* that of a leader, and *not* of a participant observer, as far as the group members are concerned. As far as they are concerned, your role is *not* that of an observer for a scientific study. Try first to have the group members take your presence in their vicinity as harmless. *Suspicion* they may manifest toward you or *resist-*

ance to establishing rapport may in fact be proportional to their solidarity, and may, therefore, indicate how closely knit the group is. But this would be only a hunch at the phase of group identification (Phase I), to be confirmed or rejected later in the study.

II
General Procedures and Precautions Throughout Observations in the Field

1. The primary precaution to heed in all observation is to insure that at no time individuals being observed and others related to them become aware that they are being studied. Laboratory studies have established that the individual's awareness of being observed, even while performing a simple task, influences behavior. A major methodological concern of this project is that give-and-take (interaction process) among the individuals studied take place as naturally as possible, uncluttered by extraneous influences, especially self-awareness of being observed with the resulting adoption of "Sunday best" manners when the observer is present. Insofar as possible, our aim is to study behavior which occurs when groups function by themselves.

1a. Because of the aim and concerns mentioned above, the observer should not take notes in the range of vision of the individuals being observed. Of course, it is frequently possible, especially in Phase I when the observer is not yet in direct contact with a group, to jot down symbols without being detected (for example, with the pretense of working a crossword puzzle or making notes for a shopping list). Later, if a specific situation calls for writing something in the individuals' presence, such as keeping score, making a list, taking "minutes," the observer can utilize the opportunity to jot down symbols without being detected.

1b. As a general rule, all observations should be written down or dictated on tape *as soon as possible* after the observation period is completed. Adherence to this rule is necessary to eliminate errors owing to forgetting. However, take ample time to write reports and avoid omitting events you remember but *think* are unimportant at the time, in order to complete a report quickly. Such incidents may prove to be significant later. Write as fully and completely as possible.

NOTE. Errors may creep into observations owing to the observer's selectivity in writing observations. For this reason, other methods will be introduced to obtain data to check the reliability of observations.

The principal investigator and/or the supervisor will specify these at the appropriate time.

2. At each phase of the study, the methods to be used in obtaining data will be specified. It is important that these specifications be followed.

2a. In Phase I, your observations of behaviors and events provide the data of interest. During Phase I, to repeat, information is not to be obtained by (a) asking questions *about the individuals* you observe from persons who know them, or (b) by questioning these individuals themselves.

2b. In later phases of the study, other methods, including certain questioning, will be used, as specified in future instructions.

3. Relationships with responsible adults in the locale of observation:

3a. If your base for observation is a public facility supervised by adults, the responsible adults should usually be informed of the purpose of your presence with the *strict condition* that they not inform others, especially the boys you are observing. This, of course, implies securing their cooperation.

3b. In securing the cooperation of adult authorities, it is essential that at no time the staff have the slightest feeling that the observer is in a rivalry situation with them in any capacity whatever, or that there is any intent to evaluate either their activities or that of the program or facilities in their charge.

3c. It is also essential that your role in the center *not* be one carrying any authority over those who use it, such as that exercised by staff members of an agency. If it is most convenient to have a role in the agency or center, put yourself in that of a "trainee" and insure that you are treated as such, for the following reasons:

To insure that you are not competing relative to the staff for prestige in the eyes of individuals studied.

To insure that you are not perceived as an authority figure in the outfit by group members.

4. Establishing a relationship with members of a group:

4a. During Phase I, while you are observing from a distance to single out a group, you should also be developing a reasonable *pretext* for being in the environs. Preferably this pretext should be one involving activities that will eventually be useful in bringing the group into contact with you (for example, the desire to use available facilities). It should be as truthful and natural as possible so that you will not become trapped by contradictions later. Above all, your presence and actions should in no way suggest that you are an investigator of any kind. People do "label" a stranger who hangs around, so insure that that label will be reasonable and harmless, *not* that of a spy, private eye, etc.

(NOTE: This point is elaborated in Instruction Set IV.)

4b. The observer's aim should be to develop a relationship with group members such that he is regarded by them as harmless, as well-wishing, as helpful on occasion, but *not* as a member of the group. In other words, the role required to obtain the needed data is that of a "big brother," not an adult supervisor, potential member, nor a strange outsider who imposes himself on them.

4c. Never initiate activities for the group you are studying *unless* such activities have been deliberately planned in the study for a particular phase.

After group members initiate activities, try to be helpful without putting yourself into rivalry with group members, especially with leaders of the groups. Complete passivity regarding what they are doing may be interpreted as disapproval on your part. Too forward attempts to help may be seen as meddling. Too effective help may arouse a rivalry situation. For example, if the members start an activity such as baseball or football, you should show interest and you may show proficiency to demonstrate that you are a regular guy and a good sport, but without *stealing the show* or competing in performance with group members. At all times, avoid showing dislike for any member or any evidence of favoritism.

4d. In gaining rapport and establishing a relationship with group members, avoid words or signs of disapproval of their attitudes or activities. However, do not identify yourself with them in such a way that they will expect support from you if they become involved in socially unacceptable activities. Without making a value judgment on them, avoid participating with them in any activity defined as illegal for their age (for example, drinking before the legal age). On the other hand, carefully note any evidence or observation of such activities in your presence. As an older person, you can evade participation without condemning, on the grounds that you are an adult with certain responsibilities (appropriate for the context). This is necessary for the conduct of this project and in order that you can obtain data on attitudes and behavior in the group you observe. Group members do not expect nonmembers to follow group customs, but they will not reveal those that might be unacceptable if you pass value judgments on members' behavior.

5. General orientation to the study of reference groups (those whose members are psychologically identified as group members) and implications for observation procedures:

5a. After using a particular site to locate a recurrent cluster of boys and as a base of operations, the importance of that site should, in general, decline in importance as the locus of observations. The reason is that the groups of particular interest in this research are *reference groups* for individual members. Any group which can be so designated is concerned not just with one activity in a particular spot suitable for that activity, but with various activities which differ in importance and in the degree of intimacy to members.

5b. The question of what activities and concerns are the focus of group interaction is an empirical one, but it cannot be answered if the observer confines his observations to one locale or one specific kind of activity (e.g., sports). We cannot hope to gain an exhaustive list of everything that concerns group members, but we can hope to delineate the major *sectors* of concern and the activities these involve. This task requires that the observer gain sufficient rapport so that he is in a position to be outside the original site of observation with them, and that they freely tell him about other activities which he may not observe at first hand. Reliability of the latter kind of data is gained by checking reports of other members, and by follow up of events and plans over time.

5c. Needless to say, the sectors of concerns and activities will vary from group to group and from time to time for the same group. These sectors have to be singled out by the observer inductively. For example, if a group meets regularly to play games, it is safe to conclude that sports is one such sector. If he finds that they watch, discuss, and talk to girls, help each other plan opportunities to be with girls, etc., this is another sector, and it may be even more important and intimate (to members) than athletic activities.

5d. At times, observers feel that because the research is focused on the study of groups, only activities involving all or an appreciable number of the members are of interest. Activities *en masse* are of interest, but there is scarcely a human group (which has patterned status relations and shared rules or norms) in which the significance of the group for the individual member can be properly assessed solely on the basis of collective activities including the whole membership. The reason that human groups are such an important topic for study is that they do affect members when they are not right in the midst of the whole membership, when they are not immediately subjected to social pressures.

5e. The pertinent evidence to establish is whether a group is a reference group for members' concerns, not just whether a group shows up at a particular place at a particular time, but also whether they are associating elsewhere, via one or more members, over the phone, etc. The evidence includes whether they make plans involving some members, whether they coordinate their activities and whereabouts, whether they *know* at given times where absent members are, whether they give and take mutual aid in matters of parties, girls, transportation, school work, etc. In short, a group may appear in one location and all together only occasionally. But, a group's absence from a place where they have been observed to associate, or a change in their activities, does not necessarily indicate that the group has become unimportant to members. It may simply indicate that the observer needs to find out what sectors are now of concern and where the related activities are carried out. He may never have the opportunity to observe directly some of these (the most intimate or secret), but he can get data and check its reliability when he has sufficient rapport with the members so that they talk freely in his presence.

III
Preparation and Form of Observational Reports

To insure uniformity of observation reports as scientific research data, it will be helpful if the report of each *observation period* is put in the following form:

1. Reports are to be numbered consecutively with the *date* and *time* of observation, which should be specified on each report.

2. A rough diagram of the place or places of interaction processes observed should accompany the report.

3. Specify the number and kind of participants observed each period.

3a. Include special mention of participants (members or nonmembers) at the start of each observation period.

3b. Note any changes of participants (members or nonmembers), giving the particular context of changes (newcomers, those who quit, etc.). Until you have learned the names of participants, use descriptive labels to refer to each. We can fill in the correct names after you learn them.

3c. Include mention of girls and adults as well as other nonmembers.

4. The main body of the observation report consists primarily of your observations concentrating on the main phase of the study at the time. The *main focus of observation,* that is, what you will be most concerned in observing at the time, is determined by the particular emphasis of each successive phase of the study plan.

The idea of a special focus of observation is to be elaborated in conference with the principal investigator and supervisor.

4a. The first focus of observation (Phase I) is *frequency of association* of participants, specifying the activities engaged in (for example, conversation, coming together, leaving together, taking sides together, etc.).

4b. After the observer gets to know the hard core of the group he has selected for intensive study on the basis of observations in Phase I, the next focus of observation is *status differentiation* (group structure or organization, Phase II). Special steps and procedures for this phase of observation will be described on a separate set of instructions and discussed with the observers.

4c. The succeeding observational steps to follow will be specified in due time after Phase I is completed and Phase II is under way.

5. Even before the observer learns the names of all group members, he will include in the report of every observation period in Phase II a tentative status ranking as explained in the instruction sheet prepared for this purpose. These status rankings are to be made on a separate sheet of paper each time.

6. It will be very desirable, from the point of view of eliminating memory distortions, to write down the observation report immediately after each observation period. Any time you can retire briefly from the sight of group members, jot down notes to be elaborated later. Preserve the *time sequence* of events in your report.

7. It is essential that we have at least three observation periods per week for each group. If there is too long a time interval between observation periods for any group, we will lose the continuity of the group functioning. Failure to locate a group should be reported, but does not constitute an observation period for purposes of data collection.

8. Include in every report under the heading *Rapport,* the efforts you make to gain acceptance and reactions of group members to you. Include:

Degree of resistance and suspicion shown by members, with supporting behavioral events.

Changes (increase or decrease) in degree of resistance and suspicion from previous reports and specific evidence of such change.

How much of the above is shared by all group members—by leader, lieutenants, low-status members—and how much is more specific to certain members.

Evidence of acceptance of the observer *outside* of the initial base of operations, especially where group members are not subject to the rules, regulations and authority of adult authorities.

NOTE: The more the observer is accepted in places and in activities that are considered by group members as intimate (exclusive group affairs), the more the observer has succeeded in establishing close rapport.

9. When reference is made to adults, officials, and staff members of an agency, specify their functions, how they treat and are treated by group members. (Do members get permission from parents to do things? Do adults help in *their* activities?)

10. Whenever the name of a group member is mentioned in any connection, *underline* it to facilitate the cumulative analysis of the reports. On the first use of real names, specify how you learned them.

11. *Indent* your own comments and interpretations. Also indent measures that you take to gain the confidence of the group. In short, be sure to separate what is actually observed and what is your own interpretation or actions you take to penetrate into the group.

12. In writing reports, do not take for granted and do not omit description of the boys' clothing, possessions (e.g., cars), relationships with parents and girls, talk about girls and "forbidden" topics, how they classify girls, other people, and social objects like cars, appliances (what is admired and what is not?), and so on. Try to become familiar with members' expressions and speech, and write down as much as you can remember. Do not censor their remarks or topics of discussion in recording them. Note their reactions to other fellows not in their group, whether they are present or absent. What do they talk *about* when they hang around together? (Avoid reporting that "they talked half an hour" without any content or indicating who took part.)

13. The purpose of this aspect of the project, intensive study of natural groups and their individual members, is a strictly scientific one. It is conceived as a basic research undertaking. Publicity is *not* desirable and is to be avoided until the study is completed and written as a scientific contribution by the principal investigator and collaborators, with proper acknowledgments, and changes of place and personal names as necessary. Data are to be regarded as confidential and for use only in scientific papers with explicit permission from the principal investigator. The

research is not carried on from sheer curiosity or to pry into the inter-personal and group relations of individuals in the groups studied. Its purpose is not at all concerned with appraising the effectiveness of the activities of the agency or agencies which provide facilities, if observation is made on community or agency facilities.

14. Since the project is a basic research undertaking, observers are to regard all material collected through observation, interview, or other methods as *confidential*. In writing the material collected for publication, no real names will be used, including names of any agencies involved. All participants in the project are to keep all data as confidential and are not to discuss them outside of the staff meetings, which will be held periodically for the purpose of clarifying the content of the observation reports and of specifying procedural steps to follow. Material in the reports or the reports themselves are not to be disclosed or used outside of these meetings.

IV
Phase II of Observation: Study of Group Structure (Organization) Through Interaction Processes Among Members

MAIN OBJECTIVE OF PHASE II

The focus of observation in Phase II is on possible patterns of inter-action among individual members in terms of their relative *positions,* in order to infer the group structure or organization. Since its objective is to delineate the group as an informal social unit and to assess the status (positions) of members, Phase II is probably the crucial one for the study of groups in this project. For adequate conduct of observations and for report writing in this phase, a thorough grasp by the observer of the properties of human groups is essential. In addition to conferences with the principal investigator and/or unit supervisor, the observer should study at least Chapters 5 and 6, *An Outline of Social Psychology* (Sherif and Sherif, Harper & Row, 1956) as preparation for Phase II.

1. Review of Observer Relationships and Procedures Necessary for Phase II.

Before the observer can effectively make the observations for Phase II, he must be accepted by the members, as a harmless and possibly helpful person whose presence as a participant in at least some of their activities is tolerated or accepted. Such rapport always implies a relationship with members in some capacity, for even young people do classify persons as to their position and role, and the intent that these imply. Therefore, the observer has to have a pretext for his presence which appears natural to group members, is acceptable to them, and is conducive to their bringing the observer into their activities as a participant (though not as a member).

1a. While the observer never aims to become a member of a group, in the sense that he competes for status within it or builds the expectation among members that he will abide by their norms which may conflict with legal or other adult rules, it is essential that group members place him in general as one of their kind, who is somewhat older. In other words, the observer's behavior (word and deed) should not convey the impression that he is socially or culturally of superior rank to the boys, excepting in matters of age, training, and experience. He should not be seen as part of the upper crust—"upper" in this case being defined as above the layer in which the group is located.

1b. One common pretext for an observer which can be adapted appropriately for different settings is this: The observer establishes his presence in a community center, park, or recreation agency with the permission and active sympathy of the official who has full authority over the locale in question. His pretext may be that he is receiving credit for field work, for participating in activities with youth, and that his *eventual* aim is to secure employment working with youth in some capacity. This pretext is often a good one, first because it does not put the observer in a position of authority in the eyes of group members; second, it carries very little possibility of contradiction by the observer or others in the course of the study; third, it does not suggest that the observer is studying the group, only that he is gaining skills himself. This pretext has been used with success in the past. However, it may have to be adapted considerably for particular situations. For some groups, an entirely different pretext may be necessary. (For example, if members are very hostile toward teachers and educated persons, the observer may not be able to gain rapport if he appears as an advanced student.)

1c. The observer's success in establishing rapport with the group is indicated by his success in moving out of the initial site of observation with members as they engage in other activities in other locations (see Instructions II). His ability to secure the observations needed in Phase II is largely dependent upon this success.

1d. If the observer is to have rapport with the group and all of its members, it is essential that he avoid critical remarks or judgments about the group, its individual members, or activities. If, because of his critical remarks, the observer arouses negative attitudes among members, this fact will certainly influence the way members behave in his presence. This is another reason for not competing with members for excellence in activities that are important to them.

1e. Once more, it should be emphasized that the observer should do his utmost not to try to steal the show or compete for prestige with adult staff members or personnel in the location, or with the leader and other members of the group, especially in activities that are important to them.

1f. The balance between being a good, regular fellow (e.g., showing interest and some skill in activities important to members) and being harmless and unthreatening to high status members (e.g., not competing for prestige) is a difficult balance requiring the observer's ingenuity. Facing the problem of achieving such a balance, an observer may detach himself from group activities entirely. Therefore, it is to be stressed that the cautions given to observers in the instructions do not imply that they are to refrain from participating in group activities. On the contrary, the observer has to be a participant in some capacity in order to make the observations in Phase II. The precautions in the instructions pertain to the attributes of this capacity, as seen by group members, not on participation as such.

For example, if the group is interested in sports or games, it is necessary for the observer to display interest in these activities and sufficient skill or learning ability to establish himself as a good, regular fellow in their eyes. The precaution not to compete should be heeded before the observer displays so much skill that his performance downgrades that of top group members. The observer is cautioned, therefore, to forego the pleasure of admiration by younger boys when he achieves this pleasure at the expense of the respect usually accorded other group members. He is also cautioned that he must participate if he is to gain rapport with the group. These precautions apply to all types of participation, including verbal discussion. If an observer talks too much, especially to the leader of a group, this action necessarily reduces the interaction between leader and other members. On the other hand, if he does not talk at all, it is impossible for him to gain sufficient rapport and this may be interpreted as a critical attitude or silent censure.

2. General guides for observation and reports in Phase II.

2a. When Phase II begins, the observer will have already gained sufficient rapport with members that they accept or tolerate his presence at least in some activities. Usually, therefore, he will know the names or nicknames of some members and will have labels for others. (He may encounter other members or new associates of the group as the study goes on, since natural groups are not static.) When Phase II begins, it is helpful for the observer to go over his previous reports and to list the boys he has observed, noting for each with whom he has been seen associating on specific occasions. From this procedure, the observer can reconstruct any possible patterns of association and can substitute real names for the tentative labels he applied earlier.

2b. Recording. When events worthy of note concerning group communication, decisions, and activities occur, the observer can watch carefully, then find an approprriate occasion (e.g., during a lull or at the completion of the event-cycle) to jot down notes and key symbols, tracing what happened, individuals involved, etc. Then these notes should be expanded immediately after leaving the group at the completion of an observation period.

2c. The notes and key symbols of an event-cycle should include at least the following:

1. Place and duration of interaction.
2. Focus of group interaction at this time (e.g., problems, activity, discussion).
3. Who makes suggestions.
4. To whom communication is addressed.
5. How suggestions are received by specific other members.
6. Decisions reached and how reached.
7. Actions taken—giving the relative duration of each of the above and of interruptions from the main track of the event-cycle.

2d. Particularly in this phase, the observer should include in every report all behaviors by members indicating increase, decrease, or change in his *rapport* with the group, as indicated on Instruction Sheet III. Specify which members are involved in these events. Report, as indented paragraphs, any efforts you make to increase acceptance. Note members' reactions to these efforts. Be sure to include any signs of resistance to you, any signs of secrecy on their part, and specify *which* members and *what* activities are involved.

3. Procedures in assessing status structure or organization:

3a. The primary dimension of interest in Phase II is *effective initiative* exhibited by members in the ongoing events of group activities. Initiative may be exhibited in terms of making suggestions, requests, orders, or giving approval to plans. It is effective when other members actually behave in line with the proposal. This means that the observations needed are necessarily over time. The actions may occur immediately afterward on the spot, or they may relate to a future event. In the latter case, the observer should report the outcome. If he cannot observe it directly, he can check it from members' conversations and reports to him (again assuming rapport with the group).

3b. Since effective initiative does not pertain simply to the frequency of suggestions made, but also to whether they are acted upon by others; who gives the approval which leads to action; deference exhibited to other members; admiration or derogation of other members in both general and specific respects—all these are closely related behavioral data. Such indications should be regularly reported in their specific contexts, whether or not members face a problem or are making a decision at the time.

3c.The data of particular value for Phase II pertain to the following: When the members face a *problem situation*, what happens and what are the outcomes over time? A problem situation might, for example, constitute trying to decide what to do now or later; making plans for some activity; trying to decide whether to take part in some activity; trying to devise means so that some or all members can participate in an activity (e.g., get dates). In such situations, the observer should report at least the following information:

1. A record of suggestions made, that is, who makes a suggestion for a choice, change of activity or a way of doing something important to the group, or how to deal with an unpleasant event or individual.
2. To whom suggestions are communicated.
3. How the suggestions are received by others and who, if anyone, takes up the suggestion.
4. The effectiveness of each suggestion: Is it acted upon at the time or at a later time? To trace this you should refer back to relevant material in earlier observatiton periods. Remember that the *outcome* determines whether suggestions are effective. Members' objections or bickerings are relevant, but what actually happens is the test of effectiveness.

5. Extent of participation in planning and in effecting action by the various group members.

6. Duration of the events.

3d. At the end of each observation period, the observer will record, on a separate sheet of paper from the report proper, a ranking or ordering of members present based primarily on effective initiative and secondarily on deference, admiration—derogation exhibited during that period. In making these rankings of status, the observer should give special weight to behaviors in activities that the particular group *usually* engages in and in activities that are *important* to group members. (Here is another reason why the observer must have rapport with the group and be able to move with them from the initial site of observation.)

Obviously, the rankings should bear a close relationship to the records of interaction process in the observation reports. Status ratings unsupported by behavior events are of doubtful value from the point of view of scientific study. At first, you may feel very uncerttain or even unable to make the ratings. Indicate your uncertainty and mention specific events in the reports which led you to order the members as you did.

3e. Method of reporting status rankings:

1. Rate the members as to status by ordering them on a separate page with the highest position at the top, that is:

    a. Highest position

    b. Second position

    · · ·

    · · ·

    · · ·

    n. Bottom position

2. To denote an individual, use a circle with his name or symbol in it until you are sure that he is a group member and you can locate him at a given position. Subsequently, use triangles to denote individual members, locating the triangles at different levels (lower to upper) to denote relative positions.

3. If you feel, on the basis of *specific behavioral evidence,* that a given individual's position is changing, indicate this by affixing an arrow to his triangle in the appropriate direction (up or down).

4. If a nonmember associates with the group, use a broken-line circle to designate him and his location relative to the group.

5. If the observer cannot, at a given time, differentiate status positions between two or more members, these may be placed horizontally, for example, as follows:

Individual b: Second position. Individual c: Second position. Continue to indicate nonmembers with broken-line circles, locating them to show their relationship with members of the group, if possible. For example, if all group members defer to him, you would locate him *above* the group.

3f. At any observation period, make status rankings for individuals actually present during the period. If an absent member is referred to in conversation in clearcut fashion indicating definite deference (e.g., "Let's don't decide until we see what X thinks") or definite derogation (e.g., "That so and so never does anything right"), this is evidence about that member's position. However, indicate that member's absence by making his *triangle* with *broken lines*.

3g. If the observer has a set of boys who get together all at once infrequently (at least in his presence), but do associate in a patterned way recurrently, the organization of the group has to be inferred from the successive and patterned associations. The burden of proof that the patterns do constitute a single organization rests on the observer's evidence. Among this evidence, the occasional gathering of all core members is, of course, a critical datum. As supplementary evidence, the observer may periodically summarize his observations and ratings for the purpose of inferring an over-all pattern of status. Such summaries are to be labeled as such and any patterns thus inferred are to be treated as hunches (hypothess) to be assessed by future evidence (observer reports and reliability checks). Such summaries are of value only if the observer supports each rating with specific behavioral evidence.

4. The criterion for establishing status arrangements in the group at the given time of study is that four successive status ratings by the observer should agree on the individuals occupying the two highest status positions and the two with the lowest status positions.

5. Reliability checks of the observer's ratings will be introduced when his ratings are stabilized as specified in the criterion. One of these checks will be observational. The second will be sociometric. Others may be introduced. The exact procedures for these checks are prepared in additional instructions for this phase and will be presented with illustrations from previous observations. Reliability checks will be introduced only following a conference with the unit supervisor to make plans and discuss procedures in detail.

V

Phase II: Independent Ratings of Status Relations

Main Objective of Procedures

The purpose of ratings of status in the group by an independent observer is to secure one of the possible checks on the reliability of the regular observer's ratings. This check is not made out of distrust for the observer, but because every observation is subject to possible selectivity and personal bias. By securing independent checks on the observations, we are in a position to conclude that regularities observed are *not* simply a subjective opinion of the observer, but can be ascertained by other methods.

1. *Guides to be Followed to Insure the Utility of Independent Ratings.* In line with the purpose of these procedures, certain guides must be followed strictly to insure that the resulting ratings are useful for the project.

1a. The independent rater must, at no time, be informed by the observer about individual members of the group he will observe. During his observation, he may learn some names, but needs only to be cautioned to devise short descriptions for each so that he can identify each boy afterwards.

1b. The independent rater must be fully instructed on the role that he is expected to play in the planned situation, as decided in advance by the observer and unit supervisor. He should be told to stay within the bounds of this role at all times while with group members.

1c. The independent rater should be informed of the general purpose and methods of study so that he knows the essentials, for example, that the boys are not to know they are being observed. Otherwise, he might betray these purposes to the boys unwittingly.

1d. In words that the independent rater can easily understand and grasp, he should be instructed by the observer and unit supervisor on the dimension that he is to rate, namely, effective initiative and allied evidence of deference, admiration, and derogation. For example, he should be told to watch who gets things started, whose words count in making a decision, who carries out actions once decided upon, who is able to make requests which are carried out, who is admired and when, who is kidded or insulted and how they react, and so forth. In this instruction, members of the group under study are not to be referred to. Any examples should come from other groups. He is to be informed that after observing them, he will be asked to rate the boys on this basis.

1e. When the independent observer makes his ratings after the events observed, he is not to do so with the regular observer, but independently of him; there should be no consultation between the two observers. Afterwards, the observer can check each label and supply correct names.

2. Planning the Event for Independent Ratings.

In general, the observer and unit supervisor should plan the event to secure independent ratings using these guides:

2a. The activity involved should be one which is important to group members, which involves all the core members, and preferably the entire membership, and which lasts for several hours, permitting the independent rater to secure adequate samples of behavior.

2b. Of such activities, the one chosen should be one in which members are faced repeatedly with (small or large) problem situations or decisions to be made. For example, if the group is interested in sports, an athletic contest with another team might be such an event, requiring planning of positions, strategies, reactions to the other team's play, etc. Or an outing, such as a picnic provides a long period of planning for food, expenditures, preparations, activities before and after eating, etc. Clearly, the choice depends on the interests of the particular group, facilities, and so on.

2c. Except for small favors that the observer has done for group members in response to their requests or wishes, this event may be the first in which he takes initiative in their activities. If an event should arise naturally in the group, and the observer could know in advance so that he could make plans, that would be preferable. However, it is usually necessary for him to throw up a suggestion. Its enthusiastic acceptance by the group depends on the observer's rapport with the group and the appeal value of the activity suggested. If it is not enthusiastically endorsed, *it should be delayed and a new opportunity created*.

2d. Once the observer has offered to arrange an event by scheduling it or providing facilities (e.g., cash), he should withdraw entirely from the planning, since this process provides data for both him and the independent rater. In other words, once the suggestion is accepted, planning should be up to the boys, within the bounds of safety and propriety already set forth in previous instructions. In order to provide a more prolonged period of observation, observers have sometimes taken boys out afterward for a meal or treat.

2e. Observer and unit supervisor will ordinarily select the independent rater with two major criteria in mind:

First, that the independent rater be capable of observing interaction with reference to the dimension in question; second, that the independent rater can take a role with the observer in the activity in a natural way and fit into the context of the group in terms of personal appearance, skills, etc. For example, this might be as referee or time-keeper at a game, or, if rapport with the group is excellent, it might be as a friend of the observer.

2f. Once an independent rating has been made, it is part of the data of the study and its importance will be discounted only if, for some reason, group members did not attend in sufficient numbers to provide an adequate sample for the rater or if the event was interrupted. In other words, precautions in selecting an independent rater, instructing him on the dimension to be rated and his role at the event must be heeded *before* the event. Once a rater has made his rankings in line with the criteria, they are data even if the regular observer disagrees with them. In this event, other independent checcks are indicated to see if the differences result from observer differences or from instabilities in the status structure from situation to situation.

VI
Phase II: Sociometric Choices

After the observer has achieved sufficient rapport with the group and has rated the status hierarchy of the group (entire core membership) in a consistent way for at least three observation periods involving the members in question, sociometric techniques can be introduced. The questions are asked *individually* of members, *in as casual and informal a way as possible.*

Popularity

1. *Question*: Who are the fellows you like to hang around with best, or whom do you like best in the group?
Who is your first choice? _____
Second choice _____
Third choice _____
Others _____
_____
_____
_____
_____
_____

NOTE TO OBSERVER: You do not have to use these exact words. Choose your wording to convey the meaning and to fit the informal situation. Report your actual words. Be sure that they mean the same thing.

Before the group member has time to mention any name, tell him to mention first the one he likes best or wants to hang around most, the next one *second,* the next *third,* and then, any others.

Use your tact and skill to get from each fellow this sort of ranked (first, second, third, and the others) choice under favorable conditions, so that you will not arouse resistance or suspicion on the part of the fellow at the time. To insure this, if necessary, use your own wording and clarification, without changing the meaning. Prepare the grounds with appropriate conversation.

2. For middle, and especially lower status members, *only*:

Who are the fellows you would like to hang around with if they accepted you as an equal?

or

Who are the fellows you would like to hang around with, if you were sure they would be eager to have you and treat you like a pal?

First choice   _____
Second choice   _____
Third choice   _____
Others   _____
                        _____
                        _____
                        _____
                        _____

NOTE TO OBSERVER: The *note to the observer* under Question 1 applies here too.

Effective Initiative

3. *Question:* Who are the fellows who usually suggest and plan activities, and see that they are carried out?

or

Who are the fellows who get your plans and activities started and see that things get done?

3a. Usually, in an over-all way, or in general:

First one   _____
Second one   _____
Third one   _____

Others   _____
           _____
           _____
           _____
           _____

3b. In fights with others:
First one   _____
Second one _____
Third one   _____
Others   _____
            _____
            _____
            _____
            _____

NOTE: If members of your group *never* fight, substitute some other "dangerous" situation involving skill which *is* meaningful to them.

3c. In other activities such as a (drinking) party or going to the movies and other entertainments:
First one   _____
Second one _____
Third one   _____
Others   _____
            _____
            _____
            _____
            _____

The intent here is to mention socializing activities which the boys really enjoy, often engage in, and regard as important.

NOTE TO THE OBSERVER: The note to the observer under Question 1 applies also to 3, 3a, 3b, and 3c.

In administering these sociometric questions and getting the choices, use the language most frequently used by the group members among themselves (English, Spanish, slang phrases, etc.).

CAUTION: The adequate completion of this procedure requires rapport with *each* member of the group. Do not try to complete it too quickly, but seize or create occasions to be alone and chat with each member. Use your skill in getting the conversation to the procedures *naturally* and in a way which will not threaten anyone. Failure to heed these cautions or starting procedures before rapport is gained can easily lead to evasive and untruthful responses.

VII
Spread of Dwellings of the Group Members

During Phase II and, if necessary, subsequent phases, you are to find out through direct observation and, when appropriate, through inquiry, the addresses of the homes of members. This information is needed for several purposes, but especially to chart the location of these dwellings in the area.

1. Obtain the home addresses of at least all of the core membership and important or frequent fringe members. Differentiate between these two kinds of members in charting the locations.

2. Prepare or obtain a city map including the streets and locations of members' dwellings. The map should be clear enough for city blocks and their sizes to be evident. Locate each member's dwelling on this map, giving the house address on an accompanying list.

3. Specify on the map the usual meeting places of members.

4. Indicate for each member the usual method of getting together (e.g., on foot, bus, car, etc.).

5. Like other data in this research, these are confidential and are to be used only for purposes of this research project.

VIII
Phase III: Study of Group Products

MAIN OBJECTIVE OF PHASE III

In Phase II, the group has been delineated as a social unit with an organization (status structure), which may range from a loose and changing association to a closely knit, stable structure. In Phase III, observation is focused on the *common* criteria for behavior, objects cherished by all members, common ways of doing things and speaking (e.g., lingo, catchwords), shared aims, and attitudes shared to some extent by all members. The data of particular interest are the common values or norms which are *distinctive* to the particular group, that is common attitudes and behaviors which differ from those of other boys in the *same* setting. However, the observer is to report all such common customs, practices, rules, mode of dress, etc. Their distinctiveness will be determined in part by other data collected in the project, as well as his observations of differences between these and other boys.

METHODS IN PHASE III

1. By Phase III, the observer should have determined, through his direct observation and conversations with the group members, the major sectors of interest and activities engaged in by the group members (see Instruction Set II). In Phase III, these sectors should be further explored. The group products of interest will pertain to activities which members regard as important (that is, which are closely related to their real concerns as adolescent boys associating regularly with other adolescent boys).

1a. As a preliminary, review all previous reports and summarize with *specific evidence in words and actions* major sectors of the members' interests and activities with other members. Note any *shared* ways of dressing, acting, regarding or treating others (members, girls, adults, school, work, authorities, other outsiders), evaluations and treatments of objects, handling of money, ways of referring in words to themselves and others, and so on. This summary should be thoroughly documented, especially with *recurring* examples.

1b. Include in the above review and summary any instances of reactions by group members to the behavior of other members as "wrong," "off the mark," objectionable, intolerable, or punishable (including as punishment reprimands, cold-shouldering, ignoring, as well as physical punishment).

2. Observations in Phase III should now focus on behaviors and events revealing (a) commonalities in the behavior of members; (b) reactions to deviations, i.e., discussion, scolding, punishments, etc.; (c) praise for behaving a certain way in line with commonly held values or goals; (d) any signs of members' evaluations of their own group and other groups.

3. Include in each report the usual information previously given (see Instruction Set III) and, in addition:

3a. Who first performed the act or words in question.

3b. How many members also conform (or use the group product) and their status.

3c. Who initiates praise or punishment for deviation.

3d. Who supports any sanctions imposed on an offending member.

3e. Other members' evaluations of the events in question, including the correctness of any punishment imposed.

4. Mention specifically any events or behaviors indicating that a certain sector of behavior (e.g., table manners, relations with parents) is *not* regulated by the group, in the sense that they are not topics of concern

to group members, so that individual variations far outweigh any possible common features.

5. Include in the focus of observations evaluations, reactions to, and relationships with the following:

5a. Other groups of boys (in neighborhood and from other parts of the city);

5b. Adults in general, parents, authorities, and police in particular;

5c. Work and jobs, now and in the future;

5d. School work, other pupils, teachers;

5e. Girls;

5f. Programs and presentations of the mass media of communications;

5g. Automobiles and other objects of value;

5h. Personal appearance, clothing, etc.;

5i. Other institutions such as church, or politics, if these are mentioned by the boys;

5j. Their own neighborhoods, homes, and facilities.

6. In conference with the principal investigators and/or unit supervisor plans for exploring specific sectors of activity and values, loyalty of members, and degree of their solidarity will be formulated to suit the particular situation of the group. These explorations will be in the form of problem situations which can be introduced by you naturally, that is, which seem to members to arise out of the "nature of things." For example, they may have been expressing a desire to do something together (e.g., compete with another team, attend an event). You might facilitate this expressed desire, but find that the event or some aspect of it conflicts with, say, members' dates with girls, or some way of behaving they customarily accept. The observations of interest, then, would pertain to their decisions and choices in such situations. Through such "arranged" situations, the observer's reports on members' loyalty or on specific norms for behavior can be checked. Therefore, they require careful advance planning.

IX
Phase IV: Member Roles and Personal Characteristics

MAIN OBJECTIVE OF PHASE IV

The final phase of observation in the study of the groups has two related objectives:

1. To specify further the roles of each member in the group structure.

2. To identify personal characteristics and modes of interacting with others which are pertinent to the individual's position in the group in terms of effective initiative and to his roles in interaction with others.

FOCUS OF OBSERVATION AND PROCEDURES, PHASE IV

Throughout the observations since Phase II, the observer has made status rankings based primarily on *effective initiative* exhibited by the individual members and on the allied treatments by others (deference, admiration—derogation). In Phase III, the major values and norms shared by the members have been delineated. Now the questions to be answered are the following:

1. How, or in what manner, does the individual maintain a particular position in the status structure? (Or, what behaviors have contributed to a *change* in this position during the period of study?)

2. What are the other members' expectations and evaluations of the individual in respects *other* than his relative effectiveness in the planning and execution of group activities? For example, is his presence actively desired by others and in what activities? What is his special contribution to the activities, other than to planning and seeing that decisions are carried out? (For example, is he amusing, tough, reliable, etc.? Does he provide some facility—backyard, money, car, ball, etc.—essential for group activities?)

3. Does the individual live up to the expectations of others usually? If not, how frequently does he *not* do so, in what sectors, and in what circumstances?

4. How does the individual member see himself in relation to the group and other members' expectations and evaluations of him?

METHODS IN PHASE IV

1. As in Phases II and III, review previous observation reports for all evidence pertinent to this phase. Summarize these in a report, citing specific events, actions, members involved, etc.

2. Continue observation focusing on the relationships among specific members, including all of the kinds of data specified in the Instruction Sets on Observer's Reports (III) and for Phase II. In this phase, however, the observations of interest concern dimensions *other than* effective

initiative (e.g., expressions of "liking," "enjoyment" of others, amusement, specific skills of members, specific facilities provided).

3. To check members' expectations of others and their own views of their relationship with others, interviews with each are now in order. Excepting the informal sociometric questions in Phase II, this is the first phase in which interview methods have been introduced.

3a. Use of interview procedures presumes close rapport with members and should not be attempted otherwise.

3b. Interview procedures are used deliberately at the end of the period of observational study, since their use may be expected to alter the observer-group relationship, to some extent.

3c. Depending upon the particular observer-group relationships, the interviewing of individual members in Phase IV (near the close) should be combined with the collection of material from them on the "natural history" of the group. Since the natural history also includes data collection from other sources, it is described on a separate Instruction Set (X).

3d. Interviews in Phase IV will vary from group to group, and from member to member, since Phase IV is more concerned with distinctive, individual contributions, and interactions. However, in general, they should aim at collecting data pertinent to the four major questions raised under *Focus of observations, Phase IV* (above). Whether or not member expectations and evaluations in specific respects are *shared* can be determined by comparing the responses of the different members.

4. When feasible, personality assessment of individual members will be made by competent professionals through appropriate tests and interviews. The observer himself, however, is to be in no way associated with such assessment when undertaken.

4a. Apart from his relationship with members, the observer and/or unit supervisor should investigate any records available in schools, public agencies, etc., which can be used with permission of the institutions involved for evaluation of the skills and performance of individual members. Such records *may* include test scores for intelligence and achievement tests, school performance, behavioral incidents, court or police records. Such records should be obtained with complete explanation to the authorities involved on the purpose of the study, anonymity of persons and places, etc., which are basic rules in this research (see Instruction Set II).

5. *Self-Radius—Goals Schedules.* The group members will be given

Self-Radius—Goal Schedules to evaluate their reference scales and the sights (goals) they set for themselves in various dimensions. As this is another interrelated aspect of the research program, the exact time of the administration of these schedules to group members and their adminis- trator (who may be a collaborator other than the observer of the group depending on the circumstances) will be determined approximately at this phase in consultation with the supervisor and the observer. The procedures and data on this aspect of the program are presented in Chap- ters 9 and 10.

X
Natural History of the Group

MAJOR OBJECTIVE

As the final step in the study of groups for the project, the supervisor and observer will obtain data *from all possible* sources on the background, origins, and development of the group studied.

METHODS

The natural history of the group is to be reconstructed on the basis of reports by members, their families, neighbors, teachers, agency officials, and legal authorities (if appropriate), as well as any extant official rec-- ords pertaining to the group or its activities. Interviews and collection of official data are the primary methods. The confidential nature of the data in this research should be carefully respected at all times during and after these procedures.

DATA NEEDED FOR NATURAL HISTORY

1. Background data on individual members, their family backgrounds, and situations.

2. Reports on the earliest associations of members, where and how they first began to associate, what their most frequent activities were, when new members arrived, etc.

3. Reports on any behaviors or events involving group members bring- ing them to the attention of neighbors, school, or community officials.

4. Any publicity received by the group or its members.

5. Reports on relationships among older brothers or other older boys in the neighborhood when this group started to form.

5a. In the event of reports of a previously existing group of just older youth when these boys started to associate, find out what has happened to that older generation? Where are the members and what are they doing?

6. In addition to observations previously reported, discover the relationships and ties between the group in question and groups of younger boys and young adults with whom they are in contact.

7. What have been the evaluations and treatments accorded to the group and its members by parents, teachers, and officials?

8. What have been the relationships between the group members and other groups of boys in neighboring areas and at school? If they are in school, what is their relative standing academically and socially?

Indexes

Index of Names

Index of Subjects